The Arts, Human Development, and Education

EDITED BY

Elliot W. Eisner
Stanford University

McCutchan Publishing Corporation
2526 Grove Street
Berkeley, California 94704

707, 1
av 7

73070

ISBN 0-8211-0414-4
Library of Congress Catalog Card Number 75-46106

Preface

The essays in this book focus upon two aspects of education in the arts: the social context in which it occurs, and the course of individual development which provides the opportunities and limits to what can occur. One function of the book is to illuminate some of the social realities that shape what we do in schools. These social realities are frequently political in character and take their form through the strictures and structures we use to give direction to schooling. For example, the allocation of funds to schools is virtually always an expression of our educational priorities. The allocation of these funds not only expresses our values; it also reinforces them by making possible educational opportunities and rewards that support the values from which the initial decisions were made. More resources for some subject areas tend to encourage us to believe, if we did not at the outset, that some curricular areas are more important than others. The point here is clear. Schools are social institutions that function in a social context. The priorities in that context and the forces, both political and economic, that animate it also bear upon the school and influence its climate and the character of its mission.

Given the fact that schools are heavily influenced by the social forces that surround them, those who wish that greater attention be given the arts in education need to recognize how these forces work so that those that are hostile to the arts in schools can be weakened and other forces more supportive can be created. The appreciation of the social and political character of educational change has not been one of the typical professional strengths of educators in the arts. All too often we have acted as if all that was needed to bring about a cultural renaissance within the school was another art or music teacher here or there. This conception of educational change is naive. The goal of bringing about change in schools in a form that significantly alters the climate of the institution and the kinds of values and life-styles that it permits and supports can be achieved by an incremental approach, but *only* if incrementalism is considered a tactic in a view of schooling that recognizes larger, more strategic goals. For example, we might begin by making more visible the achievements of our students in the arts through exhibitions, concerts, plays, and recitals. But we must not end there. More exhibitions and concerts are not, nor should we believe them to be, adequate expressions of the type of climate and program that children should have access to. All too often such beginnings become ends. Although they are given visibility within the schools, and at times within the community, too often their major function is to placate rather than to serve as a step toward significant educational change. Such events, even when given public prominence, should not be used to reassure school boards or school administrators—or even teachers of the arts—that the arts in the schools are really of central significance when in fact they are not. Nurturing illusion leads to self-deception.

Let me be even more specific. What are graduation requirements for school districts? In what fields of study do those in whose trust the schools are placed believe to be of such importance that students are required to participate in order to graduate? The issue here, incidentally, is not necessarily an argument that I am offering for prescribed courses of study at the secondary school level. I could make just the opposite argument. The fact of the matter is that some fields of study *are* required. How do the arts fare in these prescribed requirements compared to, say, the sciences? What about university entrance examinations or scholastic achievement tests? In these important rites of passage what significance is given to achievement in the arts?

Curricular requirements and the criteria for admission to further study are the symptoms of educational beliefs and values that can be used to locate the more deeply rooted sources from which they grow. Ultimately, it is these sources, the core beliefs about man and about the conditions that foster his development, that will need to be changed.

Although graduation requirements, standardized testing, and college admission criteria are the formal and empirical manifestations of educational priorities, there are other conditions in the schools, conditions that are ubiquitous and subtle that also need attention if the arts are to flourish within the structure of schooling. Take for example, the emotional-intellectual climate of the school and its disposition toward play, fantasy, and imagination. The arts are areas of human performance and experience that require a willingness to suspend the press of the "practical," to venture into the world of the imagination. To play with images, ideas, and feelings, to be able to recognize and construct the multiple meanings of events, to perceive and conceive of things from various perspectives, to be able to be a clown, a dreamer, a taker of risks—these are some of the personal inclinations that the arts require, both for their appreciation and creation. To what extent do our schools nurture such dispositions? To what extent do they stimulate them? To what extent do they, instead, encourage routine, convergent modes of thinking, beliefs in right answers, cognitive rigidity, tolerance for boredom, literalness in perception, and specificity in meaning? School programs that are hospitable to the arts will need to provide not only space and time; they will also need to create the climate that makes significant participation in the arts possible. To bring about such a change in schools is, as the authors of the chapters argue, a political as well as a pedagogical task.

The recognition of the political character of educational change is a necessary condition for bringing it about. But it is not sufficient. The realization of change in the lives of individuals requires some understanding of the course of human development and the possibilities that it presents. This brings us to the second function of this book. It is to identify some of the features of human development that will be useful for creating effective curricula and methods of teaching in the arts. What are the images of human development, growth, or progress, that we hold? What is our conception of mind, and what operations does it employ? What do we believe to be the nature of human intelligence, on what subject matters can it be exercised, and to what extent do we believe it can be nurtured?

Take as one example the meaning ascribed to that very popular word in educational discourse, "cognition." What do we consider to be cognitive? What are cognitive operations as compared to, say, affective ones? In educational discourse cognition has become associated with thinking. So far so good. But thinking has come to be associated with what children do when they use discursive or mathematical symbols to solve problems. Thinking has become identified with mental activity mediated by discourse or numbers. Thus we tend to contrast the cognitive with the affective, and the affective with the psychomotor. Although initially we created these distinctions for purposes of intellectual precision, we find ourselves trapped and blinded by the very concepts that were intended to free us through their power to illuminate.

Is it true that work in the arts is noncognitive? If work in the arts *is* cognitive or intellectual, in what way is it so? Are there such things as qualitative forms of thought and problem solving, and, if so, are the processes used for such thinking the same as those used, say, in learning to read? Are there optimal periods in a child's life for developing different modes of thought and expression? Do certain human intellectual capacities atrophy or crystallize with disuse? Questions like these provide direction for inquiry into the course of human development. The answers to such questions will, in principle at least, have profound implications for what we believe to be appropriate content for school programs. For example, if through research on the nature of human intelligence we find that the modes in which thinking occurs—visual, auditory, kinesthetic—are relatively independent and that each mode requires for its full development opportunities to utilize media and to engage in tasks that elicit and refine it, the argument for including such activities and materials in school programs is strengthened. This is especially so if we also learn that through disuse such capacities do in fact crystallize or atrophy. If we assume that mind possesses the capacity for different forms of conception, expression, and problem solving, it would appear that educational programs that seek to cultivate mind, to actualize and refine its latent capacities, will need to analyze what is now being provided and to right any significant imbalance or lack of opportunity that now exists.

In short, the study of human development provides us with an understanding of the attributes that children now possess. It also suggests what might be. The realization of what might be will require, however, more than an understanding of what is. It will require the invention of programs and educational climates that can convert the "is" to the "ought." And so we come full circle. We need to understand both the possibilities and parameters of human development. We need also to understand what needs to be changed in order to bring about change. The former provides us with a view of human potentiality. The latter provides us with a picture of the constraints upon it. These two, when married to a third party—the ability to create educational events in schools—is what is required to move from psychological and sociopolitical forms of understanding to the forms of personal realization in and through the arts that schools should hope to achieve. The chapters of this book are intended to contribute to the realization of that end.

Elliot W. Eisner

Acknowledgments

The chapters in this book were initially prepared for presentation over the course of a two-year period as part of a Public Lecture Series on the Arts in Education at Stanford University. I wish to express my gratitude to the authors for their willingness to share their ideas with an audience wider than the Stanford community. I also wish to express my gratitude to Dean Arthur Coladarci for his support and encouragement.

Contributors

H. S. Broudy, Professor Emeritus of Philosophy of Education, University of Illinois, Urbana

David W. Ecker, Professor of Art and Art Education, New York University

Junius Eddy, Consultant for Arts, Rockefeller Foundation

Arthur D. Efland, Professor of Art Education, Ohio State University

Elliot W. Eisner, Professor of Education and Art, Stanford University

Edmund Burke Feldman, Professor of Art, University of Georgia

Howard Gardner, Co-Director, Project Zero, Harvard University

Jerome J. Hausman, President, Minneapolis College of Art and Design

Al Hurwitz, Coordinator of Visual and Related Arts, Public Schools of Newton, Massachusetts

Vincent Lanier, Professor of Art Education, University of Oregon

Hilda P. Lewis, Professor of Elementary Education, San Francisco State University

Louis P. Nash, Consultant in Arts Education, California State Department of Education

Ronald H. Silverman, Professor of Art, California State University, Los Angeles

Contents

PART I

The Arts
and the
Course
of
Human Development

Introduction

The authors of the chapters in Part I direct their attention to the developmental characteristics of children's artistic activity and to the conditions that might foster its growth. Although many of the characteristics of, for example, children's visual art have been described by many investigators over an extended period of time, explanations as to why these characteristics emerge and what they mean in the course of the child's life are not so clear.

Educators who aspire to develop the artistic imagination and sensibilities of the young can, of course, be helped by an understanding of the developmental characteristics of young children and the limits that these characteristics might set for teaching and learning. At the same time, a knowledge of these characteristics is inadequate for developing instructional strategies or curricular practices. Something more must be added. That something more emanates from the contributions of the educational imagination. The task of the educator is, in a manner of speaking, to create educational events. These events always exceed the limits of what we know theoretically or empirically. No generalized type of knowledge will be perfectly appropriate for specific situations or particular children. The teacher must, somehow, artistically create circumstances that have as their

3

consequences educational outcomes. This is no less true in learning mathematics as in learning to create and respond to the arts. The chapters in this section are intended to illuminate some of the considerations through which educational events can be more effectively created.

1

What We Know about Children's Art—
and What We Need to Know

ELLIOT W. EISNER

Some Theoretical Views of Children's Art

Children's art—drawings, paintings, and sculpture—has been studied for over one hundred years, but, like other products of the human mind, it is not yet fully understood. Those who have displayed the deepest interest in this art have been psychologists and educators. The psychological interest developed in Europe with the work of E. Cleparede and in the United States with G. Stanley Hall. Hall, who was so important a figure in the child study movement, looked to children's drawings and to their stories as sources for understanding the mysteries surrounding man's evolution on earth. Children's art was a key to this mystery since it revealed, Hall believed, the unique childlike view that children employed to relate to the world. Since Hall also believed that man's evolution on earth went through the same stages that children passed through on their way to maturity, children's art broadly conceived was a prime source of evidence through which man's evolution could be explained. Other psychologists, such as Edward L. Thorndike and Alfred Binet, also took an interest in children's art. Binet used art-related tasks in his early attempts to create measures of intelligence that could be used to identify feebleminded children in French schools. For Thorndike,

5

children's drawings were yet another subject matter upon which he could exercise his prodigious skills in psychological measurement. One of the earliest and most elaborate attempts to measure children's drawings scientifically was reported by Thorndike in 1913 in the *Teachers College Record.*[1]

The psychological interest in children's art continued in the twentieth century. At Stanford University, under the influence of Lewis Terman, Florence Goodenough produced in her doctoral dissertation in 1924 the first version of the *Draw a Man Test.*[2] Later Dale Harris, a former colleague of Goodenough, expanded that test to include a *Draw a Woman Test*[3] and developed a visual scale for scoring drawings.

Sigmund Freud, Carl Jung, Herbert Read, and Rhodda Kellog are among those who have used or influenced the use of children's art as a way of discovering the hidden, covert life that lurks beneath the surface of human behavior. Unlike those more empirically orientated psychologists such as Binet and Thorndike, depth psychologists have seen in children's art a projective constellation of forms that disclose both in nonverbal and preverbal terms the anxieties, aspirations, and emotions that could not be expressed in interpersonal behavior. Alschuler and Hattwick's classic study[4] of the easel paintings of nursery school children is a prime example of how children's art has been used as data for understanding personality.

Thus, by examining the psychological literature, we can determine that within psychology itself there has been a division of interest in children's art. One group has used it as subject matter for purposes of psychological measurement, while another group has used it as a road through which the child's private life could be interpreted and understood.

The general models of mind that have been developed by psychologists in pursuit of their own professional ends have not been without consequences in the field of education. Educators, especially those working within the field of arts education, have been influenced by their models. It is with the educational views of children's art that I am most concerned.

Since the 1920's educators have, if one judges by their literature, been more influenced by the work of those psychologists on the tender-minded end of the continuum than the tough-minded end. Perhaps because of the progressive movement in education and its

efforts to liberate both the child and the school from the tight
Victorian constraints of an earlier age, educators found in the work
of Freud,[5] Sir Herbert Read,[6] and Viktor Lowenfeld[7] an invitation
to use art activities to unlock the child's creativity and to enable him
to express those feelings and images that were stifled in rigid,
authoritarian elementary school classrooms. For educators of the
1920's and 1930's, art was the vehicle that would return childhood
to the child, that would permit the child once again to be himself,
that would provide the valve needed by the child to release the
pressures built up within the conventional classroom.[8] Under the
influence of this model of mind, educators used art activities not
only as a source of rich diagnostic material but as a powerful therapeutic device to ameliorate the strains and pressures of the classroom.

Some Consequences of Theory on Practice

The practical pedagogical consequences of this view were profound for the field of art education. One such consequence was to
encourage teachers to look for meanings in children's drawings and
paintings that might not in fact be there. This, in turn, converted
their role from that of teacher—something they know how to do—to
that of psychologist—something they were not trained to do. Another
consequence was to change the teacher's role from that of teacher of
the arts to that of dispenser of art materials and fountain of emotional
support for the child, two roles that, although important, are not
sufficient to educate children in the field of art. A third consequence
of depth psychology on the beliefs of art educators and teachers
concerned the importance of art in fostering the general creative
ability of students. Because creative thinking is supposed to emanate
from the deeper levels of human mentation and because art was
believed to spring from these levels, it was reasonable to assume that
through art human creativity could be unlocked. Art activities were
the kinds of keys that opened the wellspring of human creativity
since art, by its nature, was not restricted by the linguistic baggage
and conventional expectations and rules that attended other areas
of the curriculum. Through art the creative, imaginative life of the
child could once again come to the fore.

These streams of interest—the psychological and the educational—have been important motivating forces for the study of

children's art. Yet the educational significance of art for children is not self-evident. Psychologists tend to use this art for psychological rather than educational purposes. Aside from these claims concerning the benefits to creativity and mental health, the arts do play an important role in the educational development of man.

Though one could write a lengthy treatise on the value of art in education, it is sufficient to state here that art is one of man's major avenues for the formulation and expression of his ideas, his images, and his feelings. It is through the process of working with materials that these ideas, images, and feelings are not only formulated, but clarified and shared. This process affords the individual and those receptive to his products an opportunity to understand and undergo experiences that cannot be acquired through other modes of thought. The arts, as Langer[9] has said, articulate man's feelings by their embodiment in a symbol—the particular work of art. This symbol is a form that abstracts and presents to our consciousness what man thinks, feels, or conceives. Through this form we come to feel and understand what we did not feel or understand before.

Although the particular functions art performs vary from age level during childhood, the significance of the arts needs to be conceived of in terms of their most important contributions to man's development. Children's art is a series of steps toward the goal of becoming fully human.

This brief introduction to the study of children's art and its importance in man's educational development enables us to ask what we know about its development, and, perhaps what is more important, what we need to know.

The Characteristics of Children's Art

One of the most striking features of children's art as manifested in their drawings and paintings is the regularity and stability of the so-called stages through which they pass. Since the work of E. Cleparede, G. Kerchensteiner, and others in the nineteenth century, predictable progressive stages have been identified that are highly correlated with chronological age. These stages extend from the almost random markings on paper made by two- and three-year-old children to the sophisticated use of graphic and painting techniques that convert a two-dimensional surface into a three-dimensional illusion. Changes in children's art over time demonstrate a progression that at first displays a primary interest not in the creation of a preconceived image or idea, but in the visual and kinesthetic stimulation emanating from the use of materials. The very young child uses art materials as resources for his own stimulation rather than as tools through which to construct visual images that represent some aspect of his internal reality or his perception of the forms he finds in his environment. This first general stage of development can be referred to as focusing on "function-pleasure."[10] The very young child uses materials in a consumatory, not an instrumental, fashion for the stimulation and satisfaction that their manipulation yields.

At about the age of three to four the child begins to create images that do symbolize aspects of his world. His activities with art materials are now characterized by a kind of storytelling through what might be called "pictographs"—simplified, flat, two-dimensional shapes that signify, through their rough equivalance to the objects of the world, those objects themselves. It is during this period, from ages three or four to nine or ten, that the lollipop tree, the gabled house, and the four-paned window become evident in children's drawings. This movement into the pictograph is an extremely significant one for the child because it represents two kinds of intellectual achievement. First, it represents the realization that visual materials can be used to create visual forms that convey an idea. Second, it represents on the child's part a sophisticated invention through which his ideas can be embodied in a public form.

Until the latest period of the pictographic stage, American children are on the whole, quite satisfied with the pictographic forms they create. At around nine or ten, however, these forms often cease being satisfying. Children at about this age want to acquire a more comprehensive and, in their view, a more adequate repertoire of skills that will enable them to create more visually convincing pictures.

It is during this period that the child might first experience dissatisfaction with his own best efforts and ask for the kind of assistance that goes beyond parts of assurance that he is "doing just fine." At this stage, which can be called the "representational" stage, the child wants to learn how to make the road disappear into the background, how to make the chimney look as if it is upright even though it is on a slanted roof, and how to make the house conform to the laws of perspective. The child's interests expand at this stage from not only wanting to communicate an idea, but to doing it with skill and visual persuasiveness. Making it "look right" becomes important for the first time in his artistic career.

A fourth stage of development, which is latent and of secondary importance in the previous stages of development, is one that focuses on the aesthetic and expressive aspects of the work that is done. This "aesthetic-expressive" stage begins during early adolescence, and only a small percentage of children acquire the skill necessary to realize it in its full blown-form. When we remember that what gives the arts their special power is the artist's ability to construct and organize form in a way that embodies and therefore conveys the feeling he is interested in articulating, it becomes clear that this stage gets to the heart of artistic expression. By itself there is no artistic virtue in representational drawing, even when the images are hyper-realistic. Such skill manifests itself only as technique, and, while technique is a necessary condition for the creation of art, it is not sufficient. In addition, the technical mastery of representational drawing is no longer a condition for the creation of visual art, as many of the works in our contemporary museums and galleries so loudly attest. What is significant in the creation of art, aside from significant insight and idea, is the ability to create forms that, in fact, express in nonverbal ways what cannot be conveyed in any other way. Few children achieve this highest stage of development in the visual arts.

To say that focused concern with the aesthetic and expressive aspects of visual form is rare in children's art is not to say that it is absent: aesthetic and expressive concerns are present, to some degree, in all stages. It is to say, however, that as a primary focus in the creation of visual form such concerns play a lesser role for most children than concern with use of visual stimulation for function-pleasure, with the use of form as pictograph, or with the mastery of techniques needed for persuasive representation. In each of these stages the child may attain aesthetic satisfaction: in the function-pleasure stage from the engagement itself; in the pictograph stage from the satisfaction of visual storytelling; in the representational stage from a growing sense of mastery. It is in the aesthetic-expressive stage, however, that the dominant focus centers upon the aesthetic and the expressive aspect of form, and it is at this stage that most children terminate their formal art education.

*(i)*A second feature of children's art that has been observed is the extent to which its characteristics are common cross-culturally. Children's art tends to look the same throughout the world. Indeed, the International Center for Children's Art in San Francisco has used children's art as a way of demonstrating man's common humanity. These widespread similarities have encouraged the acceptance of the naturalistic fallacy: because the characteristics of children's art are similar, there must be something "natural" in these stages. The corollary is that, since these characteristics are natural, little or nothing should be done to influence the child while he is employing these natural forms.

It may well be that the similarities in the forms of children's art are a consequence of comparable opportunities for learning in the arts. For the truth is that most schools in the United States do not provide children of elementary school age with much guidance in the acquisition of technique. Left to their own devices children tend to develop similar pictographic forms to convey their ideas, but this is no indication of what they might otherwise be able to achieve with sensitive guidance. There is some evidence that where this guidance is available the rate of their growth increases, and the sensitivity with which they can use materials expands. I am suggesting, in short, that the stages through which children pass in their visual expression need not be seen as the limits of what they are capable of achieving, but, rather, as the starting points.

*(ii)*A third observation about children's art is that children between the ages of four and ten tend to exaggerate in size those objects that are most important to them. The preoccupation with ideas or images significant to the child leads to what Piaget calls "centration"[11] and to what Arnheim refers to aptly as "local solutions."[12] The solution is local because the child neglects the relationship between his primary form and its relationship to the other, secondary or supportive, forms in the picture plane. This is not an unusual occurrence— even for adults. Indeed, one of the things that must be learned by any beginning student in painting at the university level is to see the work as a whole, to consider forms not as isolated entities but as related and interactive components. Artistic form is organic and whole, and to see it that way requires a type of perceptual distance that most children acquire only slowly. One of the contributions that arts educators can make is to enable children and adults to see these

relationships not only within their own work, but in the environment at large.

A fourth observation concerning children's development in art is that it reaches a plateau with respect to the sophistication of its graphic techniques when children are about age twelve or thirteen. From age two to thirteen there is, for example, regular and predictable development in the way children create the illusion of space in their drawings. This progression has been charted in my own research on children's drawings.[13] We can see from the patterns displayed in Figure 1-1 that the increase in children's abilities to create the illusion of space through size relationships and overlapping forms continues in a more or less upward trend until about age twelve. Beyond the age of thirteen, however, the person who does not have instruction will develop the skills acquired at earlier ages very slowly. Thus the drawings of most adults cannot be easily differentiated from those of young adolescents. It is not surprising that this should be true. Drawing and painting are, after all, the products of complex skills, and, like most complex skills, they do not develop from simple maturation. Practice and instruction facilitate their development. Since most adolescents—about 85 percent—do no formal work in the visual arts in American secondary schools, there is little reason to expect them to develop highly sophisticated graphic and painting techniques on their own.

Up to this point I have emphasized the importance of technique in children's art. This might seem strange if one values the charm and spontaneity of young children's paintings and drawings. A word should be said, therefore, about my reason for this emphasis.

All of the arts gain their significance through the development and presentation of public forms. To externalize what one feels, thinks, or imagines requires the creation of forms (in the visual arts) that will carry those feelings, thoughts, and images forward into the public world. To do this requires the transformation of a material— clay, paint, crayon, pencil, paper—into a medium, something through which those ideas, images, and feelings are embodied. To achieve this transformation of material to medium requires the use of technique, the tools and devices one employs to articulate form. The child invents or learns these techniques as he grows, and they set limits to what he is able to express in the arts. Technique is important not as an end in itself but because it expands the range of expressive options

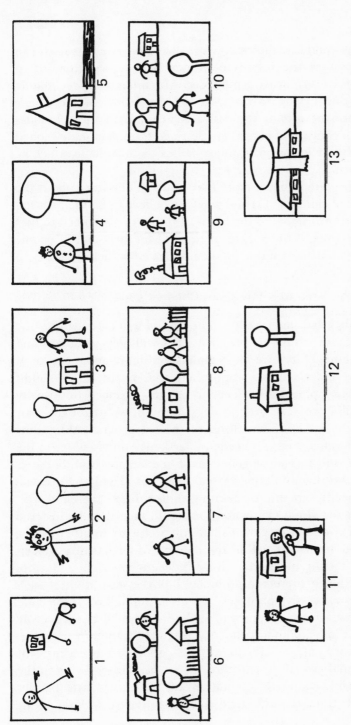

Figure 1-1. Visual examples of thirteen levels of children's treatment of space in drawing (from Elliot W. Eisner, *A Comparison of the Developmental Drawing Characteristics of Culturally Advantaged and Culturally Disadvantaged Children,* Final Report, Project No. 3086, Contract No. OE 6-10-027, U.S. Department of Health, Education, and Welfare, Office of Education, Bureau of Research [Stanford, Calif.: School of Education, Stanford University, 1967], 129)

from which the child can choose to work. The history of art itself can be looked upon as the invention of new techniques intended to realize new (or old) artistic purposes. My interest in technique, therefore, is one having to do with the expansion of the child's freedom to use the arts as expressive vehicles. Without techniques his thoughts, feelings, and images are destined to remain undeveloped or forced to find expression in those modes of thought in which he has competence.

Although there is much more that could be described about the characteristics of children's art and what we believe to be their causes, it is important to turn now to the kinds of things that we need to find out, things that might prove helpful to us as teachers and as people concerned with curriculum development in art education.

Some Things We Need to Know about Children's Art

One of the needs in arts education for children is to identify the types of structure within art programs that will help us understand at least two things. First, we must understand more about the kinds of stimulation and classroom atmosphere that facilitate the child's imaginative development, that encourage him to speculate visually and to be willing to take artistic risks. Second, we ought to know more about the kinds of structures in the art program that allow the child to develop the skills needed to articulate in visual terms the ideas, feelings, and images he generates. For example, would periods of structured and highly defined visual exercises aimed at the development of specific graphic or painting skills provide the child with more freedom for visual expression, or should such skills be fostered within a context of a more personal artistic problem? In other words, must technique be taught within the context of an artistic problem, or can it be taught more effectively independent of but in close temporal proximity to such a problem? Will the separation of such exercises from expressive purposes become meaningless for the child of eight or nine, or can these exercises be interpreted in such a way that he sees meaning of an instrumental sort within them?

The history of beliefs about the conditions necessary for fostering optimal growth in and through art has shifted between the laissez-faire, child-centered orientation of providing little besides materials and time, to the rigid subject-centered techniques of

Walter Smith,[14] who prescribed step-by-step procedures for developing artistic skill. I do not believe the "answer" resides in a middle-of-the-road policy, but in experimentation designed to determine when and under what conditions structure and open exploration are appropriate. What is the rhythm of romance, precision, and generalization, to quote Alfred North Whitehead, that develops children's confidence and competency in the visual arts? Experimentation employing different models of curriculum structure might provide some of the information needed to develop effective art programs for elementary schoolchildren.

Another thing that we need to know more about deals with what reasonable and reachable expectations are for children at various stages in their artistic development. Is there something inherent in the cognitive structure of children that sets absolute limits to their graphic or visualizing abilities? To what extent do these characteristics themselves depend upon the types of experience children have had? If, for example, children at the pictograph stage cannot, by nature, utilize tools for the creation of illusion because of a lack of development of certain cognitive abilities in general, what can they be helped to deal with that is relevant to their artistic development? Thus, if children cannot at a certain age utilize overlap or differentiation of size to create illusion, does this mean that they also cannot utilize texture, color, shape, and other aesthetically relevant components as tools for their artistic expression? In short, we need to know more about the probable limits and the possibilities for artistic growth so that we neither set artificial ceilings on their development by underestimating children's potential for growth nor overestimate their capacity to cope with certain forms of artistic problem solving. If we have erred in the general theories we have developed, and, therefore, in the schools, I believe it has been in underestimating what children are capable of learning. Education in the visual arts has been no exception. At least we should aspire to attain for all children what the most effective and sensitive art teacher can foster in the artistic development of those children with whom she comes in contact.

Still another thing that we need to know more about is the effect of focusing school art activities on nonrepresentational problems as compared to problems that deal with representational illusion. Many children become frustrated when they are not able to render a convincing image of a person, landscape, tree, or horse. They develop quite early in our culture the expectation that to be able to draw or paint means to be able to represent with verisimilitude. What would happen to children's satisfaction and their growth in the visual arts if school art programs placed much more emphasis on the abstract, on design qualities as such, and, therefore, encouraged the child to become sensitive to shape and to the character of the forms they create as forms rather than as representations of natural objects? Can young children, say between four and eight years of age, purposefully and sensitively gain satisfaction in the treatment of forms as such? If so, what will the focus on such activities over an extended period of time, for example, three or four years, do for the development of their qualitative intelligence?

These are only a few of the questions that I feel are worth asking about children's art. Many more lie beyond the scope of this chapter and the space that it would take to discuss them. There are problems dealing with the relationships among the visual and the other sensory modalities, problems regarding the use of adult works of art in relation to children's works, problems concerning the conditions that facilitate transfer of visual learning to situations outside the classroom, problems relating to the peak periods of visual development and to the possibility of visual atrophy when these periods are neglected, problems respecting the consequences of certain cultural attitudes toward the arts on the artistic self-concept of boys and girls.

Though I cannot discuss all of the problems listed above, I would be remiss if I did not mention the general neglect of the arts in American schools. This is fundamentally a political problem since educational decisions ultimately reflect values concerning the kinds of people and the kind of society a country's citizens want. We must admit that we have not given the arts much of a place in our schools. Throughout the nation only a fraction of the high schools population works in the arts, and at the elementary level the arts are marginal niceties, reserved for Friday afternoons when the "real" work of the school is done. We do not have strong art programs in elementary schools largely because we have not demanded them. We have not demanded them because as a nation we have a limited and parochial conception of the human mind and do not yet understand the role of the arts in expanding our consciousness and understanding. Art, for too many of us, is for the talented. Art is considered the beauty parlor of our civilization. But with such a view neither beauty nor our civilization can feel secure. We live at a time when we desperately need people who are sensitive, who are sympathetic, who can read the metaphorical qualities of life, who can see beneath the surface of experience. The arts have, I believe, an extremely important contribution to make in developing such human qualities. We can learn to see, feel, and understand what people like Solzhenitsyn, cummings, and Picasso have to say to us. What is more important, we ourselves can learn to construct the forms through which our own sensibilities can be expressed, in our speech, in our home, in the kinds of lives that we live. The arts in the lives of children will not guarantee the attainment of such ends, but I know of no human enterprise more centrally concerned with their realization. Art is, ultimately, not for art's sake; it is for the sake of all of us.

Notes

1. Edward L. Thorndike, "The Measurement of Achievement in Drawing," *Teachers College Record,* XIV (November 1913).
2. Florence Goodenough, "The Intellectual Factor in Children's Drawings," unpublished doctoral dissertation, Stanford University, 1924.
3. Dale Harris, *Children's Drawings as Measures of Intellectual Maturity* (New York: Harcourt, Brace and World, 1963).
4. Rose Alschuler and LaBerta Hattwick, *Painting and Personality: A Study of Young Children* (Chicago: University of Chicago Press, 1947), I and II.
5. Sigmund Freud, *The Basic Writings of Sigmund Freud* (New York: Modern Library, 1938).
6. Herbert Read, *Education through Art* (New York: Pantheon Books, 1943).
7. Viktor Lowenfeld, *Creative and Mental Growth* (New York: Macmillan, 1947).
8. For a discussion of the progressive movement and its interest in children's art, see Elliot W. Eisner, *Educating Artistic Vision* (New York: Macmillan, 1972).
9. Perhaps the most powerful exponent of this view of the functions of art is Suzanne Langer; see her book, *Problems of Art* (New York: Charles Scribner's Sons, 1957).
10. The concept "function-pleasure" was just articulated by Charlotte Buhler.
11. Jean Piaget, *The Language and Thought of the Child* (London: Paul, Trench, Trubner & Co., 1926).
12. Rudolph Arnheim, *Art and Visual Perception: The Psychology of the Creative Eye* (Berkeley: University of California Press, 1954).
13. Elliot W. Eisner, *A Comparison of the Developmental Drawing Characteristics of Culturally Advantaged and Culturally Disadvantaged Children*, Final

Report, Project No. 3086, Contract No. OE 6-10-027, U.S. Department of Health, Education, and Welfare, Office of Education, Bureau of Research (Stanford, Calif.: School of Education, Stanford University, 1967).

14. Walter Smith, *Freehand Drawing* (Boston: James R. Osgood and Co., 1875).

2

The Unseeing Eye: Critical
Consciousness and the Teaching of Art

VINCENT LANIER

The purpose of this chapter is to suggest that the teaching of art should transcend purely aesthetic concerns and move in the direction of critical moral commitment. It must be admitted that this is a controversial, if not unpopular, position, and its support requires more than a little alteration in the ways in which we look at art, the teaching of art, and, ultimately, education itself.

Most of those who read this chapter are already aware of the diversity of hypotheses regarding the nature of aesthetic experience; thus it is likely to be unnecessary to review them here. Suffice it to say that one highly cogent and, to many, very accurate explanation of aesthetic experience involves in part its functioning as self-consummatory. Such a view proposes, in effect, that the unique and principal characteristic of aesthetic response is that it has no experiential implications or consequences outside itself. Aesthetic experience can be compared to eating packaged cupcakes, which provide no appreciable nutrients and do little to satisfy hunger, but are consumed solely for the "pure" pleasure of their flavor.

Thus, in this view, aesthetic responses in general and those responses to works of art that can be characterized as aesthetic in particular can be understood best or perhaps only, if they are held separate from all other concurrent responses to the same stimulus. Peripheral contributory factors in the aesthetic transaction contaminate or confuse aesthetic analysis, acting much like what is called, in the jargon of communications theory, "noise." Needless to say, this "noise" can be both relevant and helpful, but it is not crucial. Thus, for example, elements such as those which Monroe Beardsley calls "genetic" factors (the artist's intention, or the originality or triteness of the work) may help us to know why we have had a particular aesthetic experience.[1] They do little, however, to explain the nature of that experience.

This idea of aesthetic experience as self-consummatory is a compelling landmark in describing what happens to the viewer when he looks at a work of art. One need not deny its validity or usefulness in order to propose a broader viewpoint both for the teaching of art and for art itself. It should be emphasized, in fact, that this, another, or preferably several explanations of aesthetic experience (more complete, of course, than simply the one key concept noted above) should be a vital component of a progressive art curriculum. But it must also be recognized that concepts clarifying phenomena need not be viewed as prescriptive. Even if understanding aesthetic experience requires us to isolate its "purely" aesthetic characteristics, it is still quite proper to assert that we ought or ought also attend to other concerns or elements involved in an aesthetic transaction. Further, it is reasonable to propose that the significant additional or alternative element that should be considered is the moral implication in the aesthetic transaction, when such implication is available. This is, of course, to assume that aesthetic experiences provoked by works of art are capable of stimulating moral implications, an assumption the history of the arts makes difficult to deny.

An Example of Attentiveness to Moral Implications

It might be useful to attempt to illustrate such attentiveness to the moral implications of a specific aesthetic transaction. The film *Blow-up* is by now enough of a cinema classic to provide an appropriate example. We can take from this film the scene in which its hero, the photographer, while looking for the girl he photographed in the park, walks in on a rock concert. After a few moments the guitar player on the stage, infuriated at the malfunctioning of the amplifying system, smashes his guitar and throws one broken piece to the screaming crowd. Now suddenly a part of that crowd, the hero fights frantically, like those around him, to grab the piece of guitar; he finally succeeds and, breaking away from the crowd, runs out of the building onto the street. Once there and free of the battle, he looks in surprised disgust at the piece of guitar clutched in his hand, throws it on the sidewalk, and walks away.

The aesthetic content of this scene is fairly obvious, though the primary aesthetic mechanism is dramatic rather than visual. Entering the scene on a fairly high level of tension since the hero has sighted a dim form on the street that might be the girl he is seeking, we are led to a higher pitch of excitement by the volume and beat of the music. Then the fury of the guitar player, the smashing of the instrument, and the mad battle of the crowd in which the hero unthinkingly (it would seem) takes part increase the tension until we are driven to release and closure by his escape from the building. His quick rejection of the piece of the broken guitar is a sort of recapitulation or echo of the entire scene, analagous, perhaps, to the fifth repetition of a diagonal in the background of a painting. All of this is, of course, superbly staged, photographed, and edited, a cameo Antonioni. Incidentally, although there is no lack of sound, the scene uses no words at all—if I remember correctly.

In "purely" aesthetic terms this description of some aspects of the formal content of the scene might serve to explain its singular potency as aesthetic experience—at least for me. But, as in the case of many works of art, though not all, the scene has what might be called "ideational" content as well. In almost crude dramatic symbolism, the scene (perhaps even the filmmaker) seems to be saying that many of us spend some part of our lives scrambling and battling to attain goals that turn out to be useless and unwanted once we reach them. In terms of the context of meaning of the entire film, this interpretation of the rock concert scene is quite compatible with the constant conflict and confusion between illusion and reality. Thus it is a plausible interpretation, though there may be alternatives just as or more "authentic" or true to the ideational content in the mind of the filmmaker.

This ideational content, absorbed by the viewer in an affectively powerful formal structure and language, also has transparent moral implications. Ought we join the vicious struggle of the crowd for what is, when we have it, meaningless and tasteless? What are the proper goals for people, and how do we discover them? Perhaps these are not particularly profound questions, but we need to be reminded of them from time to time.

Is Moral Attentiveness a Proper Concern for Art Education?

If the above is a reasonable illustration of attention to the moral implications of an aesthetic transaction, it is also clearly a viable pattern for content in the teaching of art, one that can be repeated with numerous works of art of all kinds—drawings, prints, paintings, sculpture, photographs, and films. Thus, the teaching of art need not avoid or dilute a vigorous concern for purely aesthetic analysis, but can, as in the above illustration, additionally involve ideas about the world and ideas of a moral character when these ideas are available in the work of art.

It is, however, quite proper and, unfortunately, even necessary to ask why art education or general education, for that matter, should concern itself with moral issues. After all, formal education in the large sense is and has been a didactic enterprise, oriented toward inculcating information, behavioral skills, and, at best, socially approved "attitudes." I submit that this is now and has been roughly since World War II the root problem of education: it does not deal with those fundamental economic, political, and social forces whose oppressive impact on our lives has become increasingly overt. All of these forces can and must be looked at as moral issues. Indeed, any relational problem concerning two or more people is, ultimately, a moral problem. Our error in the classroom seems to have been that we have avoided these problems, disguised them in aesthetic terms, diluted them beyond recognition by attending to their symptoms, or, at worst, lying about them.

Let me suggest what might be an obvious example. Although the so-called energy crisis appears to have emasculated our growing national concern with the problem of pollution, the last decade has seen this topic become a significant part of the school curriculum. Yet most of these programs—if they can be judged by a sampling—seem to restrict any examination of pollution to the necessarily superficial review of symptoms. We do not have air pollution because we drive our cars too much, or because industry must provide jobs, or because—in the case of field burning—technology has not yet provided a more economical alternative, or because the demands of public transportation require too many jet flights, or because the topography of some communities causes frequent air inversion. These are only symptoms, the root cause of which is the invariable placement of financial gain over humane concern. There is simply no alternative to air pollution as long as the unrestricted application of the profit motive and its political support remains the predominant ethical criterion of our society.

Manufacturers of motor vehicles can design and produce non-polluting engines, refiners of oil can make fuel with minimal emissions, factories can sharply curtail smoking chimneys and still provide the same number of or more jobs, farmers can refrain from burning their fields, nonpulluting alternatives to jet air travel (such as the puny but commendable beginnings of Amtrak) can be developed, and air inversion can be welcomed as desirable climatic change with little atmospheric garbage to poison its presence if—and only if—we understand the nature of the forces that deny these actions and we enforce their accomplishment through political means.

When problems of pollution are viewed in these terms, they become moral problems. We must decide whether or not it is immoral to destroy the air, the waters, the fields, and the forests that belong to all of us for the private gain of the few. It is plausible to take either side of the question, but it is unreasonable to pose the question in any other terms. How often do our schools confront such issues as pollution, population, war, inflation, and crime in this manner? It would be justified to claim that this is seldom done and that the lack of such a focus in education gives a kind of anemic futility to what the young are made to do in school. One does not have to have a Ph.D. in the social sciences to recognize, however dimly, the basic problems of existence. Neither must one be brilliant to realize that the ritualistic exercises in the first-grade study of the community or high school and college courses in political science and economics are largely unreal and pointless. What is required is a critical consciousness, an informed awareness of those social forces which oppress our lives, confine our growth, and defile our dreams, and an additional awareness of what we can do to combat them. Indeed, the central issue of education—in whatever field or on whatever level it can be confronted—is to clarify the ways in which the social, political, and economic world works and how it can be improved.

Should the arts as they are taught in our schools contribute to such an effort? It is clear that, if education is seen in any measure as the development of a critical consciousness, then art education should foster that enterprise. Can art education contribute to this end? There is little doubt that art education can contribute to this end. It can be structured to do so if there is a collective recognition of its obligation. An illustration might again be helpful. We shall continue to use pollution as our content, and the following, by now almost traditional, curriculum idea might demonstrate some possibilities.

Let us envision a required art class in a junior high school in which the classroom is miraculously equipped with a cassette videotape recorder and camera. Let us envision further an art teacher at least adequately trained to deal with newer media (the technology involved is far from complex) and imbued with that necessary zeal to provoke a confrontation and investigation of some of the substantial problems of our present society. Such a teacher and class might prepare and film a documentary, or simulated dramatic videotape, exploring one or several local instances of pollution and inquiring as sharply as possible into the causes of that pollution. The emphasis here will have to be at least the most significant information available on the problem and its origins and at best some substantive indication of how the affected public can act to control the problem. The first without the second is merely a reflection of the kind of liberal journalism already a part of our cultural response to pollution, although it may still be of value to repeat it within the context of the school.

Some may respond to this rather simple suggestion by insisting that such a procedure in the classroom is more properly the province of the social studies teacher. Perhaps this is true. It is, nevertheless, usually the art teacher who can best supply a concern for visual aesthetic qualities in what is, at least in part, a visual medium. Without careful attention to the affective impact of these visual qualities, a film or videotape has less chance of engaging the emotional and intellectual response of those who view it as well as those who make it. In other words, one historically verifiable and currently exploitable function of the visual arts is their capacity to invest ideational content with, as it were, affective charges. When this ideational content is contemporary and insightful (that is, basic rather than superficial), both the producer and the viewer tend to regard it with sharpened intensity, and it creates a greater chance of influencing subsequent action.

Thus, as in the case of the scene from *Blow-up* discussed above, emotion-eliciting presentation of moral issues through the medium of an art form is no do-gooder's fantasy; nor is it a conspiracy to reduce all art to propaganda; nor is it even the manifestation of emotionalist aesthetic theory as in the writings of Véron or Tolstoy or Ducasse. Not only is this kind of curricular emphasis a plausible direction for art education, but it is a direction that is likely to help rescue education in general from its present inadequacy.

In addition to this moral function, the kind of classroom art activity recommended here has other significant implications for the teaching of art. The choice of the film medium (I use the term "film" to include videotape, despite the McLuhanistic distinctions in that context) was, of course, no accident. It is precisely the contemporary media of the arts, and the popular media at that, which possess the capabilities for rescuing the teaching of art from its present doldrums.

Conditions for Progress in Art Education

A digression from my pleading for moral commitment seems appropriate. I would suggest that art education has much to learn from the world, both inside and outside the school. It must learn that as unimaginative and uninspiring as art may often be in the classroom, it is magnificently virile outside of it—not in the effete, elitist, middle-class galleries and museums, but in movie houses, dress shops, magazines, sides of buildings and subway cars, and on television screens. We do not have to teach aesthetic response; the young of today already have it, more, perhaps, than their elders.

Art education must learn that of all the available contemporary visual media, motion pictures and television appear to be the most powerful stimulators of vigorous response, no small part of which is aesthetic in character, almost regardless of how one describes the nature of aesthetic response. The reasons put forward for this unique power of the film media are many and diverse, and one would have to be a scholar in the field of film to select the most accurate from among them. Because the potency of film is increasingly recognizable, it is extremely unfortunate that art teachers and the teachers of art teachers have not in general been able to make use of film media to support the learnings they envision.

Art education must also learn that in a healthy society (it is obvious that I am preaching moral commitment because we do not presently live in a healthy society) the study of art needs no rationale other than that visual aesthetic experience is an important part of living and that understanding the nature of one's aesthetic response and expanding its parameters is the birthright of every child. It does not matter whether or not the study of art makes one "creative," cures one's hang-ups, sharpens one's visual acuity, makes one a Sunday potter when he or she retires on a pension, helps one rearrange a bedroom, a classroom, or a poolroom. Art is vital preeminently because it is art and needs no other justification under wholesome social circumstances. This is what Elliot Eisner calls an "essentialist" position and what I have called the intrinsic value of art education.[2] Instead of creating artists, we should be developing, for the most part, "literate" citizens, with knowledge of and affection for the full range of visual arts available today.

Art educators should also learn, as this chapter attempts to suggest, that these unwholesome times demand the commitment described here. In so doing, the teaching of art assumes a position of extrinsic value, or, to use Eisner's second, contrasting term, a "contextualist" position. There is no inconsistency in moving from intrinsic to extrinsic concepts of value, given the dictates of social need. It is unnecessary, furthermore, to have any limitation of age level in planning or teaching a critical moral consciousness through art. Art educators appear to have undergone a kind of self-inflicted intellectual acupuncture, deadening themselves to human potential by questionable if not demonstrably false limitations by age level (as in child development levels in art), by socioeconomic levels (as in the case of the so-called "disadvantaged"), and by intellectual stratification (as in the kinds of simple to complex developmental curricula we usually design). To paraphrase Bernadette Devlin, people are stupid only because they are lied to by their leaders. Perhaps we should apply this idea to education; thus, many children find school unreal and unrewarding only because they are shortchanged by their teachers.

Those in art education will also learn—but, apparently, not very soon—that a realistic appraisal of their educational functions requires a kind of humility foreign to the professional history of the field. As a field of study art education is truly peripheral, granted the primacy of the social, economic, and political concerns noted above. As shocking as such a conception might be, there is no avoiding the fact that visual images are notoriously inaccurate conveyors of information and ideas, even of emotion. If we wish to transmit anything more complex than a primitive or rudimentary concept or datum and desire some accuracy in that transmission, we always use words, never pictures alone. Indeed, one might say that the ancient adage should be reversed and that, in truth, "one word is worth a thousand pictures." This is, incidentally, one of the reasons for the power of film media. Not only do they provide the additional dimension of occurring over time, which is unavailable to most of the visual arts, but contain the mechanism of words, with which complex ideas can be negotiated.

The field is also peripheral because some of the arrogant assumptions of universality one finds in the literature dwindle appreciably when they are examined with objectivity and care. It is still claimed, for example, that the study of art trains one to see; thus, terms such as "visual literacy" or "perceptual skill" mean a kind of all-embracing visual and even social competence. It is much more reasonable to insist that the study of art teaches one to see art, and not everything else in the world, with greater efficiency. After all, if activity in art did promote this overall skill, the lives of artists would reveal a far higher level of general perceptiveness than is generally the case.

The same debilitating assessment is appropriate to the concept of creativity, so long the lion in the zoo of beliefs held by art educators. As conceptually inadequate an idea as it is, creativity— especially in the sense of its transfer from art to other activities—has been monopolized by art educators as if no other human behavior could promote it as vigorously or ensure its absorption as a pattern of response. Perhaps, in view of art's perpetually tenuous hold on the edge of the school curriculum, this pride is pardonable. It is, however, certainly no help to us or to others in revealing the significant role that art can play in the process of education.

If it is agreed that all of the above is a reasonable argument and that art educators should do what has been described, then why has it not been done? There are, of course, a number of significant reasons for this situation in the areas of education and the arts in general and in the teaching of art in particular. Since, however, both education and the arts seem to be, or actually are, beyond our influence as individuals, we might most profitably look at the teaching of art to see why the kind of moral recognition described here has been and is now almost universally absent. Perhaps the main reason is that, ever since its inception (even if we go back to 1871 and Walter Smith), the art teacher has been obsessively preoccupied with studio production and the model of the artist. Despite the ingenious conceptual acrobatics of our theorists, classroom art teachers, with only infrequent exceptions, promote a curriculum whose end subordinates all else in favor of the creation of individual studio art products. Those who publish in the art education journals have written exhaustively of all kinds of values purportedly inherent in art activities inside and outside of the classroom. They include the development of creativity in art and, by transfer, general creativity, the growth of visual literacy, therapy for emotional problems, the promotion of supraverbal communications skills, the development of aesthetic information, and, ultimately, aesthetic criteria. Some of these concepts of value involving redirection of goals and curriculum in teaching art have intellectual merit; others are inadequately conceived, to say the least. Not one of them, however, appears to have influenced in any significant measure the day-to-day activities in the classroom. It is as if the theoreticians in the field, or those who write at least, inhabit some sort of shadow world imperviously separate from the real world of the school.

There are, of course, other reasons why the moral role of art education remains unrecognized. Disinterest in social issues, the hallmark of today's artistic production, which is consciously or unconsciously aped by the majority of those in art education, may be one reason. A lofty neutrality toward forces in the social arena conditioned by traditional academic and scientific attitudes might be another. Fear of personal or vocational reprisals or confusion about available data on moral issues could be very understandable reasons. The almost total lack of support for this recognition within the field is certainly another. But, whatever the reasons, the moral vacuum in art education exists as it exists in most of the educational establishment. Indeed, it might be said that the lack of moral concern in education is itself a reflection of much the same condition in our society in general.

It has been suggested here that the teaching of art should promote critical consciousness, that it can do so, and that there are some potent pressures keeping it from doing so. Perhaps one last question needs to be asked and answered. Will art education begin to move in this direction at some not too distant time? It is unfortunate that there is no realistic option but to answer in the negative. It may be that we need a modicum of critical consciousness to know that we must teach it to the young, and there are lamentably few signs of such awareness on the American scene today. The most optimistic we can be is to recognize that change comes quickly in our contemporary culture; thus, the answer to that question might be different tomorrow.

Notes

1. Monroe C. Beardsley, "Critical Evaluation," in *Aesthetics and Criticism in Art Education*, ed. Ralph A. Smith (Chicago: Rand McNally, 1966), 318.
2. Elliot W. Eisner, *Educating Artistic Vision* (New York: Macmillan, 1972), 2.

3

Goals and Roles in the Art
Education of Children

RONALD H. SILVERMAN

It seems obvious that any attempt to examine the goals and roles associated with the art education of children must, in this age of emphases upon behavioral objectives and systems approaches to teaching, appear as an excursion into pedantic excessiveness. It is essential, therefore, to provide a brief explanation for my having selected a topic that has often been dealt with in the literature, if not the practice, of education for more than a decade.

My interest in this topic stems simply from the nature of my involvement in the field of art education. I am primarily concerned with the preparation of art teachers. This means that I attempt to acquaint future teachers with the nature of art education and to provide them with insights and experiences that will contribute to transforming them from art students into art teachers. Almost every week during the academic year I visit schools to observe, evaluate, and assist student teachers in coping with the realities of classroom teaching. I try to help them provide learning experiences in art that are relevant to their pupils' interests and needs and that reflect a comprehensive view of the visual arts as a subject to be studied.

These frequent visits to the "firing line" serve to remind me constantly to focus upon what I believe are the key variables in effective teaching: knowledge of one's subject, pupils, and social milieu; the ability to formulate heuristic and specific teaching plans; and the knowledge and skills required to implement and evaluate such plans and to develop and utilize valid measures of pupil growth and development. My professional task is to provide the guidance that will enable my students to deal with these variables.

I have been performing this role for almost twenty years. And, after observing literally hundreds of situations in art teaching, I have come to believe that, in addition to certain personality factors that are cumulative from birth and that are not amenable to change within teacher education programs, effective teaching is directly related to clearly conceptualizing the nature of goals and roles as they pertain to art education. In my view, the extent to which any teacher is able to increase pupils' understanding of art and skill in its production is directly related to one's ability to think through what he or she intends to teach and how to go about doing it.

Empirical Basis for Concern about Goals and Roles

The above assertion does not merely reflect impressions gathered over many years of working with student teachers. It is also based upon empirical verification. During the school year 1967-1968 I directed a controlled experimental study that involved over a thousand seventh-grade pupils and their art teachers. We were attempting to investigate the role of art in the education of economically and socially disadvantaged youth.[1]

The study provided opportunities for teachers of our experimental groups to be informed about the disadvantaged and alternative descriptions of the structure of art; utilize an experimental text written especially for disadvantaged seventh graders; acquire fifty reproductions related to this text and the interests of seventh graders; and develop lesson plans designed to reflect what the students had learned and acquired.

Ten evaluative instruments were utilized in a pre- and posttest format with an intervening semester of study between testing periods. These instruments included three perceptual tests designed to measure visual speed and accuracy and spatial orientation and spatial visualization aptitudes; two cognitive tests that dealt with abstract reasoning abilities and an understanding of general vocabulary; attitudinal measures concerned with self-image, use of leisure time, and mature reactions to stress situations; and art aptitude scales that measured drawing ability and an understanding of art vocabulary.

Experimental and control group teachers were randomly selected from a pool of seventh-grade art teachers working in schools that were eligible for Title I funds for poverty areas as stipulated by the U.S. Office of Education. Our groups were taught by art teachers who participated in a six-week seminar during the summer of 1967. Control groups were taught by art teachers who had a two-week orientation session. We also had several non-art control groups made up of seventh graders not enrolled in art. Both control and experimental group art teachers were required to formulate semester plans that were subsequently evaluated by two outstanding seventh-grade art teachers who were not involved in the experiment.

A matrix of twenty-seven variables associated with the investigation provided the statistical basis for making inferences about art education for disadvantaged seventh graders. Among these inferences was the finding that taking art in the seventh grade, whether under experimental or control conditions, results in a significant increase in the ability to make rapid and accurate visual discriminations. Other changes in behavior, however, were more related to the variables of teachers' experience and competency than to whether or not a pupil had taken art or was in a control or experimental group situation. It was found, for instance, that the number of college units in art taken by the teacher and the years of experience in teaching the disadvantaged were correlated significantly with pupils' growth in both visual speed and accuracy and the development of drawing skill. In addition, those teachers who were most effective in bringing about improvements in important behaviors tended to rely less upon teaching devices that others had developed. It was also found that the teachers judged most capable in formulating comprehensive and specific lesson plans were also superior in developing aptitudes in spatial orientation and an understanding of art vocabulary.

These kinds of empirical data reinforce my belief in the necessity for those who are to provide art education experiences for children and youth to have proper education, pertinent experience, and sound judgment. Though effective teaching does indeed require an understanding of one's subject and experience in working with pupils, these qualifications alone are not sufficient to alter the behavior of children toward the development of expressive and appreciative skills. It is also essential for teachers to think clearly about how and what they wish to accomplish. A coherent exposition of roles and goals is thus required.[2]

Having explained my concern with roles and goals, I shall be more specific in my discussion of the topic. I shall first attempt to clarify the meaning of the term "goal" and then discuss several ways of making statements concerning goals that have varying degrees of potential for effecting growth in pupils. This will be followed by an explanation of the term "role" and an examination of alternative teaching roles that reflect variations in orientation and disposition, as well as differences in readiness of pupils. This last discussion will take place within a context of organizing aesthetic judgment curricula for primary-grade children.

The Meaning of Goals in Art Education

What are goals for art education? They are simply verbal statements identifying anticipated outcomes that should accrue as a consequence of someone's being involved in learning experiences in art. Such statements are referred to as goals, aims, purposes, or objectives. Some educational theoreticians would distinguish goals from objectives by asserting that the former concern a field generally and that the latter relate to a particular aspect of a subject.[3] But, regardless of the terminology, verbalizing what one hopes to accomplish should function as a predisposing force that directs the art teacher to seek out needed information, implement particular teaching strategies, and utilize relevant measurement devices. It is unfortunate that many statements of goals are couched in such vague terms that their influence as a catalyst to action is minimal.

For example, can the statement "art education should develop aesthetic sensibilities" be expected to point a teacher toward the actions required to achieve such a purpose? Though this type of statement may be laudable for all levels of education in all of the arts, it is not sufficiently specific to enable a junior high school art teacher, for instance, to decide what kinds of information and media need to be acquired or what form of art activity should be utilized to affect the development of which aspects of aesthetic sensibility.

Before formulating more specific statements of goals, one should decide whether to do so on the basis of some kind of an organization of the goals themselves or upon an examination of the nature of the subject to be taught.

Organization of Goals

A prominent example of the organization of goals without reference to a particular subject is the Taxonomy of Educational Objectives in the Cognitive and Affective Domains developed by Bloom, Krathwol, and their associates.[4] One can take their listings, which move essentially from simple to more complex behaviors, and place under each heading items associated with the visual arts. I have tried this exercise and have found it worthwhile. One is forced to think about his subject in terms of specific categories and, as a result, speculates about aspects of the visual arts that might otherwise remain undiscovered. A few examples of this forced speculation, within the Cognitive Domain, under the heading "Knowledge of Conventions," are knowing the characteristic ways of treating and presenting ideas and phenomena such as objects in drawing and painting, symbols in posters, designing procedures, and care of tools and materials. Within the Affective Domain, under the heading "Commitment to a Value," conviction and full involvement in a cause, principle, or doctrine are demonstrated by writing letters to the editor protesting the low status of the arts.

While these examples may suggest the value of categorizing behavior in a general way, that is, not specific to any one field, I have found their lack of direct relevance to the visual arts to be a source of frustration when one attempts to develop a comprehensive listing of learning behaviors in art. In addition, because of their complexity, these taxonomies would be exceedingly difficult for the classroom teacher to employ to any great advantage. Perhaps full-time curriculum developers can use such listings, but it has been my experience that art teachers lack the time or the incentive to sort out behaviors in art that can be readily associated with the categories identified in the Cognitive and Affective Domains. Perhaps their greatest value is placing before the educational profession a coherent listing of the kinds of behaviors it must be cognizant of and try to develop, which was, of course, the purpose of Bloom and his associates.

Another, different, approach to organizing goals in relation to a general framework suited to all subjects is the elaborate scheme developed by educational psychologist, Asahel Woodruff. In 1968-1969 he directed a series of training institutes for art educators that were held in various parts of the nation. These meetings were sponsored by the National Art Education Association and funded by the U.S. Office of Education.

Woodruff's formulations were modeled on conceptual structures that are closely akin to cybernetic and industrial systems. His purpose was to make educators as proficient at producing truly educated citizens as industry is in manufacturing commodities efficiently and profitably. One example of Woodruff's approach is his "Independent Instructional Variables within a Quality Control Model." Within this model he delineates the need to consider the incoming student, pretreatment diagnosis and prescribed placement, a host of treatment variables, post treatment measurement, and student output. Under "treatment variables" are considered the nature of the task and factors associated with it such as media and learning climate.

The task is characterized as a "carrier task" because it carries learning with it by requiring the learner to acquire concepts and competencies he does not initially possess, but without which he cannot complete the task. The attempt to identify relevant carrier tasks associated with the visual arts results in a listing of educational goals. They may range from general statements such as "producing a product" to specific concerns such as "producing a space divider suitable for use in the school cafeteria."

Woodruff's categories were utilized by participants in training institutes with varying degrees of success as they attempted to develop sample art curricula in response to his conceptual scheme.[5] And attendance at one of his institutes did provide opportunities to think about and question the necessity to develop more logical approaches to the formulation of goals for art education. It is my contention, however, that neither a general systems approach to stating goals, such as Woodruff's, nor an all-encompassing but nevertheless general taxonomy can be of immediate value to the classroom teacher. Such ventures are highly suited to the endeavors of curriculum developers and text writers. Because of their complexity and lack of immediate relevance to the subject matter of the visual arts, they cannot be too productive in aiding the teacher with the task of formulating goals that will ultimately result in significant learning.

Organizing Goals in Relation to the Subject

I believe a more satisfactory solution lies in the examination of the subject itself. The nature of visual arts education should be the basis for identifying and classifying goals to be attained and not some general structure into which one shoves statements about what knowledge, skills, and attitudes are to be acquired.

There are, of course, many ways to categorize the visual arts so that they may be taught effectively. Examples might include the limited conception developed by Dow at the turn of the century wherein visual forms were classified as the elements and principles of art, or the more comprehensive view reflected in California's Framework for Art Education, adopted by the State Board of Education in 1970. The latter, which serves as a guide to curriculum development, calls for the inclusion of four basic components in all art programs: experiences to develop perceptual skills; art activities to develop expressive skills; schooling to develop an understanding of our cultural heritage; and nurturing abilities for making aesthetic judgments.

Although these schemes attempt to delineate the subject itself, they do not offer the classroom teacher the kind of breakdown of the subject matter that facilitates specific forms of stating goals. Dow's system is limited because of his rather primitive conception of formalism, which, unfortunately, has been adopted as dogma by too many art teachers. And the California Framework suffers because of its brevity and its neglect of the specific terms associated with the visual arts.

An exhaustive listing of such terms, which, however, would become a burden to the teacher because of its complexity, is the very formidable *Guidelines for Curriculum Development for Aesthetic Education,* developed under the sponsorship of the Central Midwestern Regional Educational Laboratory in 1970.[6] It offers specific listings of both art terms and the outcomes of art instruction, and has proven to be exceedingly valuable in identifying subject-matter constituents.

Another helpful conception of the visual arts is provided by Laura Chapman in an article titled simply "Subject Matter for the Study of Art."[7] In it she delineates concerns that are relevant when one is dealing with art as a subject to be studied, rather than when one is focusing upon art as a developmental activity, which seems to characterize theorizing about art education in past generations.

The topics to be studied in the art class would include producers called artists and objects and events called art; sources that artists employ for their ideas and visual studies such as social events, myths, dreams and fantasies, and views of land, sea, animals, and people; the ways artists interpret their ideas; the materials and techniques utilized to produce visual qualities; the ways artists improvise upon, extend, and refine their ideas; the feelings and meanings that can be evoked by varying arrangements of visual qualities; and the factors that both influence the character of works and affect judgments about them.

Listings such as Chapman's are, of course, invaluable to the teacher of art because they provide a basis for deciding what to teach; it is from this aspect of the decision-making process that significant statements of goals should flow.

The final example of utilizing the structuring of subject matter as a basis for stating goals is my own formulation. I organized the scheme initially as a response to the request of the Center for the Study of Evaluation at U.C.L.A. They asked me to evaluate and modify a listing of hierarichal goals in art education for elementary schools that they had developed. At their suggestion, I put forth my ideas in the form of a flowchart, which was based upon what I conceive as the three basic outcomes of art education: learning how to produce, think about, and appreciate art.

Producing art consists of two fundamental aptitudes: interpretative skills, which are concerned with abilities for producing surface and representational qualities; and creative skills, which reflect the use of imagination, fluency, and flexibility in approach and the ability to produce original works. Behavioral attributes associated with these aptitudes are also delineated to provide examples of how goals can flow from a concern with a general dimension of art education to specific instances of goal-related behavior. The flowchart having to do with goals for making art appears in Figure 3-1.

Goals related to comprehending the visual arts are broken down into discussing and examining the physical and social aspects of art, and reading about the roles of art and artists to acquire a historical perspective. The behavior emanating from these activities is also listed: identifying and describing pervasive qualities such as angularity and symmetry; recognizing styles and periods in works of art associated with various times and places; and identifying how art carries ideas

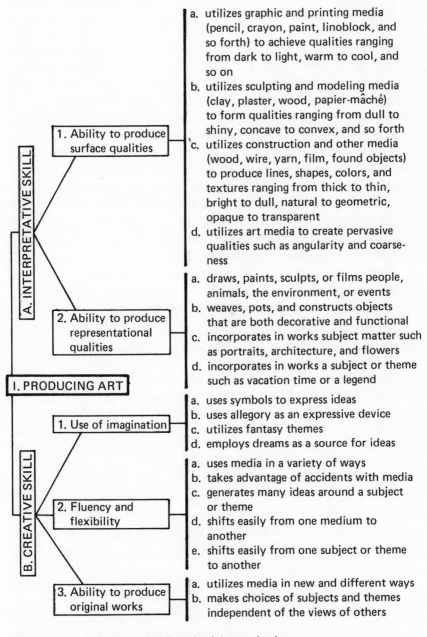

I. PRODUCING ART

A. INTERPRETATIVE SKILL

1. Ability to produce surface qualities

a. utilizes graphic and printing media (pencil, crayon, paint, linoblock, and so forth) to achieve qualities ranging from dark to light, warm to cool, and so on
b. utilizes sculpting and modeling media (clay, plaster, wood, papier-mâché) to form qualities ranging from dull to shiny, concave to convex, and so forth
c. utilizes construction and other media (wood, wire, yarn, film, found objects) to produce lines, shapes, colors, and textures ranging from thick to thin, bright to dull, natural to geometric, opaque to transparent
d. utilizes art media to create pervasive qualities such as angularity and coarseness

2. Ability to produce representational qualities

a. draws, paints, sculpts, or films people, animals, the environment, or events
b. weaves, pots, and constructs objects that are both decorative and functional
c. incorporates in works subject matter such as portraits, architecture, and flowers
d. incorporates in works a subject or theme such as vacation time or a legend

B. CREATIVE SKILL

1. Use of imagination

a. uses symbols to express ideas
b. uses allegory as an expressive device
c. utilizes fantasy themes
d. employs dreams as a source for ideas

2. Fluency and flexibility

a. uses media in a variety of ways
b. takes advantage of accidents with media
c. generates many ideas around a subject or theme
d. shifts easily from one medium to another
e. shifts easily from one subject or theme to another

3. Ability to produce original works

a. utilizes media in new and different ways
b. makes choices of subjects and themes independent of the views of others

Figure 3-1. Variables associated with producing art

from generation to generation and gives form to important ideas and events. Figure 3-2 presents many of the cognitive factors about the visual arts that need to be studied.

The belief that art is important is reflected in abilities to make critical judgments and in the appreciation of visual forms. These abilities, are, in turn, related to being capable of evaluating works of art through making both social and aesthetic appraisals and to being aware of relevant environmental and historical factors, as well as wanting to be involved personally in producing and evaluating art. The behaviors that flow from such goals appear in Figure 3-3.

I have found the above approach to stating goals particularly valuable in working with pre- and in-service teachers. It results, of course, from my digesting the approaches of many of my colleagues to which I have already alluded. But, because my scheme reflects the obvious domains of art education and contains listings of easily understood examples of behaviors associated with its basic goals, teachers of art can readily put it into operation.

Having explored several alternatives for thinking about and developing goals for art education, I shall now turn to the roles of teachers as they affect the practice of art education.

The Meaning and Significance of Roles

Roles are conceptions of what is done—the series of acts one performs—to achieve some aim, purpose, or goal. In sociological terms, roles are played or practiced in order to maintain one's status in social space. When the school is considered as a social institution, as it should be, many strata of status may be identified, and different roles may be distinguished that facilitate separating one stratum from another. It may be assumed, for example, that the principal has the highest status within the school, and he or she must fulfill role expectations if that status is to be maintained. Teachers have a somewhat lower status than the principal but a higher status than an attendance clerk, providing the teachers perform their roles as expected.

The primary tasks of teachers are to deal effectively with subject matter and to develop understandings and skills that are relevant to particular subjects and that will enable their pupils to function eventually as independent and contributing members of society.

It is obvious that teachers who successfully develop the aptitudes of their pupils have little difficulty in maintaining their status within the school's social hierarchy.

In our secondary schools, teachers usually function within the limits of a particular subject. And the relationships among their knowledge of the field, the status of the subject itself, and the status of the particular teacher within the school are often very evident. For example, an outstanding teacher of a low-status subject may have higher status within the school than a poor teacher of a high-status subject. Thus, it is extremely important that the teaching role be performed adequately, especially for the teacher of a low-status subject. The fact is significant within the field of art education because of the considerable number of data that establish it as a low-status subject within the secondary school (art is a graduation requirement in fewer than 10 percent of American high schools).

Elementary teachers are also concerned with the relationship between role and status, even though they must teach approximately twelve different subjects. Few elementary teachers have any depth of background in the visual arts. It would be foolish, therefore, to expect them to devote time and energy to teaching a subject that does not enjoy a high status and that they will probably teach poorly. Such actions would only contribute to diluting their role and to a subsequent loss of status. The obvious but difficult solution to this dilemma is to provide elementary teachers with many worthwhile art education materials plus inducements to utilize them effectively so that they may perform their role as effectively in the area of art as they do in other fields.

Roles as They Relate to Goals

Roles can also be conceived in ways that are useful in establishing the goals of art education. This view is reflected in the practice of organizing the subject on the basis of the roles performed by those who are involved in the production and analyses of art. Playing the roles of artist, art historian, and art critic will make up the content of the art course. Stated in other terms, when studying art in school, children should behave as artists do as they work with tools and materials; they should analyze works of art in terms of their historical consequences just as art historians would; and they should perform

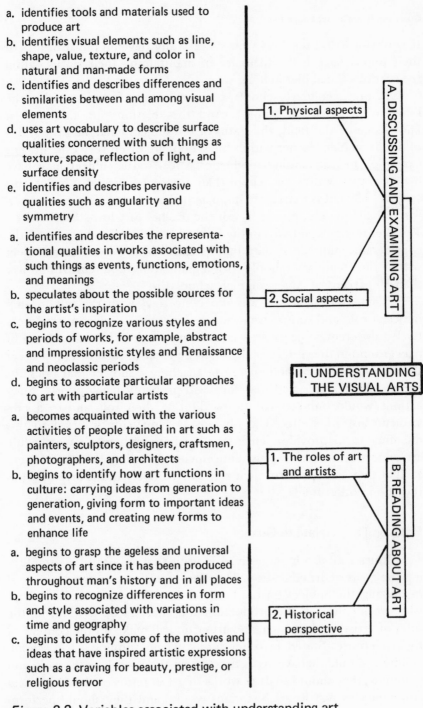

a. identifies tools and materials used to produce art
b. identifies visual elements such as line, shape, value, texture, and color in natural and man-made forms
c. identifies and describes differences and similarities between and among visual elements
d. uses art vocabulary to describe surface qualities concerned with such things as texture, space, reflection of light, and surface density
e. identifies and describes pervasive qualities such as angularity and symmetry

a. identifies and describes the representational qualities in works associated with such things as events, functions, emotions, and meanings
b. speculates about the possible sources for the artist's inspiration
c. begins to recognize various styles and periods of works, for example, abstract and impressionistic styles and Renaissance and neoclassic periods
d. begins to associate particular approaches to art with particular artists

a. becomes acquainted with the various activities of people trained in art such as painters, sculptors, designers, craftsmen, photographers, and architects
b. begins to identify how art functions in culture: carrying ideas from generation to generation, giving form to important ideas and events, and creating new forms to enhance life

a. begins to grasp the ageless and universal aspects of art since it has been produced throughout man's history and in all places
b. begins to recognize differences in form and style associated with variations in time and geography
c. begins to identify some of the motives and ideas that have inspired artistic expressions such as a craving for beauty, prestige, or religious fervor

1. Physical aspects

2. Social aspects

A. DISCUSSING AND EXAMINING ART

II. UNDERSTANDING THE VISUAL ARTS

1. The roles of art and artists

2. Historical perspective

B. READING ABOUT ART

Figure 3-2. Variables associated with understanding art

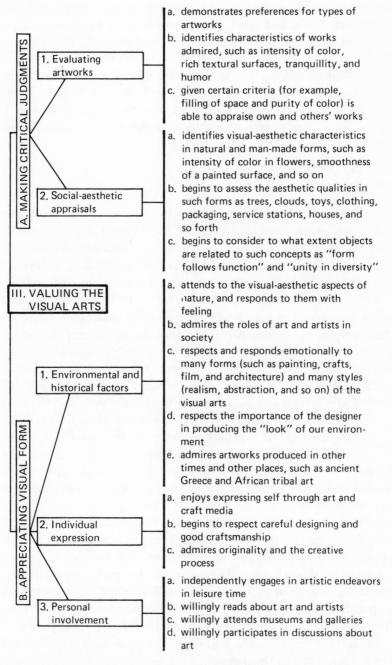

Figure 3-3. Variables associated with valuing art

as art critics when identifying and evaluating the meanings and merits in their own works and in all manner of visual aesthetic phenomena.

There is nothing revolutionary in relating goals and roles. But, if a delineation of roles is to have a meaningful effect upon the development of worthy goals, deliberate efforts will have to be made to answer in great detail several deceptively easy questions: How do artists behave? What is the nature of historical inquiry in art? And how do art critics function as they describe and evaluate the visual arts?

Roles and Teaching Styles

Another alternative for considering the concept of role is derived from psychology. In addition to defining roles in terms of social status or speculating about their relationships to the goals of art education, roles can also be considered as reflecting idiosyncratic tendencies associated with individual behavior. Every individual exhibits behavior that is rooted in heredity and in experiences undergone in the pursuit of solutions to problematic situations. He acquires behavioral patterns that affect the ways in which stimuli and tasks are perceived. Individual teachers also adopt ways of performing roles that reflect such behavior patterns. What they do is, therefore, a consequence of the nature of the milieu in which the task exists, the typical expectations associated with the role required to perform the task, and the personal behavior patterns exhibited by a teacher as he or she perceives the situation and performs accordingly. Since this chapter has emphasized the importance of the teacher's role in art education, it should prove worthwhile to stress how particular patterns of behavior may affect the ways roles are performed when one is teaching art.

To facilitate this discussion of teaching styles it is necessary to relate *how* one teaches to *what* is being taught. I shall use as an example the global goal of developing aesthetic sensibilities, referred to earlier in this chapter. This goal can be made somewhat more specific by stating that the teacher will attempt to develop within her pupils abilities for making aesthetic judgments. When dealing with goals and roles, we must also consider the level of sophistication of pupils. Our example will pertain to the primary level of schooling from kindergarten to third grade.

Before describing several alternative conceptions of teaching roles and how they may manifest themselves when one is attempting to develop aesthetic sensibilities, it is essential to clarify my conception of aesthetic judgment as it is used in this chapter.

The Meaning of Aesthetic Judgment

One of the four major components of art instruction identified in California's Framework for Art Education is the development of aesthetic judgment, which is defined as follows: "Aesthetic judgment involves the study of the visual, intellectual, and philosophical bases for understanding art and for making judgments about its form, content, technique, and purpose. Students' concern for their visual environment is enhanced as they learn to recognize, talk about, and work with the underlying structure of art. They also come to understand issues and to develop criteria for appraising visual forms and for arriving at personal preferences and opinions." While this definition delineates some of the tasks and outcomes associated with aesthetic judgment, it does not make explicit what occurs when one makes such judgments or how they differ from other kinds of judgments.

One can infer from Good's *Dictionary of Education* that aesthetic judgments are neither declaratory, related to a declaration of rights of parties or individuals; ethical, concerned with conduct and means and ends in relation to established norms and principles; nor moral, involving choices among principles, policies, or courses of action made in relation to some criterion of proper conduct.[9]

Aesthetic judgments are actually a form of value judgment. As such they constitute decisions about both the nature of experienced objects and those factors that regulate the formation of desires, affections, and enjoyments.[10] To distinguish between value judgments that are aesthetic and those that are not, it is necessary to define the term "aesthetic."

The term "aesthetic" has traditionally been viewed as an adjective that pertains to the beautiful quality of an object or event. It is a quality that is experienced immediately in contrast to what is arrived at through inference or reflective thought.[11] Aesthetic judgment refers, therefore, to a decision about the extent to which an object or event is adjudged beautiful.

The problem with this definition is the limitations of the term "beautiful" and other commonplace adjectives usually associated with it such as lovely, handsome, and pretty. To enlarge our view of what is aesthetic, we must go beyond dictionary definitions and attempt to describe its experiential variables. Such descriptions are essential in order to prepare curricula and evaluative instruments designed to develop and test abilities for making aesthetic judgments.

The Nature of Aesthetic Experience

When one looks at an object and assesses how it will help to accomplish a particular task, he is judging the instrumental value of the object. But when one looks at an object and responds to its inherent qualities of shape, texture, color, and scale, concern for the object itself is being expressed. Thus, for example, judging a painting on the basis of its relative merits as a monetary investment is very different from judging it as an object that evokes a sense of pleasure because of its celestial blue sky or the richness of its surface texture. Both responses are value judgments but the experiences associated with each are quite different.

Objects or events that are viewed in relation to their instrumental value include consideration of such factors as costs and profits and how an object or event will contribute to one's social status or aid in resolving problematic situations. Aesthetic experiences, in contrast, are characterized by their dependence upon the qualities inherent in the object or the event itself. For instance, one examines a suit or dress and responds to a felt relationship between the texture of the fabric and the shape or style of the garment; they appear to complement each other, and one is pleased to observe such coherence.

Other examples of aesthetic experiences might include responding with a sense of awe to the redness in the western sky at sunset, gasping at the fantastic scale of the Grand Canyon, being delighted by the reflections in a patent leather shoe, or being transformed into a state of euphoria while observing the exquisite delicacy of line and color in Botticelli's *Birth of Venus*. These examples have been limited to the pleasure one feels while responding to the physical qualities in well-organized or unusual visual situations. Other types of aesthetic response, however, strain the traditional definitions of the term aesthetic. One can encounter, for example, a work of art whose subject is the horror of war such as the series of etchings by that title created by Goya or Picasso's *Guernica*. Although it is true that one can focus on the beauty of line, the shape, or the value relationships in these works, what of the deep sense of horror and revulsion evoked by their subject? Such feelings cannot merely be attributed to the subject being depicted. These deeply felt responses occur because of the way formal qualities—lines, shapes, value, space, and so forth—are organized and the associations made with content that render a work meaningful to the viewer.

Aesthetic experience encompasses, then, not only responses to the physical attributes of objects or events. It also includes the cognitive act of drawing relationships between ideas and values acquired through prior experiences and the forms and meanings represented in current stimuli. This is the way, in fact, that Monroe C. Beardsley, the aesthetician, actually defines aesthetic experiences. He believes such experiences occur when formal interests (responses to color, shape, and texture) and commemorative interests (concern for things considered important or valuable) merge.[12]

Whether one is reacting to beauty, horror, or formal qualities, it is clear, however, that aesthetic responses are made to objects or events that are actually experienced. It can be concluded, therefore, that aesthetic judgments are those acts which establish the relative merits of physical phenomena as they are encountered by the senses and filtered through the intellect. This includes, of course, a vast variety of forms existing in nature and produced by man, in addition to those accorded the status of art. And many decisions about the value of these forms are made without special schooling. In other words, everyone, whether educated to do so or not, is making aesthetic judgments all the time. But what of the quality of these decisions? Are they all of the same magnitude? Do they all result in significantly enriched experiences?

Naive and Sophisticated Aesthetic Judgments

It is when one is contemplating the background required to respond deeply to the complexity in the works of a Botticelli, a Goya, or a Picasso that the necessity for being educated to make aesthetic judgments emerges. Looking at Grand Canyon and deciding that the scale of its formations and negative space is overwhelming can, in all probability, be accomplished simply as a consequence of maturing in an urban environment wherein such grandeur is rarely if ever observed and where popular standards, or cultural norms, as to what constitutes enormous size prevail. When one contrasts the Grand Canyon and what he has previously experienced, it does indeed stagger the imagination.

But how does one regard the fragility of the small yellow wild flower that grows on the rim of the canyon? Or, can popular norms provide the insights needed to respond to the linear qualities in the *Birth of Venus* and make judgments about the extent to which such qualities relate to its subject and theme? The differences between naive, culturally determined aesthetic responses and educated, aesthetic perception are eloquently stated in the following passage from Gotshalk.

If an object is markedly displeasing to him, the naive percipient is usually quick to push it aside or to take himself from its presence. If the object is very pleasing, he usually lapses intermittently into sentimental reflections upon it or into reveries, nostalgic, sexual, or heroic, depending on the subject matter. A thin line of pure aesthetic response or intrinsic perceptual appreciation usually runs through his experience, but the line is not only thin but usually broken in many places . . . .

Disciplined aesthetic experience is in most fundamental respects the exact opposite of naive aesthetic experience. Perhaps its most basic difference is in orientation. Disciplined aesthetic experience begins by taking a work of art not as a natural object momentarily viewed aesthetically, but as a work of art, a special type of creation. It is aware of the general character of art, its possibilities and limitations, and is not easily surprised or offended by a work simply because it differs from a natural object in perceptual appearance . . . .

Moreover, disciplined aesthetic experience is usually deeper as well as wider, since it is ordinarily much more analytical and brings to bear upon a work a much larger volume of relevant knowledge and training. Its appraisals also are usually far less dogmatic. It allows the work itself to speak out more fully, and its critical decisions customarily come as precipitates of a voluminous experience of apprehension rather than as a consequence of an instantaneous interaction between the object and fixed preconceptions that often have little to do with art or art criticism. Finally, disciplined aesthetic experience is ordinarily much more pure, sustained, and active than naive experience. At its best, it treats the work of art with the single-mindedness, seriousness, vigor, and respect that the creative artist presumably bestowed on it.[13]

Thus, to recapitulate, aesthetic judgments are decisions about the extent to which qualities and meanings associated with experienced objects or events evoke significant affective responses. Everyone makes aesthetic judgments, but there is a distinct difference between commonplace responses and those which are informed through educational processes designed to develop aesthetic literacy.

Alternative Approaches to Developing Educated Aesthetic Judgments

Curriculum makers could, of course, develop a list of sequential experiences designed to help children make better aesthetic judgments, and such a list could indeed reflect the behavior displayed by art critics as they perform their role. But the extent to which curriculum prescriptions are implemented is a function, at least in part, of the degree of compatability between the approach being advocated and a particular teacher's perceptual or teaching style. To clarify this point, I shall describe three somewhat different emphases in planning for the development of aesthetic sensibility in primary-grade children.

These alternatives reflect three types of teacher: the artistic-intuitive teacher who feels most comfortable when providing her pupils with opportunities to handle art media because of her familiarity with art processes and her belief in the virtues of manipulative experiences; the formalist-analytical teacher who is confident in her verbal abilities as well as her understanding of art processes and who seeks to acquaint her pupils with the elements of visual form and the principles of their organization; and the humanist-verbal teacher who has been "liberally educated" so that she comprehends something of the history of art and can verbalize about aspects of its social reality, but who lacks sufficient experience to emphasize studio activities within her classroom.

I have developed a series of charts that reflect these differences in orientation for both kindergarten and first-grade and for second- and third-grade teachers. Distinctions in grade level are based upon the variations in cognitive functioning between five- and six-year-olds and those who are seven and eight, as identified by Piaget.

Five- and six-year-olds are classified as "preoperational." They are, therefore, expected to cope with the physical world on the basis of sensorimotor activities and perceptual adaptations to stimuli. Their symbol representations are highly dependent upon direct experiences. Seven- to eight-year-olds are in the "operational" stage of

Table 3-1. Aesthetic judgment plan for the artistic-intuitive kindergarten or first-grade teacher

Pupils' objectives	Pupils' activities	Teacher's strategies
Explore opaque water color and discover that the intensity of colors can be altered by adding water. Describe variations in color intensity by using such terms as bright, dull, strong, and weak.	Paint with a large brush, three colors, and water, and make a variety of painted stripes, dots, and strokes using more or less water. Identify the differences in the qualities produced using appropriate art vocabulary.	Provide for each pupil three premixed colors, one dark and dull, one light and bright, and one of middle value and intensity (such as a blue mixed with black and a bit of orange, a bright yellow mixed with white, and a green straight from the container), a ¾" bristle brush, a container of water, and 18" x 24" newsprint or manila paper. Pupils should be encouraged to experiment with their paints, adding more or less water to create various effects.
Produce variations in the intensity of crayon colors and their dark and light qualities by utilizing more or less finger pressure as they draw. Identify verbally the variations produced while using such words as bright, dull, strong, weak, dark, and light.	Use primary crayons to produce strokes, dots, and circles while using more or less finger pressure to create thick and thin lines of varying intensity and value (dark and light).	Distribute 12" x 16" manila or fiber-tone paper, red, yellow, and blue primary crayons, and encourage pupils to produce a variety of effects. After the experimental period, a verbal review will be conducted that focuses attention upon an accurate description of the surface qualities produced.

Use colored chalks to produce a variety of lines and then describe them in terms such as straight, curved, thick, thin, up and down or side to side in direction.

Moisten their paper and then use three different colors of primary chalks to produce a variety of linear qualities. After their experimentation is concluded, they will tell about the visual effects they have discovered.

Provide for each pupil 12" x 16" colored construction paper (gray or tan), a wide-bristle brush, a container of water, and three sticks of primary chalks. Pupils will be directed to cover their paper with water, to create as many different kinds of lines as possible, and to attempt to identify variations in visual qualities they have created.

Manipulate clay and, after rolling, pinching, and pulling exercises, identify verbally the variations in dark and light qualities created as well as differences in surface texture.

Use a ball of soft clay, roll it around on a smooth surface, push and pound it with the palm of the hand, and pinch and pull it with thumb and forefinger. Employ words such as dark and light to describe differences in surfaces that have been pushed in or out, and rough and smooth for areas that are dimpled or lightly touched by one's fingers.

Prepare balls of buff clay for six to eight pupils and encourage pupils to experiment with the clay. Pupils will be told to use their palms and fingers to see how many different shapes and textures they can make. Pupils will be asked to describe the results of their explorations so that variations in surface qualities they have created will become apparent.

Produce simple animal forms out of clay by pulling out head and legs from torso core and then create textural variations with fingers or sticks that have relevance to the scale of the animal form.

Hold a ball of soft clay in one hand, pinch clay with thumb and forefinger of the other while pulling out legs and head. If animal is large and gross in form, pupils will make textures using finger pressure; if small, sticks will be used to create textural variations.

Prepare balls of clay for six to eight pupils at a time and demonstrate how to pull legs, head, or tail from central ball. Pupils should be allowed to practice "pulling" technique. They should be able to observe simple teacher-made demonstration pieces—one large clay form, the other small—that display the use of fingers or small sticks to create textural surfaces. Pupils should be asked to decide whether to use fingers or sticks to ...ure their animal forms.

Table 3-2. Aesthetic judgment plan for the artistic-intuitive second- or third-grade teacher

Pupils' objectives	Pupils' activities	Teacher's strategies
Create a visually rhythmic pattern by alternating thick and thin chalk lines drawn across wet paper and then describe both the linear variations created and the different feelings engendered in the works of fellow pupils.	Moisten paper and stroke across it with colored chalks using group-ings of thick and thin lines. Talk about their composition using terms such as thin, thick, fuzzy, and sharp and discuss feelings evoked by different arrangements of lines such as excited, calm, and pleased.	Provide each pupil with a 12″ x 16″ sheet of colored construction paper, water container, and brush. Pupils will be asked to select three colors of chalk, and their decisions should be based upon the color of the paper and the feelings they want to evoke; for example, yellow, orange, and red lines on a gray paper will generate excite-ment while light blue, medium blue, and green lines on the same paper will evoke a sense of calmness.
Make crayon portraits altering crayon pressure to control the intensity of the colors utilized in order to focus attention on particular facial features or expressions.	Draw either self-portraits using a mirror or sketch their fellow pupils. Emphasize facial features judged un-usual by utilizing the point of the crayon with greater finger pressure to produce more intense and darker colors; subtle areas can be rendered by using the side of crayons with slight finger pressure.	Allow each pupil to draw himself or someone else and provide crayons of five colors (yellow, red, blue, brown, and black) that have been broken in half with the paper removed and 9″ x 12″ or 12″ x 16″ fibertone paper. Pupils will experiment briefly using the point and side of their crayons; this will be followed by teacher's demon-stration of how to emphasize facial features through varying degrees of crayon pressure.

Paint an outdoor scene and alter intensity of colors to create variations in dark and light and dull and bright qualities associated with the theme of the painting.

Use opaque water colors to create a painting wherein colors are selected because they are relevant to a pre-determined theme such as sunny or cloudy day, celebration, or fantasy.

Provide tempera paints in primary colors and black and white within egg cartons. Pupils should be encouraged to experiment with mixing color—primaries making secondary colors, white for tinting colors, black for shading, and using water to dilute the intensity of colors. This will be followed by painting an outdoor subject on 18" x 24" manila paper in relation to a theme chosen by the pupil. Alternative examples will have to be shown to or demonstrated for pupils; for example, the subject of one's backyard can be painted in dull and shaded colors (cloudy day), strong and tinted colors (sunny day), or colors unrelated to nature (fantasy).

Experiment with buff and terra-cotta clays and note differences in their color, texture, and structural properties. Create a sculptural form using fingers to produce negative spaces and surface textures.

Work with two types of clay and carefully examine similarities and differences. Create two forms that are similar, utilizing buff clay for one and terra-cotta for the other. Spatial and textural qualities will be appraised, and variations will be identified that are due to the nature of the two clay bodies, such as more light being reflected off the buff clay piece and the tactile texture or terra-cotta being more coarse.

Encourage pupils to explore each clay body thoroughly while answering such questions as: Which one is easier to push, pull, twist, or pinch? Which one seems stronger? Which is most flexible? Which is smoother? Pupils should be asked to use terms such as "negative space" to describe the openings they create in clay and "solid" or "volume" for the actual clay areas they produce.

Table 3-3. Aesthetic judgment plan for the formalist-analytical kindergarten or first-grade teacher

Pupils' objectives	Pupils' activities	Teacher's strategy
Draw an abstract line picture using a variety of lines to delineate objects; construct a "shapes-only" abstract picture using cut-paper shapes. Linear qualities and variations in shapes thus produced will be identified and listed.	Use crayons to draw a picture consisting of lines only and cut from colored construction paper shapes that will be pasted down on another sheet of paper to form a cut-paper composition. They will be asked to identify lines and shapes using such adjectives as straight, curved, zigzag, round, oval, vertical, horizontal, large, and small.	Provide pupils with crayons and 12" x 16" newsprint or manila paper, and scissors, paste, three pieces of 6" x 6" colored construction paper, and one piece of 12" x 16" manila paper. Pupils should be encouraged to explore the fullest range of possibilities without regard for making a literal, pictorial statement.
Observe their classroom environment and discuss its characteristics by identifying variations in line, shape, texture, dark and light qualities, color, size, and space.	Identify visual qualities in their classroom distinguishing between the size and shape of doors, windows, and bulletin board; the colors and textures of walls and woodwork; and spaces between and within objects.	Direct the attention of pupils to the visual qualities in the classroom while asking questions such as: Where is the brightest blue in the room? Where is the largest rectangle? Where is the roughest texture? Where is a shape that is repeated again and again, but that may differ in size?

Take a nature walk and identify variations in color (range of greens in trees and shrubs), texture (surfaces of tree bark, brick walls), and shapes (flowers, trees, doors, windows, buildings, cars).

Examine visual qualities as they exist in nature and man-made environment and observe the diversity of colors, textures, and shapes and how they are altered in appearance by the action of direct and reflected light and shade.

Prepare pupils for nature walks by informing them that they are to identify the "nature" of things: the shapes, colors, and textures in buildings and cars, as well as colors in the sky, and the shapes, colors, and textures in trees and flowers. Pupils should be shown examples of what is meant by such variations prior to their walk.

Create a variety of patterns with cut paper by alternating rectangular and curved shapes and dark and light qualities, identify differences in visual qualities in their own and other pupils' works, and speculate about the different feelings evoked by alternative arrangements.

Cut out of colored construction paper a series of geometric patterns (dittoed) and group them so that a rhythmical pattern is created, such as two circles, a bar, two circles, a bar, and so on. They should strive to complete a full page that reflects consistent patterning of angular and curved shapes. They need to verbalize about the differences they observe between their own and others' works.

Prepare dittoed colored construction paper sheets, distribute scissors, and demonstrate how shapes can be cut by turning paper as one cuts. Provide paste and sheet of 12" x 16" manila paper. Pupils should be directed to describe the differences between their own works and those of their peers in terms of variations in visual qualities such as angular or curved shapes being most important because of size or color, and so forth.

Table 3-4. Aesthetic judgment plan for the formalist-analytical second- or third-grade teacher

Pupil's objectives	Pupils' activities	Teacher's strategy
Create abstract works using only lines or only shapes in response to a requirement to reflect certain ideas, feelings, or moods in their composition, such as making a line composition called "in a boat" or "walking to school" and constructing a shape picture with cut-out construction paper titled "buildings" or "jumping around."	Paint or crayon sketch a line composition or a picture using only shapes that emphasize a mood or feeling one associates with a subject, object, or activity, such as using wavy, undulating lines of varying thickness to convey the feeling of movement; making straight, curved, and angular lines associated with walking in on a sidewalk, down a curb, around a tree, and up several steps; placing many rectangles together to simulate a cityscape; or placing rectangles haphazardly to simulate the agitation of jumping.	Provide paints or crayons in limited colors—three per pupil—to allow one to focus attention on qualities of line and shape. Pupils should be confronted with a series of teacher-made charts that show how lines and shapes can be organized to convey different feelings.
Observe their environments at home and school and develop lists of art terms that describe the visual qualities encountered: for example, dark brown, roughly textured roof, red-orange brick wall, huge palm tree with brown, hairy texture bark and sharply pointed green leaves that look like lines coming out of a central core.	Make a list of art terms that describe the qualities of the visual phenomena encountered in their environments. They will share their lists with their fellow pupils in order to enlarge their functional vocabularies.	Require listings of visual qualities from pupils and set up a room display that incorporates the terms they have utilized; for example, tack up several pupil-made lists of visual qualities along with a display of photographs and reproductions and then attach colored yarn from a given word or phrase to its visual counterpart.

Collect all kinds of "found" objects and classify them according to similarities in shape, texture, and color; for instance, round and smooth objects can be placed together, as can all cool-colored objects or warm-colored and rough-textured objects.

Discriminate between large-small dark-light, dull-bright, rough-smooth, and warm-cool qualities in their own works, the works of others, and objects in the environment. Begin to describe the ideas generated and feelings experienced when visual qualities are encountered, such as the sense of sharpness conveyed by a rectangular, cool blue shape, the feeling of mystery associated with a series of dark green shapes painted on a blue-green background, or the elegance reflected in strong vertical columns resting on a horizontal base.

Make a collection of a variety of items ranging from buttons and seashells to bits of tree bark and string, and organize them in relation to their visual qualities; charts and box displays can be employed in order to share "collections" with classmates.

Make judgments about the extent to which observed visual elements are experienced aesthetically; thus, shapes are felt because of their angularity or roundness, line movements because of their stability or agility, colors because of their warmth, brightness, or coolness, and textures because of their smoothness and hardness, roughness and softness. Pupils will begin also to use qualifying terms to describe their feelings when experiencing, for instance, a bright but small red dot against a pale blue background in contrast to a huge orange square placed upon a gray background.

Encourage pupils to develop a collection of found objects and supervise the organization and display of items brought to class.

Develop a series of charts or a felt board display that shows visual elements occurring in various relationships, such as curling black lines over a large lemon yellow circle and vice versa. Photographs of nature and reproductions of artworks should also be collected and displayed. Pupils will be encouraged to describe the visual elements in these pieces and make judgments about the kinds of feelings and ideas they generate.

Table 3-5. Aesthetic judgment plan for the humanist-verbal kindergarten or first-grade teacher

Pupils' objectives	Pupils' activities	Teacher's strategy
Match visual qualities in artworks with those they have produced themselves.	Examine their own works and select a particular quality such as a strong red or round shape and then attempt to identify a similar quality within works being exhibited.	Mount an exhibition of reproductions and demonstrate how to find visual qualities in one's own work and in the works of others.
View reproductions of artworks and identify verbally variations in color, line, and spatial qualities such as strong or weak, bright or dull, and dark and light colors, and thick or thin, straight, curved, or angular lines and shapes.	Look at reproductions of paintings and identify which work possesses the strongest blue and greatest variety of lines (Pollock), many angular shapes (Picasso), and the brightest red and many textures (Marin). View each work and describe its obvious surface qualities.	Display reproductions such as: *Composition* by Pollock, *Man with a Pipe* by Picasso, and *From the Bridge* by Marin. Pupils should be directed to identify obvious qualities in each work.

View photographs of sculptural forms and identify verbally obvious light and dark areas and textural variations created by alterations in negative and positive space and surface treatment.

Examine photographs of sculptural works and select the work that possesses the greatest dark-light contrast because of its deep space (Moore), least textural contrast because of its smooth surface (Brancusi), and repeated linear movements because of the way stone is carved to show hair and the folds in clothing (Mestrovic).

Display photographs of works such as: *Madonna and Child* by Moore, *Bird in Flight* by Brancusi, and *My Mother* by Mestrovic. Pupils should be asked to examine photographs carefully and then respond to questions about visual qualities that seem to contribute to their aesthetic impact.

Identify from an exhibit of reproductions and photographs works that meet the following criteria: a happy scene; very strong dark and light contrast; a lonely scene; a feeling of strength and power; a peaceful scene.

View reproductions and make judgments about visual qualities and their meanings such as: bright colors in the "happy" painting by Prendergast, the strongly shaded areas in the "stormy" scene by Innes, subdued colors and sense of loneliness in a work by Wyeth, strong diagonals and vertical movements in the powerful painting by Stella; and empty space and stillness in the work by Homer.

Provide opportunities for pupils to make judgments while viewing works such as: *Central Park* by Prendergast, *Coming Storm* by Innes, *April Wind* by Wyeth, *The Brooklyn Bridge* by Stella, and *Boys in the Pasture* by Homer.

Table 3-6. Aesthetic judgment plan for the humanist-verbal first- or second-grade teacher

Pupils' objectives	Pupils' activities	Teacher's strategy
Observe reproductions of paintings and identify variations in surface qualities such as color intensities, dark and light areas, and visual textures. Begin to interpret meanings in such works by attempting to describe expressive qualities such as happiness, tension, sadness, anger, and loneliness.	Examine reproductions and locate visual qualities and interpret such meanings as clear colors and sharp value contrast in a happy painting by Grandma Moses, strong dark and light contrasts and opposing linear movements in a tense work by Delacroix, somber colors and subdued contrasts in a sad and moody work by Rembrandt, stark dark and light contrast and tortured shapes in an angry painting by Picasso, and static movement in a quiet and lonely work devoid of people by Hopper.	Provide reproductions that include *Joy Ride* by Grandma Moses, *Frightened Horse* by Delacroix, *Study of an Old Man* by Rembrandt, *Guernica* by Picasso, and *Seven A.M.* by Hopper. Encourage pupils to be specific when identifying surface qualities and to think carefully about the kinds of events they have experienced so that appropriate associations can be made when speculating about ideas and feelings engendered by artworks.
Examine several photographs of sculpture, select a particular work, and discuss the material used, its formal characteristics, and its possible meanings.	Observe photographs of sculptural forms from ancient Egypt, tribal Africa, or pre-Columbian America. Identify the medium used and variations in dark and light and textural qualities using such terms as stone, deep space-absorbed light, shallow space-reflected light (Egyptian cat); carved wood, rough texture (Baluba mask); terra-cotta clay, smooth texture (Colima dog). Pupils will also note differences in the ideas conveyed by such diverse forms as the elegance of the Egyptian cat, the dramatic strength in the Baluba mask, and the playful humor in the Mexican dog.	Arrange a display of photographs of sculptural forms and ask pupils to identify variations in media and spatial and textural qualities and to speculate about how such qualities make them feel when, for instance, they are making comparisons between the smoothness of the Egyptian cat and the Mexican dog and the deep rhythmic carving in the Baluba mask.

Examine reproductions or artworks, select a particular work, identify its form and the medium used, and describe its most obvious surface qualities and its subject and theme.

Begin to make a more complete analysis of artworks. Identify the form (drawing, painting, print); the medium employed (pencil, chalk, oil paint, watercolor, woodblock, copper plate); obvious surface qualities (colors, shapes, textures); subject matter (landscape, still life, portrait, historical event); and theme (storm, elegance, power, war).

Develop charts and display relevant examples to help explain how art forms, media, surface qualities, subject, and theme can be identified.

View sculptural works and make judgments about what appear to be the essence of a work in terms of its most characteristic visual qualities.

Examine examples of sculptural works and make judgments about their most obvious visual qualities and the ideas and feelings that they might convey; for instance, soft curves and slight depressions add up to a calm and peaceful feeling in a sculptural portrait of a young Buddha; angular qualities and strong diagonals convey a sense of both strength and gracefulness in a statuette of a draped Greek warrior; or a mobile by Calder with its soft angular and brightly colored shapes that are repeated with subtle alterations while moving constantly may provoke a sense of fantasy, easy variation, and a feeling of pleasure.

Provide a display of photographs of sculptural works. Ask pupils to identify qualities and interpret meanings in relation to both the forms observed and the objects and events they had experienced previously.

Examine photographs of architecture and identify obvious formal qualities (rectangular, square, curvilinear, smooth, transluscent, opaque) and apparent functions (domestic, commercial, industrial, educational).

Look at an exhibit of architectural objects and make simple judgments about their form and function, such as identifying the pointed, soaring arches in a Gothic cathedral as a device for calling attention to the "paradise" existing in the sky; noting the interlocking triangles in a geodesic dome designed to enclose space without any other internal vertical supports; describing the rectangular purity of a glass-covered skyscraper that reflects both light and images and thereby provides an enclosure for space that is ever changing in appearance; and identifying in the design of an airport terminal the graceful curve in the roof and the diagonal columns that support it, which, together, convey a sense of lightness and strength associated with the airplane.

Organize a display of architectural forms such as the interior of Chartres Cathedral, the geodesic dome of the American Pavilion at Expo '67 designed by Fuller, the Seagram Building designed by Mies van der Rohe, and Dulles Airport designed by Saarinen. Charts or blackboard drawings that diagram various architectural forms should also be provided.

their development. They are capable of ranging mentally forward and backward in time but only in relation to concrete, existing objects and people. Neither they nor their five- and six-year-old schoolmates are capable of dealing with abstract theories and propositions, according to Piaget.[14]

Table 3-1 represents a plan suited to the kindergarten or first-grade teacher who would rely primarily upon art activities to nurture aesthetic sensibilities. Her pupils would explore a variety of basic art-making media to discover visual qualities that would be identified and codified into concepts and terminology utilized when one is making aesthetic judgments.[15]

Table 3-2 presents a plan for the same type of teacher but at the second- or third-grade level. The emphasis is still upon manipulating art media, but activities would generate more complex vocabulary, and pupils would be expected to utilize images acquired through previous sensory encounters.

The plans for teachers in kindergarten and the first grade and those in the second or third grade who would emphasize analyzing the formal elements associated with visual phenomena are represented in Tables 3-3 and 3-4. Such teachers would utilize art activities and careful observation of the environment as the vehicles for identifying and reflecting upon the visual constituents that contribute to the formulation of aesthetic judgments.

And Tables 3-5 and 3-6 indicate the approaches that may be utilized by these two groups of teachers who are inclined to focus upon existing art works. They would have their pupils range over a wide variety of forms and guide them toward identifying visual qualities as well as interpreting their possible meanings.

Thus, in conclusion, it seems obvious that a well-prepared teacher could incorporate the suggestions within all of these charts and, thereby, provide a comprehensive program for her pupils. In so doing she would also be developing perceptual and expressive skills, an understanding of art history, and abilities for making aesthetic judgments. But my purpose in developing these charts was to demonstrate that there are alternative roads to developing aesthetic sensibilities; that one need not be an artist, historian, or critic to do so; and that significant *goals* for the nurturing of children's artistic behavior can be formulated while one is performing teaching roles that reflect variations in background and disposition.

Notes

1. A detailed description of this study is provided in Ronald Silverman and Ralph Hoepfner, *Developing and Evaluating Art Curricula Specifically Designed for Disadvantaged Youth*, Final Report, Project No. 6-1657 (Washington, D.C.: Office of Education, 1969).

2. Further support for this view is provided in a review of related research reported in Ronald H. Silverman, "What Research Tells Us about Motivating Students for Art Activity," *Art Education*, XXIV (May 1971), 27-31.

3. A brief but excellent article that delineates distinctions among aims, goals, and objectives is Arthur Efland, "Evaluating Goals for Art Education," *Art Education*, XXVII (February 1974), 8-10.

4. A review and critique of these taxonomies are provided in Daniel Tanner, *Using Behavioral Objectives in the Classroom* (New York: Macmillan, 1972).

5. One example of an interpretation of Woodruff's conception produced by a participant in the NAEA Training Institutes is Virginia Brouch, *Art Education: A Matrix System for Writing Behavioral Objectives* (Phoenix: Arbo Publishing Co., 1973).

6. Manuel Barkan, Laura Chapman, and Evan Kern, *Guidelines for Curriculum Development for Aesthetic Education* (St. Ann, Mo.: CEMREL, 1970).

7. Laura Chapman, "Subject Matter for the Study of Art," *Art Education*, XX (February 1967), 20-22.

8. California State Department of Education, *Art Education Framework* (Sacramento: Bureau of Publications, 1971), 7.

9. *Dictionary of Education*, ed. Carter Good (New York: McGraw-Hill, 1959), 305.

10. *Ibid.*, 594.

11. *Webster's New World Dictionary* (New York: World Publishing Co., 1957), 18.

12. Monroe C. Beardsley, "Art and the Arts," *World Book Encyclopedia* (Chicago: Field Enterprises Educational Corp., 1965), I, 710-714.

13. D. W. Gotshalk, *Art and the Social Order* (New York: Dover Publications, 1962), 160-161.

14. Mary Ann Pulaski, *Understanding Piaget* (New York: Harper and Row, 1971).

15. These plans were initially developed pursuant to a contract with the Office of the Los Angeles County Superintendent of Schools for "Developing and Implementing Aesthetic Judgment Curricula for the Primary Grades."

4

Changing Views of Children's Artistic Development: Their Impact on Curriculum and Instruction

ARTHUR D. EFLAND

In the autumn of 1973 I came upon a draft copy of the doctoral dissertation of my late colleague Manuel Barkan written in 1951.[1] I was interested in his approach to theory development for art education. The dissertation was eclectic in approach, drawing upon knowledge and generalizations from a variety of fields such as sociology, psychology, philosophy, and anthropology. It attempted to synthesize these into a foundation that could more adequately provide a rational basis for the practice of art education than had heretofore been available. Following are some of the questions that occurred to me.

First, could we today proceed to develop a framework or foundation either by the approach he used, or some refinement of it? Is the knowledge pertaining to our field sufficiently clear to permit a coherent synthesis of views, or are there too many confounding facts and conflicting values to allow for the formation of a foundation or a framework rationalizing our practice?

Second, if we assume that a foundation could be formulated with the current knowledge we possess, what would it look like? How would it differ or be similar to his synthesis of twenty-three years ago?

Finally, how would such a framework or foundation serve us today? Will it lessen the gap between practice and theory? Will it make the task of rationalizing our goals easier? Will it accord the field of art education the status of a discipline?

Answers to such questions would require either a far more ambitious analysis or a more foolhardy speculation than I could undertake in this chapter. For that reason I have decided to ignore these questions for the moment. I shall, instead, deal with a small piece of the problem, that is, I shall examine a concept that recurs in different forms in various views or theories of art education including that of Barkan's: the concept of the "child" and the nature of his artistic activity. The various views of the child, children's art, and the explanations offered of what this development entails form one of the fundamental underpinnings of a theory of art education. It is necessary to distinguish, at the outset, between a theory of children's art and a theory of art education. The first tries to describe a phenomenon such as children's drawing and explain why children draw the way they do, or why they respond to certain artistic stimuli and not others. It tries to explain the facts pertaining to artistic behavior in children. The second may contain a theory of children's art, but it does more. It attempts to prescribe desirable teaching methods, content of art instruction, and appropriate activities. A theory of art education tries to answer the basic curriculum questions: what to teach, how to teach, and to whom to teach. It deals with the questions of when to teach and, in some cases, whether to teach at all. It may attempt to arrive at answers to these questions by examining contending views of the nature of art, the creative process by which art is produced, and views regarding the response to art. It seeks to locate the place of the visual arts within the cultural heritage in general and within contemporary society in particular, for purposes of arguing for its place within the school curriculum.

As stated above, a theory of art education would offer prescriptions in the form of goals and objectives and may indicate content and activities through which such content is pursued. Such goals ultimately rest upon certain assumptions concerning the worth of the individual, beliefs about the nature of art, and the view of society held by the writers of the theory.

A theory of art education makes little or no pretense at being scientific in the sense that it can explain or predict events with the certitude of a physical law. That is not its primary purpose. Rather, it is an attempt to develop a network of knowledge, beliefs, values, and opinions constructed by means of facts and arguments into a coherent conceptual structure that has as its primary purpose to provide the members of a profession with common definitions, terminology, concepts, and patterns of discourse. It provides the members of a profession with an agenda and a basis for communication upon common problems. The value of a theory of art education lies primarily in its communicative utility.

Childhood Concepts in the History of Art Education

Around the end of the nineteenth century, views regarding the nature of childhood began to influence the practice of art teaching. Art was previously taught by means that were derived more or less from prevailing conceptions of art—conceptions such as those developed by European academies or views of art developed by a particular teacher. Walter Smith was invited by the Massachusetts legislature to establish the Massachusetts Normal Art School in 1871.[2] His methodology evolved without the least reference to the nature of child development. The system of instruction consisted of a series of copy exercises.[3] It differed from academic methods of drawing instruction that entailed the use of drawing from live models. The exercises were sequenced in an order of increasing complexity. Training was for the purpose of developing proper visual and motor habits.[4] His curriculum was geared to the production of "masters of industrial drawing" rather than the production of art for an aesthetic purpose. This rigorously utilitarian concept of art dictated the character of his curriculum rather than a concept of child development. It should be remembered, though, that his methods were not intended for use with children. Logan quoted a passage from Smith's *Industrial Drawing* to show that his young daughter did not agree with him on the proper mode of representation. He wrote: "She is wildly indignant with me at any faults I point out, and simply turns and thrashes me if I point out a faulty line." His daughter had every right to protest since his methodology was not fashioned for children of her age.

The prevailing nineteenth-century explanation of why children draw the way they do was a naive view based upon the supposition that children were simply untrained and untutored in the use of the proper skills and that they had not developed good habits of observation to produce drawings that exhibited correct proportions and perspective. The prevailing style of art was naturalism or realism in which the work of art was conceived of as a mirror held up to nature. The artist was a camera. Later theories concerning children's art attempted to use psychological explanations to account for the characteristics found in their drawings. Some examples of these early psychological views are given by Arnheim in his book *Art and Visual Perception*.[5] But, in the last decades of the nineteenth century, such views were not yet available.

A writer who was to have an enormous influence upon early childhood education in the twentieth century, reveals much the same view regarding children's art.

Even the smallest children try spontaneously to draw outlines of objects which they see, but the hideous drawings which are exhibited in the common schools as "free drawings," "characteristic" of childhood, are not found among our children. These horrible daubs so carefully collected, observed and catalogued by modern psychologists as "documents of the infant mind" are nothing but monstrous expressions of intellectual lawlessness; they show only that the eye of the child is uneducated, the hand inert, the mind insensible alike to the beautiful and the ugly, blind to the true as well as to the false. Like most documents collected by psychologists who study the children of our schools, they reveal not the soul, but the errors of the soul; and these drawings, with their monstrous deformities, show simply what the uneducated human being is like. Such things are not "free drawings" by children. Free drawings are only possible when we have a free child who has been allowed to grow and perfect himself in the assimilation of his surroundings and in mechanical reproduction; and who, when left to create and express himself, actually does create and express himself.[6]

That polemic attacking untutored child art and psychologists who deign to study such things was made by Madame Montessori. Though she was generally regarded as an advocate of spontaneous expression in children, she seems to reject such manifestations when they occur, apparently on aesthetic and moral grounds. Only when certain mechanical procedures were imposed upon the eye and the hand was the child deemed free to produce art that is "spontaneous" or, rather, art that conforms to her expectations of what art is.

Another dominating personality who was to have an enormous influence upon art education in the early part of the century was Arthur Wesley Dow. Dow's concepts of teaching were also derived from his views regarding the nature of art rather than from a particular conception of children's artistic development. As a young man studying in Paris he became dissatisfied with the sterile academicism of European schools. With the help of the curator of the Boston Museum, Fenollosa, he developed a method of art instruction that he was later to call a "synthetic"[7] approach as distinguished from the academic approaches favored in the art academies. He maintained that there are a few fundamental ideas common to all fine arts and that the function of instruction is to use these elements and principles to create progressively complex compositions, beginning with simple harmonies of lines. At the heart of his doctrine was the formalism of Clive Bell.[8] Munro wrote of Dow's approach in 1929, seven years after his death.

To a mature and scientific mind such a schematic analysis of art is undeniably interesting, and to the teacher, it may be helpful as a reference map of the field. But to suppose it as a method of creating beautiful forms is to reveal a decided lack of familiarity with the psychology of aesthetic creation. New and vital plastic forms are rarely, if ever, conceived through such a course of plodding synthesis, but rather all at once as a new vision, the product, largely impulsive and automatic, of many experiences in looking at nature and art with a selective and reconstructive eye.[9]

Smith and Dow illustrate the fact that some of the early views of teaching art made almost no reference to the nature of childhood and to the nature of the accommodations that might be necessary in order that school-age children might benefit from art instruction. The feeling that children had some special needs to which educators should give attention began to occur with the advent of the kindergarten and the child study movements, which were then getting under way. Kindergarten education was given great impetus in the United States by Elizabeth Peabody.[10] She had visited Froebel in Germany and after seeing his work became one of his ardent disciples. For the first time the creative impulse in children was recognized and given encouragement. The emphasis in teaching slowly began to shift from the subject to the child. Related to this movement in education was the manual training movement in which simple crafts and constructive activities were introduced into the elementary classroom. In a book entitled *What and How* Palen and Henderson describe and advocate such activities as clay modeling, sewing, papercraft, and sticklaying: "We place in their fingers pencils with which to draw apples or form letters before they have the finger control to guide the pencil or the training of the eye to see intelligently that which is set before them . . . . Give him instead a nice soft piece of clay. Now watch the transformation. Now he smiles over this pliable mass! How careful the touch and pat! How proud of the finished product!"[11] Their concept of handwork and of learning through the senses was not as profound as that of Froebel, who thought that sensory learning was actually superior to book learning for early childhood. For Palen and Henderson craftwork was simply a nice transition from the "freedom of the home to the restraint of the classroom," but one can cite this book and others of the period as evidence of a changing climate of opinion regarding the nature of childhood. There was a greater effort to tailor learning activities to children's abilities and interests, and this tendency led some art educators to question the heretofore logical and systematic approaches to instruction advocated by Smith and Dow.

In 1881 G. Stanley Hall had established the first child study center at Johns Hopkins University.[12] He and his followers discovered that the child had an emotional life as well as a corporeal existence and that his education depended upon expression as well as impression. The effect of this concept was to broaden the scope of content and to begin to shift the emphasis in art education from the product to the child.

Of this development Henry Turner Bailey, one of the key figures in art education at the turn of the century, was to write: "Paidology (the science of the child) is revealing much to us. We are beginning to follow the lead of the child in education. When unrestrained, he has always expressed himself by means of drawing almost the first day in school. Such free expression has been disregarded or discountenanced; now it is fostered and studied, for it is the germ of artistic graphic expression, and the basis for technical instruction."[13]

In the period between the turn of the century and World War I, many educators began to fit the insights of Froebel with those gleaned from child study in what was to become known as the "child-centered school." Francis Wayland Parker was one of the first to plead for a curriculum that capitalized upon the natural spontaneity of children. "Every child has the artist element born in him; he loves to model objects out of sand and clay. Paint is a perfect delight to children, bright colors charm them. Give a child a paint brush, and though his expression will be very crude, it will be very satisfactory to him; he will paint any object with the greatest confidence."[14]

Cizek and His Followers

After World War I, the progressive education movement was growing in America. Many of Parker's and Dewey's ideas were put into practice. Dow's simple exercises in composition and arrangement were supplanted by a new and more potent influence: the teachings of Franz Cizek, whose interest in children's art began with his observations of the children of a carpenter's family with whom he lodged as an art student. Watching and encouraging their efforts, he noted that all children draw with some similarity but not schematically. Only adults are schematic in the sense that they have learned to accept certain visual conventions such as linear perspective. On journeys to other countries he found again and again that children draw many of the same things and in the same way, and it seemed that they followed unconsciously certain eternal laws of form.[15] What interested American progressive educators were Cizek's statements about his methods: "Method poisons art . . . . In his class he makes no suggestions to the children unless they ask for them. He gives no orders. What he does is give sympathy and understanding to stimulate the childish imaginations."[16] Rugg reported that Cizek would answer the puzzled queries of visitors to his studio: "I take off the lid and other art masters clap the lid on—that is the only difference."[17]

According to Munro, Cizek was against having children copy from nature or go to museums to look at the work of great artists of the past. He believed that creative expression must come from within. In his critique of Cizek, Munro noticed that certain "unconscious influences" had been at work influencing the children. "The teacher himself, first of all, was doing more than he realized; in no other way could the marked likenesses between the pictures be explained . . . pictures exhibited on the walls are imitated, especially when thought to represent the teacher's preference . . . . Finally, the student is sure to see current art outside the school."[18] Munro observed quite correctly that neither the conscious removal of directive influences nor the unconscious effects of haphazard ones provided the student with a means of continuous growth. "A few years of undirected toying with art materials had been enough to exhaust its attractiveness, and he (the student) had come to demand something more substantial to bite down on mentally, some intellectual food for his growing curiosity about the world. For this next step in development the free expression method had no help to offer him: nothing but the vague advice to keep on being himself, and doing whatever he wanted."[19]

The work of Cizek had undeniable appeal. What is more, it seemingly required nothing from the teacher except the directive of "taking off the lid." The typical progressive educator, felt, therefore, that it was the ideal method of teaching art to children. This was particularly true of the teacher who knew little or nothing about art. All one had to do was give the child complete freedom, and he would create masterpieces.

MacDonald writes that three factors contributed to the recognition of children's art: studies in psychology regarding children's artistic development, the growth of interest in primitive art, and the appreciation of the characteristics of modern art.

The downfall of academic high art at the end of the nineteenth century, the inrush of colorful post-impressionist work shortly afterwards, made possible for the first time a comparison between child and adult art. Child art, primitive art, tribal art, western Asiatic art were no longer regarded as crude, but rather as sensitive and expressive forms of art. Sir Herbert Read rightly stated that it was a growing appreciation of primitive art and revolutionary developments in painting which helped to bring children's art within the general range of aesthetic appreciation.[20]

Montessori, as discussed earlier, could not look at children's art as it was, because she was not able to look at modern painting. Cizek's career reveals the presence of the three elements that contributed to his strong advocacy of children's art. At the time he entered the *Akademie der Bilden Kunste* in Vienna, the beginnings of such modern stirrings were being felt. He studied and worked with a group of designers and architects who were influenced by the arts and crafts movement of England and who were becoming attracted to art nouveau. As a group they abhorred academic art and felt the need for a more creative modern art. The group founded the *Sezession* movement in 1897, and they were highly influenced by the antirealist tendencies of Klimt, whose pictures were filled with the pattern and symbolic shapes associated with art nouveau.[21]

It should be noted that the German name for art nouveau was *Jugendstil*, which is translated literally as "the style of the young." Cizek's ideas gained currency because he saw children's art "as an art which only a child can produce," to be cherished for its own aesthetic qualities. It was Klimt and his circle who, according to MacDonald, urged Cizek to seek permission to create his *Jugend Kunst Klasse*, which was founded in 1897 and lasted until the Nazi occupation of Austria in 1938. Other artists such as Klee studied children's art in the same way that Picasso and Modigliani studied and borrowed from African sculpture. Robert Goldwater notes that Kandinsky saw in the art of the child "a direct expression of the interior essence of things," a quality he conceived of as important to all art, but he suggested also that the work of Klee provided the opportunity "to examine paintings in which the art of the child is the predominant influence."[22]

Some of the first psychological studies of children's art were published by George Kershensteiner in 1905.[23] He observed that various "schema" produced by children appear to undergo a process of development through differentiation in their formal attributes. This seemed to provide the necessary empirical underpinning for Cizek's view that "children have their own laws which they must obey."[24] MacDonald also points out that Froebel's ideas were in the air during Cizek's youth. Froebel believed that everything had an inherent self-active drive to develop itself along certain lines appropriate to its nature. "Development of everything, including the child, comes from within, using the thought which is innate in everything that has come out of God's creative mind."[25]

My wife's parents were born and educated in Vienna, and my mother-in-law studied with Cizek at the *Kunstgewerbeschule,* but the methods of teaching that she described[26] were not at all like those of the Papa Cizek described in copious detail in Wilhelm Viola's book *Child Art.*[27] The methods, as she describes them, involved a rigorous and demanding exploration of design elements and principles, more akin to Dow's "synthetic approach" than to free expression. It should not be forgotten that Dow and Cizek were contemporaries who were doing their major work at almost the same time in history.

Vienna in the early twentieth century was a place of both great intellectual ferment and of social turmoil. The Austro-Hungarian Empire came to an end after an existence of nine hundred years. There was a break with past aesthetic traditions. Historical styles, subjects, and themes lost their appeal, and one felt the need of a new beginning. Freud was evolving his theory of the unconscious, while at almost the same time Schoenberg was developing atonal music. Cizek's insistence upon shielding the child from his historical traditions was understandable for the child was the harbinger of a new and pure style. The past was bankrupt, and the child was to be the carrier of a new beginning. Cizek, as far as I can tell, did not see the artistic development of children as a therapeutic or intellectual good. He was not primarily concerned with their mental growth. This view had to await the ideas of another Viennese named Viktor Lowenfeld.

Lowenfeld's Creative and Mental Growth

Lowenfeld's approach to children's art and its development was shaped by many of the same cultural elements that had earlier affected Cizek. Prominent among them was Freudian psychoanalytic theory, which viewed art and dreams as an expression of the hidden drives that exist in the subconscious. The work of art can be read as an indicator of the psychological health of the artist, and self-expression in art, like psychoanalysis itself, was seen as a kind of therapy enabling the individual to put himself in touch with the sources of inner drives. It was also seen as a process by which the individual put himself in touch with experiences outside the self. Both of these tendencies made it possible for the individual to identify what was innermost in his being, thus allowing him to develop an integrated personality. If the *Jugendstil* or art nouveau was the background style that provided the context for Cizek, then for Lowenfeld the styles that were part of the scene while his ideas were formed were the German expressionist and surrealist styles, both of which owe their existence to the recognition of the subconscious as a force to be reckoned with in human affairs.

Lowenfeld's ideas were also shaped by the political events between the two world wars, especially the rise of anti-Semitism and the German occupation of 1938. I believe that these political events combined with his psychological insights influenced his particular conception of children's artistic development. In the preface of his second edition he says: "Having experienced the devastating effect of rigid dogmatism and disrespect for individual differences, I know that force does not solve problems, and that the basis for human relationships is usually created in the homes and kindergartens. I feel strongly that without the imposed discipline common in German family lives and schools the acceptance of totalitarianism would have been impossible. Without it, this world might have been saved from the most devastating of wars."[28]

It is ironic that this passage did not appear in the first edition, which was written while the war was in progress. The first edition refers to the need to improve the teaching of art and indicates that the book was written to help guide teachers in this task. It opens with a passage that is often quoted both by Lowenfeld's proponents and critics.

If children developed without any interference from the outside world, no special stimulation for their creative work would be necessary. Every child would use his deeply rooted creative impulse without inhibition, confident in his own kind of expression. We find this creative confidence clearly demonstrated by those people who live in remote sections of our country and who have not been inhibited by the influences of advertisements, funny books, and "education." Among these folk are found the most beautiful, natural, and clearest examples of children's art. What civilization has buried we must try to regain by recreating the natural base necessary for such creation.[29]

Art for the child is merely a means for expression. Since the child's thinking is different from that of adults his expression must also be different. Out of this discrepancy between the adult's "taste" and the way in which a child expresses himself arise most of the difficulties and interferences in art teaching.[30]

Don't impose your own images on a child! All modes of expression but the child's own are foreign to him. We should neither influence nor stimulate the child's imagination in any direction which is not appropriate to his thinking and perception. The child has his own world of experiences and expression.[31]

The disunity between art and society [and] between education and environment represents one of the factors from which our present time suffers. On the other side, this disunity is clearly expressed by an art expression which because of its extreme individualistic character almost loses its communicative meaning. Two extreme antipodes can be found within this one culture: the tendency toward a conformation of traditional patterns, and the extreme individualistic trend in contemporary art.[32]

Putting these views of the child, art, and society together we see society described in images of discord and disunity, while the child is a potential integrating force, provided that "education" and other forms of adult influence could be minimized or eliminated. The creative and mental growth proceeds with its own inherent order finding its way to integration provided that it is not seduced and corrupted by the forces of socialization, forces that tend to make children more alike rather than nurture their uniqueness. In this process art is merely an instrument. One is left with the unmistakable conviction that in Lowenfeld's view a healthy society in the future could only come about through the education of individuals whose creativity is not impaired by the educative processes that should be nurturing it. In this view the child is the redeemer of a sick society, with art and education serving as instruments to that end. Teaching is a midwifely task involving "anticipation" and "motivation." The teacher anticipates children's artistic needs by recognizing the stages of expression exhibited by their creative products and by providing appropriate media to facilitate the desired expression at each stage. The teacher later provides for the stimulation, encouragement, and nurture of children who exhibit different emerging creative styles. Some children, according to Lowenfeld, develop a visual and others a haptic style, and, in his view, each deserves to be encouraged by the teacher.

The kernel of Froebelian idealism that was noted in Cizek can also be found in Lowenfeld. His convictions about artistic development were certainly more profound than Cizek's. For Cizek, the child existed for art's sake to produce a kind of art that only the child can make. For Lowenfeld, art existed for the child's sake.

Read's Educational Theory

An English contemporary of Lowenfeld was Herbert Read. Both men developed ways of describing stylistic differences in the work of children, and they both saw art as an instrument for personality integration. Read held a more positive view of society than did Lowenfeld. He saw the need for the reciprocal development of the individual's uniqueness and his social consciousness. "Education must be a process not only of individuation but also of *integration* which is the reconciliation of individual uniqueness to social unity. From this point of view the individual will be good in the degree that his individuality is realized within the organic wholeness of the community . . . . "[33]

Although both writers used the concept of integration, it had a different meaning for each. Lowenfeld used the term to describe the healthy personality, which was characterized by the intellect and feeling being in some kind of harmony. The lack of such integration, was, on the other hand, symptomatic of neurosis. Read's concept of integration involved these dimensions of the personality, but it also included the individual's orientation to society and to the cosmos. "Art is mankind's effort to achieve integration with the universe and the organic rhythms of life." Hence, art is more than a therapeutic agency; it is based upon aesthetic principles anchored in the order that is found in the universe and that can be found in the structure of matter itself. Man in his natural state (prior to the corruption of civilization) can perceive this underlying order and respond to it. Primitive man is, thus, unconsciously integrated with nature, as is the child. Therefore, the child "should be educated to become what he already is."[34] And so aesthetic education is: "The education of the senses upon which consciousness and ultimately the intelligence and judgment of the human individual are based. It is only insofar as these senses are brought into harmonious and habitual relationship with the external world that an integrated personality is built up."[35] Read's concept of self-expression resembles a process such as play, which is engaged in by the child for his personal satisfaction. It is an important means by which his psychic equilibrium is maintained. Self-expression also includes any spontaneous elaboration of fantasy and teaching, which, in Read's view, consists of "watching objectively the development of any fragment of fantasy."[36] His psychology draws heavily on Jung and his view of the collective unconscious, which is likened to a "universal mind" consisting of half-forgotten imagery that recurs in art throughout the world. He collected many drawings of one such symbol, the mandala. In a study of English schoolchildren's drawings of mandalas he concluded that the children producing those with greater elaboration and in brighter colors usually had more integrated personalities. In a remarkable passage, he summarizes with great eloquence and vehemence the relation between creative expression in art and the prospects for a healthy society:

We are down to the fundamental formulas of life, in the individual and society, and there we find our aesthetic principle presiding. There is no escape from it. It is the principle of whatever design and purpose our wisdom can discern in the

universe, and to ignore it, or deny it is to plunge mankind into the chaos of
ineptitude so often realized in our discordant history . . . . The gigantic catas-
trophes that threaten us are not elemental happenings of a physical or biological
kind, but are psychic events. We are threatened in a fearful way by wars and
revolutions that are nothing else but psychic epidemics.

    . . . The secret of all our collective ills is to be traced to the suppression of
spontaneous creative ability in the individual . . . . *Destructiveness is the outcome
of unlived life!*[37]

    Both Read and Lowenfeld saw art education as a potential force
working for the redemption of mankind. The freedom with which a
child expresses his inner self and the capacity to respond innocently,
albeit naively, to the world outside was a symbol of freedom everywhere. Both men lived at a time when the struggle for freedom from
political bondage was uppermost in everyone's mind. Lowenfeld saw
redemption for the social order tied to the child's creative potential.
Read saw it in the repository of symbols in the universal mind, the
collective unconscious, in the unity that transcends the diversity and
that could serve as a basis for the reconstruction of the social order.

Barkan and the Emergence of Postwar Thought

    In the years preceding the Second World War the study of child
psychology depended heavily on psychoanalytic theory. By the end
of the war other psychological trends began to emerge. Among them
was one that was to have a strong impact upon Manuel Barkan: the
transactional psychology of Ames and Cantril. In this view knowledge
results from an individual's interaction or transaction with his environment. Knowledge is a construction made of the world rather
than a series of discoveries. Prominent among an individual's transactions are the concepts one has built up about the world in his
previous experiences. The experimentalism of Dewey provides the
epistemic foundation for this psychological orientation. His *Art as
Experience*[38] provided Barkan with a transactional aesthetic doctrine
whereby the aesthetic experience is explained as the result of transactions between the work of art and the viewer. The philosophical
doctrines of Stephen Pepper also influenced Barkan's thought.[39] Both
Dewey's and Pepper's philosophic orientations avoid the formulation
of absolute laws of art or beauty. They suggest that no two persons
viewing the work of art are likely to see it and derive meaning from

it in quite the same way. Each individual brings something different to it as a consequence of his previous experiences. The intellectual climate of the early 1950's could be characterized as relativist in character. Different views were not only tolerated; they were considered desirable. At the time that Barkan was writing his dissertation and his book, Ohio State University developed an elaborate collection of exhibits using the devices of Ames and Cantril. Among them were demonstrations of such things as autokinetic phenomena and the famous distorted room. They tend to illustrate the view that our approach to reality depends in large part on the understandings we have formed in our past experiences. For example, most of our experiences involving vision in rooms have repeatedly confirmed the hypothesis that a room is rectangular in shape. It is difficult to accept a contrary hypothesis that the room we are looking at is misshapen in some way. It is only by altering our point of vision that we begin to receive cues that force us to modify our original hypotheses about reality. Transactional ideas such as this were part of the intellectual climate. Some of the same transactional views of reality were permeating Barkan's view of childhood and of society.

Children do not develop in a vacuum. They grow up within a culture and assimilate the variety of current cultural life patterns. To understand their educational needs is to see these children in terms of the ways of life that surrounds them. "The first lesson of modern sociology is that the individual cannot understand his own experience or gauge his own faith without locating himself within the trends of his epoch. . . ." Current cultural attitudes toward experience in the arts are essential elements in a foundation for art education. *Experience in the arts pertains to the lives of people, the way they act, and the kinds of things they consider valuable.*[40]

Barkan's concept of the child is that of a growing organism developing through interaction with the environment. It is quite different from the views of Read and Lowenfeld in which the child is seen as an organism developing from within, where the environment is considered a source of potential corruption rather than nurture. They felt that personality was established early and set for life. Art was a form of self-expression that served to reveal inner needs and to relieve tensions. By contrast, Barkan draws upon the psychology of George Mead, who stated:

"The self is something which has a development; it is not initially there, at birth but arises in the process of social experience and activity . . . ."[41]

"An individual's communications are social actions which he performs by expressing himself through language. When a person makes a gesture or a comment, he evokes a response from those who see or hear him. It is *in the responses from others* [italics Barkan's] that the meaning of the individual's original comment is clarified. . . . In this process the individual achieves awareness of himself . . . ."[42]

Unlike Freud, Mead views personality as an entity that is open to change with the learning that occurs through successive interactions with people and with the environment. For Barkan "Personality is the individual's characteristic pattern of interpreting events for the purpose of acting in terms of them. His personality is his particular readiness to act."[43]

The view of the child's personality development and the role of the arts in this process was one cut from new cloth. Art in Barkan's view was an instrument of communication: "The visual arts are a language through which people express their ideas, feelings, and understandings of the things they see in their world."[44]

Art was viewed as an instrument rather than an end. But his conception of art was strongly related to his conception of learning, which he described as an organizing process through which individuals create meaningful images. Quoting from Kepes, he stated: "To perceive an image is to participate in a forming process; it is a creative act."[45]

For Barkan, then, the teaching of art cannot proceed from the needs of the child alone, but must take into account social and cultural factors as well. The child does not develop independently of his environment, and the visual arts are a part of that environment, providing a means of communication. Children's art in Barkan's view was not an end in itself as it was in Cizek's; nor was it a means for creating a healthy personality as it was in Lowenfeld's view, but was, rather, a means for helping the individual to become integrated in his society. He summarizes this view: "The innovator of a language of form creates the new form out of a personal need *to organize his sensations and ideas into a coherent aesthetic structure in order to communicate his newly conceived ideas to others.* This also means that language forms are communicable only insofar as other individuals are able to share the ideas embodied in the person who produces them . . . . Without a social reference personal expression becomes aimless."[46]

Conclusions

This look at Barkan's *Foundation for Art Education* concludes my analysis of the concept of children's artistic development. I could have extended the analysis to include Schaeffer-Simmern, Arnheim, Kellogg, Lansing, and McFee, but I believe that my present discussion has been sufficient to demonstrate that children's art and children's artistic development have meant different things at different times. Sometimes it was not considered at all in the teaching of art. At other times it was seen as an end in itself, more often it was seen as an instrument serving the growth and personality needs of the individual. This then is my first conclusion: that, as a concept, children's artistic development does not operate as a precise, standard term in our literature.

A second conclusion concerns the fact that the term children's artistic development is frequently elucidated by the use of certain metaphors. One of the first of these metaphors is referred to by Israel Scheffler[47] as the molding metaphor. The child is like a lump of clay being pressed into a mold, which is the curriculum. Certainly this describes the practices of Smith and Dow discussed earlier in the chapter. Another is the growth metaphor. The growing child is like a plant or a flower. The teacher is the gardener who provides nurture and care. She cannot create the flower, but she can help it unfold. Cizek said, for example: "Nothing here is made; it has grown like flowers." On another occasion he stated: "Make your schools into gardens where flowers may grow in the garden of God."[48] Still another metaphor is what Scheffler describes as the organic. This one played an important role in Read, Lowenfeld, and Barkan. In some of the writers, however, the metaphors sometimes become confused. Both Lowenfeld and Read seem to utilize a metaphor of social redemption where the child plays the role of a messiah. The problem with all such metaphors is that they do not always apply in art education. Nor should we feel that we are free of metaphors today. A military metaphor began to creep into the literature on curriculum during the 1960's. Academic programs or curriculum development projects were "operations," and planners were "task-force teams." Elliot Eisner and Ralph Smith have on recent occasions criticized the use of a "production" metaphor in which students are producers of behaviors, which can be monitored and evaluated like goods on an assembly line.

A third conclusion has to do with the way concepts operate within the theories of art education. In some theories children's artistic development is the central tenet upon which all the other terms rest, as was the case in Read and Lowenfeld. When this happens all other aspects become subservient to it. Art becomes merely an instrument for the child's development rather than a component of his cultural heritage. Teaching recedes into the background. No longer the intentional behavior of a professional, teaching becomes "gardening" and the curriculum so much fertilizer. Society is a potential source of pollution waiting to impair the unfolding of the plant.

There have been times when views of the child played little or no role in shaping teaching practices, as can be seen in the discussion of the teachings of Smith and Dow. But, in the not so distant past we seemed for a time to be returning to a version of that view. By the middle 1960's many art educators would have agreed with Barkan when he wrote: "The primary purpose for the study of art by elementary school children rests in the humane and aesthetic values to be derived . . . . Developmental characteristics in themselves are not the end goals of art education nor are they the end goals of any other field. Rather, developmental needs, capacities, and achievements are instruments used by the teacher . . . ."[49]

If children's needs become instruments, what then becomes the end? Is it the subject matter, or is it the society? In the same decade when Barkan wrote that passage, competence in subject matter had social relevance, and social necessities made some subjects more important and others less. In the 1960's art was perceived as having less value while science and mathematics were seen as having more. There is, in addition, always the danger that both the child and the subject matter will become instruments of society rather than the reverse. Who decides how society's interests are best served? How is the public interest defined, and at what cost to the individuals being processed by the educational system? These kinds of questions also underscore the fact that, when societal interests or those of the subject tend to dominate curriculum considerations, the decisions affecting the welfare of the individual student are in danger of being subverted in some way.

A fourth conclusion concerns the development of a theory of art education today. From what was hinted at in the third conclusion, it would seem that a theory of art education cannot draw all of its strength from a conception of childhood, as can be seen in most theory-making attempts in the past. It cannot be derived from conceptions of the nature of art, and it cannot postulate goals and objectives without some explicit recognition that individuals do more than just develop personalities; they also develop into members of social groups. A theory of art education has to strike a balance among children's needs, the nature of the subject, and societal interests. Writers in curriculum theory such as Tyler and Taba have said this many times, but the development of such a theory is no simple matter. Elliot Eisner characterized the problem well in the opening lines of the preface to *Educating Artistic Vision* when he used the image of putting together the pieces of an intellectual puzzle. He is right in saying that "The puzzle is not yet complete and probably never will be."[50] The nature of childhood, art, and education always seems to elude precise definition, not only because more facts are constantly coming to light, but because they are open concepts. To define them once and for all is not the function of theory, for to do that is to foreclose the future.

Notes

1. Manuel Barkan, "Toward a Foundation of Art Education," doctoral dissertation, Ohio State University, 1951.
2. James Beck Green, "The Introduction of Art as a General Education Subject in American Schools," doctoral dissertation, Stanford University, 1948.
3. Walter Smith, *The Drawing Book* (Boston: James R. Osgood and Co., 1872).
4. Frederick Logan, *Growth of Art in the Public Schools* (New York: Harper and Brothers, 1955), 70.
5. Rudolph Arnheim, *Art and Visual Perception* (Berkeley: University of California Press, 1954), Chapter 3. The view that is termed "naive realism" seems to be descriptive of the views that prevailed at the end of the nineteenth century.
6. Maria Montessori, *The Advanced Montessori Method* (London: Arthur Livingston, Publishers, 1918), II, 304-306, quoted in Herbert Read, *Education through Art*, 2d ed. (New York: Pantheon Books, 1945), 113-115.
7. George J. Cox, "The Horizon of A. W. Dow," *International Studio*, LXXVII (June 1923), 189-193.
8. Clive Bell, *Art* (London: Chatto and Windus, 1914).
9. Thomas Munro, "The Dow Method and Public School Art," in John Dewey *et al.*, *Art and Education* (Philadelphia: Barnes Foundation Press, 1929).
10. Logan, *Growth of Art in the Public Schools.*

11. Anna Wilson Henderson and H. O. Palen, *What and How* (Springfield, Mass.: Milton Bradley Co., 1908).

12. Green, "Art as a General Education Subject," 315.

13. *Ibid.*

14. Logan, *Growth of Art in the Public Schools*, 107. Quoted from Francis Wayland Parker, *Talks on Pedagogics: An Outline of the Theory of Concentration*, ed. Elsie A. Wygant and Flora Cooke (New York: Progressive Education Association, 1937).

15. Wilhelm Viola, *Child Art* (New York: John Day Co., 1936).

16. Allan Ross MacDougall, "Developing Artists through the Imagination," *Arts and Decoration*, XXIV (January 1926), quoted in Green, "Art as a General Education Subject."

17. Harold Rugg and Ann Schumacher, *The Child Centered School* (Yonkers on Hudson, N.Y.: World Book Co., 1928).

18. Thomas Munro, "Franz Cizek and the Free Expression Method," in Dewey et al., *Art and Education*, 313-314.

19. *Ibid.*

20. Stuart MacDonald, *The History and Philosophy of Art Education* (New York: American Elsevier Publishing Co., 1970), 320.

21. *Ibid.*, 340-341.

22. Robert Goldwater, *Primitivism in Modern Art* (New York: Harper and Brothers, 1938).

23. MacDonald, *History and Philosophy of Art Education.*

24. *Ibid.*, 344.

25. *Ibid.*

26. Personal communication with Mrs. Hermine Floch.

27. Viola, *Child Art.*

28. Viktor Lowenfeld, *Creative and Mental Growth*, 2d ed. (New York: Macmillan, 1952), ix.

29. *Ibid.*, 1.

30. *Ibid.*, 1-2.

31. *Ibid.*, 3.

32. *Ibid.*, 21.

33. Herbert Read, *Education through Art* (New York: Pantheon Books, 1945), 5.

34. *Ibid.*, 2.

35. *Ibid.*, 7.

36. *Ibid.*, 194.

37. *Ibid.*, 201-202.

38. John Dewey, *Art as Experience* (New York: Minton Balch Co., 1934).

39. Stephen Pepper, *The Basis for Criticism of the Arts* (Cambridge, Mass.: Harvard University Press, 1946).

40. Manuel Barkan, *A Foundation for Art Education* (New York: Ronald Press, 1955), 19.

41. *Ibid.*, 156. Reprinted from George Herbert Mead, *Mind, Self, and Society* (Chicago: University of Chicago Press, 1934), 135.

42. *Ibid.*, 156.

43. *Ibid.*, 152.
44. *Ibid.*, 17.
45. *Ibid.*, 55. Quoted from Gyorgy Kepes, *Language of Vision* (Chicago: Paul Theobald, 1944), 15.
46. *Ibid.*, 167.
47. Israel Scheffler, *The Language of Education* (Champaign, Ill.: Thomas Publishers, 1961).
48. McDonald, *History and Philosophy of Art Education*, 343.
49. Manuel Barkan, "Art in the Elementary Schools," *Report of the Commission on Art Education* (Washington, D.C.: National Art Education Association, 1964).
50. Elliot Eisner, *Educating Artistic Vision* (New York: Macmillan, 1972), v.

5

Impression and Expression in Artistic Development

H. S. BROUDY

Any theory that purports to have discovered stages of human development is highly valued by educators. The reason—or at least one of
the reasons—for this is that if we understood the natural or even the
regular sequence of changes in the child, we would try to capitalize
on them in pacing instruction. We would use to advantage those
times when the pupil learns most easily and refrain from pressing
upon him activities for which he is not ready. Rousseau, for example,
believed that the best education was negative, permitting the person
to go through natural developmental states without interference
from the distortions of an artificial and corrupt society. Education as
growth or unfolding has a long history, as has the metaphor of the
teacher as a wise and sensitive gardener. My ignorance of artistic
development in this quasi-genetic sense is virtually total, although
there is no lack of interesting literature on the subject.

I do not wish to deny that there are stages of development or to
belittle their value for limiting or facilitating the effects of instruction.
Nor do I wish to denigrate the value of inquiries that link aesthetic
experience with various stages in personality development, such as
developments in self-concept. I simply do not know enough about
such studies to be able to judge their relative plausibility, let alone
their scientific validity.

There is, nevertheless, no way of entirely avoiding certain questions about the origin of aesthetic experience, for it is a peculiar sort of experience, indeed. How does a sensory image in any medium—sound, color, gesture, texture, movement—come to acquire, or embody, or express human import? For example, how does a tree acquire the appearance of strength, loneliness, majesty? How does the painting of a tree take on such qualities? Why would anyone "see" or "hear" natural objects in this fashion? Why would anyone contrive objects to be "seen" or "heard" in this manner?

There are several answers. One is that sensorimotor-affective stimuli can fuse into a single significant image. For example, how does a dark gray cloud come to look threatening? One might hypothesize that repeated experiences with visual images of dark gray clouds in close conjunction with rain, spoiled picnics, and getting drenched would in time fuse into a visual quality called "threatening." From his experience the individual would, therefore, form the generalization that a dark cloud "threatens" unpleasant consequences. This constitutes a bit of empirical knowledge about the weather and its relation to life. But knowing this does not necessarily constitute an aesthetic experience. In order to make the experience aesthetic it is necessary that the dark cloud not merely refer to consequences but that it present some of the qualities of those consequences as an image, on its face, so to speak. The dark cloud must *look* threatening as well as serving as a signal of unpleasant events to come.

Another way in which dark clouds come to look threatening is by our learning the usual meanings of a set of more or less standardized images. Folklore, folk art, and folk language teach us that a certain cast of facial features is the image of shiftiness; that chins look strong or weak; that some musical patterns are martial while others are romantic. Television commercials display to the nation innumerable times a day what masculinity and femininity are supposed to look and sound like. The image of youthful vigor is captured in pictures of sleek bodies moving rapidly through water or on horses or motorbikes, while gleeful faces are tilted upward toward a bottle of cola.

So powerful is the influence of conventional imagery that if the image is not right, the thing is not right either. Some people cannot believe that dirty blue jeans and long hair might cover clean thinking and decent feeling. To this day the assassination of John F. Kennedy as explained by the Warren Commission is dramatically implausible to those who are convinced that there must have been a great conspiracy. Whatever the facts may turn out to be, the public will be dissatisfied if the aesthetic image of the event does not express or match the importance of the event. The same may be said of Watergate. One day these events will be given the right aesthetic image by a genius of the theater.

With age, sensory perception enables one to build a store of images whereby appearances are perceived to be reflections of human feeling—"the forms of feeling," to use Susanne Langer's term. That store can be augmented by absorbing the imagery of the arts and by exercising one's own imagination—the image-making power.

Imagination is the matrix of both thinking and freedom because it conjures up images of what might be. Out of what might be come hypotheses and theories about what is or must be the case and of states of affairs that could be otherwise and more consonant with our wishes. Imagination creates possibilities and therewith the image of freedom itself. From very early childhood, we are told, the world of make-believe vies with the real world for our assent. This, then, may well be the origin of aesthetic experience, but in its developed form the origins are no longer conscious. We are, on the contrary, at our aesthetic best when our consciousness is completely filled by the image itself, when, as D. W. Gotshalk put it, the image is compellingly "interesting to perception."[1] This state is sometimes referred to as the aesthetic attitude.

Why are certain images interesting to perception? I shall not rehearse the theories of art that purport to give answers to this question. I am inclined to the view that the fascination of art lies in the indirectness with which an image intimates human import. All aesthetic experience involves perceiving a metaphor or analogy, that is, a nonliteral communication of significance. Rhythm, balance, contrast, theme and variation, subordination, unity in complexity, when applied to images of human feeling or import, produce works of art.[2] Such portrayals of feeling when contemplated aesthetically do not necessarily produce the feelings they portray; they do, however, provide us with an *insight* into their nature and possibilities. If this is so, then the distinctive goal of general aesthetic education is to develop the skill of perceiving such portrayals. These are the skills of artistic impression, skills that are correlative to but not identical with those needed to create such portrayals—the skills of expression. The strategy of aesthetic education or designs for aesthetic education is concerned with the relation between these two types of skills.

With respect to both types of skills a person can be characterized as having the innocent eye, ear, or hand; the conventional or stereotyped eye, ear, or hand; or the cultivated eye, ear, or hand. It may be convenient to call these stages of development, although I have no evidence that this sequence is universal or necessary and some evidence that it is not. In my view it is sufficient to note that for formal aesthetic education the third stage is the primary goal; this means regaining the first stage in a cultivated form after its sojourn in the second stage. But the third stage may never be reached by some; there are, in fact, those in arts education who, like Rousseau, would concentrate their efforts on preserving the innocence of the first stage, thus protecting students from contamination by all stereotypes, cultivated or otherwise.

The first stage is marked by spontaneity and is unhampered by knowledge or social inhibitions. Clichés of language and perception have not yet intervened to prevent a five-year-old from calling eraser rubbings "mistake dust" or movies "dreams in the air." Viktor Lowenfeld observed that for the young child at a certain stage the size of a given element in his drawings represents the importance of the object rather than its physical dimensions. The conventions of linear perspective have not yet inhibited his mode of expression. Neither have various conventions deprived him of the dance, poetry, drama, and fiction as spontaneous forms of expression. I would assume that the same sort of freedom from stereotype characterizes innocent impression also.

In both types of innocence we value the spontaneity, which is also the mark of honesty and creativity. This spontaneity is often identified with creativity and accounts for the reluctance of many arts educators to interfere with it. The reluctance takes the form of denying the validity of external standards both in impression and expression; thus, whatever the innocent eye, ear, or hand perceives or does is to be regarded as good simply because it issues from the child himself. The artistically good is equated with authenticity.

However, if aesthetic perception is a distinctive sort of perception—the perception of human import in sensory images (images or portraits of feeling)—then it does not follow that all authentic impressions or expressions are equally sensitive or discriminating aesthetically. One can perceive the object noting fewer or more differences in fewer or more dimensions. Indeed, some authentic perceptions may not be aesthetic at all; they may be quite practical, as when the lumberman perceives the lone pine tree not as lonely but as so many board feet of building materials. But who knows whether the infant fixating the colored beads dangling in his crib is interested in their appearance as such or as possible additions to his diet? The scribblings of the very young child who announces confidently that "this is a horse" may be no less or more authentic than the crayon drawings of his later years purporting to depict a horse, but must we say that there is no difference in artistic quality between them? The advocates of free activity in arts education do not, I believe, deny the difference either; they merely want to urge that the standards be internal to the pupil, not imposed upon him by someone else, such as the teacher.

Spontaneity, originality owing to lack of constraints imposed by experience and knowledge, and honesty unspoiled by the desire to please others—these are the very attributes that Adam and Eve were supposed to have had and to have appreciated in the Garden. The familiar injunctions to be as a little child, to allow little children to approach important people, and the almost irresistible appeal of the short span in which children are not self-conscious of their own charm—these all attest to the importance of the age of innocence in the aesthetic field as in the moral one.

As the person grows older, the aesthetic categories of the popular arts begin to determine impression and expression. Popular music, poetry, fiction, painting, and dance, in both the folk or commercial versions, standardize the images of feeling. Each age has its fashions of appropriateness of appearance in persons, landscapes, speech, and clothing; each decade has its standardized images of masculinity, femininity, heroism, love, courage, good, and evil. They are as automatic and pervasive in their influence as the syntax of spoken language. We use them long before we study them, and we use them without thinking about them. They are the aesthetic mores of an age.

Variations from the stereotypes are permissible, and there is no lack of them, but they are variations within fairly narrow limits as a study of the top tunes, top movies, or top television programs will show.

Stereotyping of perception and execution is not confined to the popular arts. Gombrich has argued that all artists produce only what their skills and techniques permit them to. "The artist will be attracted by motifs which can be rendered in his idiom. As he scans the landscape, the sights which can be matched successfully with the schemata he has learned to handle will leap forward as centers of attention. The style, like the medium, creates a mental set which makes the artist look for certain aspects in the scene around him that he can render. Painting is an activity, and the artist will therefore tend to see what he paints rather than to paint what he sees."[3]

Some uniformities of perception and expression are unavoidable. Without categorial frameworks that ensure some such uniformity our experience would be so idiosyncratic that communication of any kind would be impossible. But categorial frameworks may or may not be congruent with reality. For example, the categorial framework by which we construe experience in terms of responsible moral agents persists even though it does not fit the consumer-seller-producer relationship in our complex society, where it is almost impossible to fix responsibility for anything on anybody.

Education replaces categories of common sense with categories of knowledge. Scholarship and scholarly inquiry frequently do not simplify life; in fact, they introduce more problems than they solve. And yet faith in education is faith that in the long run the search for more refined maps of life is worthwhile and that to incorporate such maps into one's thought and feeling is the road to self-perfection. Education is the institutional version of the Socratic dictum that the unexamined life is not worth living, or, to put it more moderately, the uncultivated person does not know what he is missing.

There is no way of avoiding the second stage if we are to live in society at all, and it is possible for many, if not most, individuals to live out their entire lives at this level of mass culture and the uniformity it so often demands. In a modern technological society, however, it is unlikely that we shall find many persons who do not have a special expertise in something. Usually it is in their occupation; often it is in a hobby. In these areas they are cultivated and live by categories different from the standardized ones. They use the categories of the connoisseur, of the expert, of the buff; they have reached the third stage. The case, it seems to me, is no different in the realm of art and the aesthetic than it is in science, in collecting antique bottles, or in piloting jet airplanes.

The move from mass stereotypes to categories of the connoisseur is a move from social habituation to cultivation; it is the recovery of childhood innocence, but in a cultivated form. Baudelaire said that "genius is nothing more than childhood recovered at will—a childhood now equipped for self-expression."[4] Most of us cannot recover the naturalness of childhood at will and are not equipped to express that happy state if we did.

To recover the innocent eye, ear, and hand once childhood is past requires effort and help. To suspend our practical and cognitive concerns long enough to be impressed fully by the work of art calls for practice and instruction. As Benedetto Croce pointed out, ordinary perception notes just enough of the object to index it for some purpose. Witness the difficulty in doing a self-portrait, even though we look at the subject with tedious regularity. Aesthetic perception is complete, not selective; it is intensive, confined within the borders of the work of art. If artists, all of whom I suppose make some claim to genius, can recover their childhood and express it, can their works help us do the same? They can, if we achieve or approximate artistic impression and expression. At this juncture a tax-conscious citizen might ask some pertinent questions. For example, how important is instruction in artistic impression? The popular arts are perceived easily and adequately without it. Indeed, art can have mass appeal only if it can be perceived (enjoyed) without study. Artistic expression is another problem altogether, for approximating the skill of the artist is virtually impossible for those without talent and a strong desire to become an artist. Therefore, for most of the school population, instruction in order to achieve some approximation to artistic levels of impression and expression is either unnecessary or impossible.

If we are to argue that aesthetic education is necessary and possible for all pupils, we must do so on the ground that the skills of impression are needed for the perception of the serious arts and that they can be taught to everyone. This conclusion runs into several difficulties. One is that arts education programs traditionally have been performance oriented. Another is that the standard approach to serious art has been to give courses in appreciation, which emphasize knowledge about art rather the skills of perception. Still another is that the distinction between popular and serious art must be made usable and defensible. Finally, the question remains as to why skill in perceiving serious art is worth insisting on for everybody—or anybody.

The difficulty with the performance-oriented approach is that, as the technical standards become more demanding, only the talented and the ambitious pupils persist. In the approach emphasizing appreciation historical and critical knowledge about works of art is substituted for the direct perception of them, which often results in conventional judgments and taste. If aesthetic education is to be a part of general education, the skills of expression need to be developed, but the technical standards may have to be relaxed to the point where the individual decides how much technique he wishes to acquire. I believe a case could be made for a general requirement that all pupils get some experience in art performance, especially in the elementary grades. Such opportunities are not usually available outside the schools, and with technical standards relaxed so as not to exceed individual needs or wishes, such courses would provide personal satisfaction in a variety of ways both at the elementary and secondary levels.

Such experiences would preserve especially the willingness of the individual to express himself in the various media—most of which he abandons by the onset of adolescence. It is fortunate that nonrepresentational work in the visual arts and the greater freedom now displayed in contemporary theater, dance, poetry, and music can protect the individual longer from invidious comparisons with the professional and the talented amateur. For the nonartist one might, therefore, defend the proposition that a performance is "good" if it satisfies the performer's need for expression, and the school might acquiesce in this approach. It would limit itself to providing materials and opportunities for work in the various media and such instruction as the individual might wish to receive.

With regard to the skills of impression the case is quite different. As has been said, popular art needs no formal instruction for its appreciation. Some might object, however, to the distinction between popular and serious art. How are they to be distinguished, and on what grounds is one "better" than the other?

By serious art I mean nothing more pretentious than that it is thought worthy of study and cherishing *as* art by artists, critics, and historians of art. By this standard jazz is now as much serious art as electronic music and Bach fugues. Not all important art is serious, if importance is judged by social impact. The song "Over There" had a considerable effect on patriotism during World War I, while some of the most serious music may have no discernible social impact. Nor are serious and solemn synonymous. The works of Mozart are regarded as serious, but many of them are not solemn. Serious art requires instruction for its proper perception as well as for its creation or performance. Instruction is also necessary because serious art tends to be esoteric, complex, artificial, and sophisticated, and the talk about it equally so. Because it tends to employ a strange idiom and unfamiliar forms, it usually eludes those who are not privy to what counts in perceiving and judging it. The stylistic properties of popular music are absorbed as they develop; the stylistic properties of complex symphonies and operas are not immediately discernible.

Because serious art, especially in its classical exemplars, is supposed to be "good" art, it creates feelings of guilt and anxiety in the layman if he does not know what makes it good or great, especially if he does not like it. Contemporary serious art that is experimental bothers him even more, partly because it is less familiar than favorite masterpieces, and partly because experimental art tends to deviate radically from the perceptual stereotypes. Thus aleatoric music puzzles and even irritates the layman. Once he discerns the formal design behind this kind of composition, however, the irritation and frustration are diminished, although he may still not like it.

To perceive serious art, as the artist does, therefore, involves more than staring or listening. It may mean directed looking and listening so that the formal properties and stylistic characteristics become visible and audible. It may mean listening long enough to be able to detect harmonies, rhythms, and tonal colorations. A long period of directed listening by the learner may be necessary in order for him to listen as the musician listens. Whether the pupils need to know the history of a particular composition, the life of the composer, and the critics' analysis of it is open to question, but that the teacher has to know some of this information is beyond question. Knowledge about music is no substitute for the proper perception of it, but knowledge may prevent improper perception, and if checked continuously against what is heard in the music, knowledge about it will not be mistaken for the direct aesthetic experience of it. The same holds true for the other arts.

According to this view, therefore, development in aesthetic competence means acquiring enough of the skills of impression and expression so that one can engage in transactions with serious art as well as with the popular variety, especially the sensitive and fairly confident perception of it. I realize, of course, that current theories in art education are far more subtle than this and make broader claims for it: creativity, self-expression, and humanism in general. All these values, as well as worthy use of leisure time, hobbies, and even mental health, may be the result of aesthetic education, and I do not dispute their worth either to the individual or to society. Hopes of achieving these goals, furthermore, have created new constituencies that favor more attention to the arts in the schools. But for a school to make aesthetic education an integral part of its curriculum requires that it contribute something to the aesthetic capabilities of the pupil that other agencies such as museums, the mass media, and the informal activities of the community cannot. This "something" is the skill of perceiving serious art in the manner of the artist.

But how do we justify the study of serious art at all, or for that matter the serious study of anything? I would suggest that we do so on the same basis that we justify the study of science, history, mathematics, geography, or any other discipline. Every one of these disciplines is a refined version of ordinary experience. There is a common sense science, and there is an educated science; there is the ordinary use of language, and there is the educated use of it; there is a popular astronomy, and there is a refined version. If there is value in acquiring the cultivated or studied or refined versions of these modes of experience, then there is value in achieving the cultivated forms of the arts. And if the cultivated versions of these diverse disciplines have a place in the school curriculum because without instruction they would not be picked up informally, then serious art should be the object of study in the schools for the same reason. As to whether it is better to be cultivated than not, one can only appeal for testimony to those who have experienced both. I know of no way of convincing anyone that he ought to be cultivated if he chooses not to be, or if he prefers his children not to be. But it is clear that schools were not established for such persons, and not a little of the current rebellion against the school is generated by them.

For a number of reasons artistic perception seems to me to be the most promising approach to a strong development of arts education in the public schools. First of all, it does not alienate art teachers, who are properly suspicious of generalists and watered down music or art appreciation courses. Secondly, general classroom teachers and pupils can be taught the skills of artistic perception much more readily than they can be taught adequate skills of performance. Finally, once we learn to perceive in the manner of the artist—with the painter's eye and the musician's ear—we have a solid base for enlarging indefinitely both the skills of impression and expression. Our pupils will have the necessary, albeit not the sufficient, conditions for becoming critics and improving their taste if they wish, but, in any event, they will not be looking or listening for the wrong things.

Notes

1. D. W. Gotshalk, *Art and the Social Order,* 2d ed. (New York: Dover Publications, 1962).
2. These principles of artistic form are described by DeWitt Parker in *The Analysis of Art* (New Haven, Conn.: Yale University Press, 1924).
3. E. H. Gombrich, *Art and Illusion* (New York: Pantheon, 1960), excerpted in *A Modern Book of Esthetics,* 3d ed., ed. Melvin Rader (New York: Holt, Rinehart and Winston, 1966), 45.
4. Quoted by Robert Hughes, *Time,* April 15, 1974.

6

Unfolding or Teaching: On the Optimal Training of Artistic Skills

HOWARD GARDNER

Two widely diverging views can be found on the optimal means for developing artistic talent, for fostering creative artists, performers, and perceivers in the visual arts as well as other aesthetic domains. One view might be termed the "unfolding" or "natural" perspective. The child is viewed as a seed, which, though small and fragile, contains within its husk all necessary "germs" for eventual artistic virtuosity. The role of the naturalist or gardener is primarily preventive: to shield the young shoots from malevolent influences—violent winds, fiendish crows—so that the seeds have the opportunity, on their own, to unfold into uniquely beautiful flowers.

By analogy, in the field of art education, every normal child is seen as (at least potentially) a productive and imaginative practitioner of the arts. The art teacher must play the role of a Rousseauean tutor—shielding the innocent and fragile young child from pernicious forces in the society so that his inborn talents can flower. Other than providing a comfortable setting and minimally equipping the child with paints, clay, or blocks, the teacher does little that is active; his or her task is preventive rather than prescriptive.

Preparation of this chapter was supported by the National Institute of Education, through Grant No. G-00-3-0169 to Harvard Project Zero, and by the Spencer Foundation. I thank Ellen Winner and Dennie Wolf for their comments on an earlier draft.

The opposite point of view, if somewhat less in favor today, is no less familiar to those who have toiled in the fields of the arts and education. This perspective, which can be termed the "training," "directive," or "skills" approach, holds that, at the very minimum, unfolding is not enough. Like a young seedling abandoned on the shady side of the hill, the child artist, left alone, will never achieve his or her potential. Special cultivation or perhaps even transplantation is necessary if the immature plant is to survive or thrive. By the same token, the young child, even one displaying considerable promise, will come to nought without firm guidance and active intervention on the part of more knowledgeable adults. Proficiency in the arts entails the attainment of many highly intricate skills, ones that can be acquired only under the direction of a gifted teacher or practicing artist.

It is an established ploy, in teaching, writing, and even thinking, to set up two such antipodes—or straw men—and then to declare, sagely and with a tug on one's beard, that both sides have a point and that the truth lies in a golden mean, located just about midway between equally untenable extremes. I will succumb to this spineless stance to the extent of affirming that both positions have a solid point in their favor. Yet I hope to go beyond the obvious, by insisting that a deeper understanding of both views—unfolding as well as training—may emerge from a developmental perspective and, indeed, that questions in art education in general benefit from such an examination.

Developmental studies are today much in vogue. Almost everyone quotes Jean Piaget or Jerome Bruner or Erik Erikson,[1] whether or not they agree with or even understand them. This is not the occasion for a minicourse on child development, but it may be opportune to offer a few asides regarding the developmental perspective. To be specific, one is not being "developmental" simply by looking at children, nor by noting the ways they change over time. To say that the average three-year-old is thirty-three inches in height and that the average twenty-year-old is sixty-six inches in height is to make statements about children and their growth, but to abjure a developmental approach. Only when one begins to focus on questions like the rate of growth, the meaning of spurts in growth, the organization of physiological systems, and, most centrally, on the possibility that physical growth in two periods of life, such as infancy and adolescence, may be mediated by different physiological mechanisms and affect different portions of the body has one focused on developmental issues. For it is the burden of developmental psychology to discern qualitatively different stages in physical, intellectual, and affective growth, the fundamental units and operations entailed in each stage, the factors contributing to the growth and differentiation of each, and the interrelations and organization among them.

It is no more possible to give a capsule summary of the "state of knowledge" in developmental psychology than a foolproof definition of the field but, again, a schematic description taken from the work of Piaget[2] may help to orient our inquiry. Piaget sees intellectual development as consisting of four broad stages: a "sensorimotor stage," occupying the first two years of life, during which the child gains a practical knowledge of the physical world about him,[3] coming to understand, for example, that objects have a permanent existence within a framework of space and time; an "intuitive" or "semiotic" stage, covering the period from ages two to six or seven, during which the child explores various kinds of symbols and images representing the world, but does not yet do so in a systematic or logical way; a "concrete operational" stage, extending from about the age of seven to the age of twelve, wherein the subject becomes able to think logically about objects, to classify them consistently, and to appreciate their continuity despite alterations in their momentary appearance; a "formal operational stage," commencing in early adolescence, at which time the child becomes able to reason logically using words and other symbols so that he can create a world and make deductions about it, without departing from the "abstract" or "theoretical" level.

Piaget's work is absolutely fundamental to any study of children and their minds. This is true even if one has not yet been converted to his developmental perspective, even if one does not share his convictions that each stage represents a qualitatively different way of thinking about the world, indeed of thinking altogether, or that each stage follows logically after its predecessor, in turn becoming the necessary ingredient for progress to subsequent stages. To conduct research in the area without knowing about Piaget is about as sensible as pursuing biological studies without taking note of recent developments in genetics and molecular biology or of pursuing physics while ignoring Einstein's conceptual breakthroughs.

Having thus praised Piaget, let me add that I think his view can be seriously misleading to those of us involved in art education. Piaget's model of mature adult thought, as implied above, involves scientific thinking in the manner of the physicist or chemist. Piaget explicitly states—and his candor is refreshing in this eclectic era—that he is not interested in creativity, as it is usually defined, or in the arts. It is quite possible, however, that if "involvement in the arts" is seen as a final stage of development, one might arrive at a rather different set of elements and stages, which, while not directly contradicting Piaget's works, possess a strikingly different flavor.

My own work has been devoted largely to the building of an informal model of artistic development.[4] Portions of the model are based upon empirical research conducted by many investigators, including those of us associated with Harvard Project Zero;[5] large portions of the model are based on my own observations, impressions, and intuitions as a parent, teacher, and reader. No doubt the model will be tinkered with and revised in the years to come, and that is to the good. I feel that the model casts some light on the central question raised at the outset, and for that reason I propose to sketch it briefly for you.

During the opening years of life, as Piaget has brilliantly shown, the child is indeed involved in the development of basic sensory and motor capacities and in the parallel enterprise of constructing knowledge about the physical and social world. These activities are evidently a prerequisite for artistic activity, for instance, in awakening the child to various means of communication, but are not in any powerful sense involved with the arts. That is because, in my view, the arts are integrally and uniquely involved with symbol systems—with the manipulation and understanding of various sounds, lines, colors, shapes, objects, forms, patterns—all of which have the potential to refer, to exemplify, or to express some aspect of the world.[6]

Coming to grips with the world of symbols, a world in large part designed by the culture, is the principal challenge of the years following infancy. The most familiar example is, of course, language, where, in the course of two or three years, the child catapults from a phase where he can utter or understand a mere word or two to one in which he can effortlessly issue sentences of almost any length, understanding as well a dizzying variety of structures and messages. But equally stunning progress occurs on all other symbolic fronts.

Children with a musical flair can sing long and complicated pieces of music, assimilate the basic components of a musical style, and, in some cases, even compose works of interest. And by the time they enter school most children have also advanced from the merest capacity to scribble and form simple geometric patterns to the ability to make complex and aesthetically satisfying paintings.[7]

I view the period of ages two to seven, then, as a time during which the child's capacity to use, manipulate, transform, and comprehend various symbols is maturing at a ferocious pace. These processes can be seen in at least two ways: in watching the same child over a period of many months, as he advances from simple forms and patterns to complex configurations with many integrated portions; and, within a briefer interval, as he explores the potentials and possibilities of particular graphic patterns, often making inferences not apparent initially or combining the pattern with another scheme on which he has also been working. This kind of rapid "microgenetic development" is, in its own way, as amazing as the more leisurely "ontogenetic development," or evolution over a matter of months or years.

What is most striking, however, about the events of this period is that they seem to be similar in most children and that specific instruction has relatively little effect on what the child does. Let me be clear about what is meant here. There are indeed differences in children. Some favor one medium over another. For example, some children have an extremely verbal approach to all media; they prefer to tell stories, treating pictures as an excuse for narrative. Other children may have an orientation that is pictorial or visual-graphic; they prefer to express themselves nonverbally, and their pictures exhibit an intensive preoccupation with the visual properties and potentials of a configuration. Moreover, children also differ in the kinds of schemes they come to fix on, in the various set ideas or themes that recur in the works, and even in the extent to which these themes are beneficial or counterproductive.[8]

Yet, over and above these differences in style and preferences, the principal stages affecting young children across cultures, and across media, are persuasively similar. And, as far as we know, this parallel artistic development occurs despite the fact that educational procedures in various cultures may differ enormously. My best guess is that during this symbolic period the child is propelled by a dynamism all his own. Like the seed with its own plan for development, the child is following the inner logic dictated by his own sensorimotor development and the nature of the particular symbols with which he is working; external interference and efforts at instruction rarely prove valuable or productive.

By the age of seven or eight, and sometimes earlier, the child has achieved an initial grasp on the major symbolic media of his culture. In our society, for example, a child of this age understands what makes a story (and what does not), and he can produce a literary work that, at least in its broad lines, conforms to the general cultural model. He has a sense of what occurs within a piece of music and, in many cases, can combine fragments in order to produce a new piece on the basis of a familiar style. Finally, his works in the visual or plastic arts also exhibit a sense of composition, balance, and construction, which indicates an awareness of the constituents of executed works of art, and he has long since learned to "read" the various representations contained in pictorial productions.

With what I hope will be regarded as benign exaggeration, I have suggested that the young child of this age is an incipient artist. By this I mean that he now possesses the raw materials to become involved in the artistic process: a notion of how symbols work in a raft of symbolic media, some knowledge of how to construe a work, some capacity to construct one on his own. Indeed, he can enact the roles of performer, artist, and member of an audience. Only when it comes to the task of being a critic—who, like Piaget's formal operator, must be able to reason on the level of words or logical propositions— is the young schoolchild significantly deficient.[9] It would be absurd, of course, to view the child of seven or eight as a mature artist. He requires, at the very least, additional knowledge about the medium, more understanding of the culture in which he lives, increased flexibility in the way he regards artistic objects, and greater psychological insight about human nature, as well as superior technical skill permitting him to realize desired effects in particular media. Indeed, becoming acquainted with all the potentials of the medium, the multifarious ways in which it has been and can be employed, is perhaps the central task of artistic development and the one that most clearly differentiates this form of development from other realms, including those detailed by Piaget. It is my feeling, however, that these tasks involve quantitative rather than qualitative change. That is, while the acquiring of technique, of cultural understanding, of knowledge of feelings and thought may well require a lifetime, probably a very full and complete one, no new level of cognitive operation is required. The seven- or eight-year-old has the mental equipment to become an artist, and he need not pass through qualitatively different stages in order to participate fully in the artistic process. Here, then, I part company with Piaget. While he highlights the advent of concrete and formal operational thought, rightly perceiving these forms as central to the achievement of the scientist, he does not focus on other forms of thought, and so he does not confront the possibility that concrete and formal operations are not directly relevant to the artist's task nor the contention that versatility with a medium represents an extremely sophisticated cognitive achievement.

This point is very controversial, and for this reason, many people do not concur with my conclusion. Two worthwhile points may nonetheless emerge from this controversy. First, there is renewed recognition that artistry is not just "less-developed" science, but rather involves different processes of thought with their own evolution; artistic cognition may not involve qualitative changes after early childhood, but it continues to deepen and evolve for many years. Second, this perspective helps to explain why individuals in other cultures, including the so-called primitive societies, who do not exhibit types of thought crucial to Western science, nonetheless produce artistic works and exhibit an aesthetic awareness commensurate with, if not superior to, our own. We must acknowledge forms and intensities of thought other than those upheld by Piaget; the particular genius of "medium knowledge" and "symbol use" has to be recognized.

We find, then, that the seven-year-old has gained enough of an intuitive familiarity with symbol systems that he can work with them adequately. However, he knows little and can accomplish little that is subtle and complex. At the same time, he is superbly equipped to learn. Throughout the world, schooling commences at about this time, and during the years from approximately age seven to thirteen, the major lessons of the society are transmitted to offspring. The child of this age seems superbly equipped to learn just about everything, not merely reading, writing, and arithmetic, not merely farming, fishing, and hunting, not merely reasoning, religion, and rhetoric. As V. S. Pritchett has pointed out, "That eager period between ten and fourteen is the one in which one can learn anything. Even in the time when most children had no schooling at all, they could be experts in a trade. The children who went up chimneys, worked in cotton mills, packed coster barrows, may have been sick, exhausted, ill-fed but they were at a temporary height of their intelligence and power."[10] If one has any doubts about the particular learning genius of this period, he should travel with a preadolescent to the South seas and note who picks up the language of the islanders—without a trace of an accent.

Many of our data about children's artistic capacities describe this period of life. Since much of this research has been published, I shall not dwell on it here. We have found, basically, that children around the age of seven or eight suffer from a number of woeful aesthetic misconceptions or impairments, which, fortunately, prove to be quite reparable.[11] Youngsters of this age do not, for example, exhibit sensitivity to painting style: they view paintings chiefly in terms of subject matter. A few weeks of training in which children look at paintings and are directed to notice stylistic features produces, however, a dramatic increase in their sensitivity to painting styles.[12] Indeed, so fertile are the minds of these subjects that their sensitivity to style is enhanced even if they are merely drilled in grouping together animals of the same phylogenetic group.

We also find that children of this age display little tendency to produce metaphoric figures of speech in tasks where they are requested to produce such figures. Indeed, their responses exhibit a literal, concrete, trite, or realistic trend. Again, however, a majority of these youngsters can be trained within just a few weeks both to recognize and produce metaphoric language.[13]

Finally, I should mention an informal study by Judy Burton, who has worked intensively over a period of weeks with sixth and seventh graders. She finds that such preadolescents initially possess little sense of how to produce a third dimension, overlapping surfaces, and a sense of space or perspective in their drawing. However, after some experimentation with various two- and three-dimensional materials such as paper, wire, or lines, and after some guided practice in producing the subject matter of greatest interest to them—the human figure—the youngsters undergo a quantum leap in their artistic productions. In a matter of weeks they become sensitive to the details of the human figure, and to the potential for producing depth relations, in a way previously inaccessible to them. Children of this age generally exhibit a tremendous ability to acquire within a short time new skills in the arts; they enjoy doing so; they are not overly distraught by terminology, by errors, or by empty verbalisms. They are ready to plunge in, to forge ahead, to gain mastery.

And it is in this respect that they differ so demonstrably from other children just a few years older. It is not that adolescents are in some absolute sense less intelligent, or even necessarily less motivated. But for a reason that we do not yet completely understand, enthusiasm about acquiring skills in the arts and the ready capacity to immerse oneself fully in an expressive medium seem lacking in most adolescents, especially in our culture.[14]

Piaget may have uncovered one reason for this. During adolescence the child is developing his critical reasoning skills to a new level. For this very reason he may adopt a much more critical opinion of his own work, comparing it unfavorably with what highly skilled individuals are accomplishing. If he finds his own capacities inadequate in comparison, he is no longer motivated to continue producing. And he remains, at most, a perceiver of the arts. Here, then, we encounter an important lesson for art education. If we are to prevent this decline of interest (and possible decline in skill), our pedagogical efforts during the preadolescent period become extremely important. Sufficient progress in teaching or training should, therefore, be realized so that, when the child finally gains in critical acumen, his works will not seem so inadequate that he quits in despair.

At least two steps would seem helpful. First, skills should be developed to a sufficiently high level so that the child's work will, objectively, possess merit; he will then feel less need to reject what he has done. Second, and of equal importance, the child should be encouraged, gently but definitely, to take a somewhat more critical stance toward his work during preadolescence. He can be presented with problems,[15] exposed to various solutions, and given practice in evaluating and improving them. By such measures he gains familiarity with the practice of criticism; he employs it himself; he benefits from it. When he enters adolescence, criticism is already a familiar tool that he can now apply by himself as well as accept graciously. In the cultivation of this critical capacity, I think, lies our best hope of preventing the army of child artists from narrowing into one lonely platoon—of maintaining a garden of young painters instead of a barren row of survivors—during the interval from childhood to adult-hood.

Perhaps, in a sense, Piaget has been vindicated. In the end I have returned to his scheme to explain one of the most striking and troublesome events in artistic development: the frequent decline of artistry during adolescence. But it should be noticed that what, for Piaget, is a clearly beneficent event—the advent of formal logical operations—proves severely problematic for the child. Indeed, some of our studies have even indicated a high point in artistic creativity *before* adolescence, with the reasoning capacities of this later period proving more of a hindrance than a boon.[16]

There is, then, a central enigma pervading the development of the child. While, in the sciences, development is completely linear and progressive, at least through adolescence, in the arts, the picture is rather different. There is, if anything, a kind of golden period during the first years of life in which every child can be regarded, in a meaningful sense, as a young artist. And, while many children continue to participate in the arts in middle childhood, it is often with much less of a sense of inner direction, with much more of a searching for a model, and a considerable amount of mindless repetition and pointless stylization when no inspiring teacher is present. The development of scientific capacity is, generally speaking, a straight line upward; the lifeline of artistic development is punctuated by ups and downs.

Yet, if the emerging picture of artistic development is less simple than one would have liked, our developmental analysis does provide one potentially useful prescription. As already suggested, the early years of life constitute a time of natural development of artistic competence. And during this period the approach of unfold-ing, of giving full rein to natural development, seems indicated. During middle childhood, however, a more active type of inter-vention is called for. Rigid exercises are not necessary, but rather ones that give the child tools for achieving the effects he wants, that open up rather than foreclose possibilities. He should have some questions to ask and some ways for trying to answer them and an incipient acquaintance with standards and with criticisms. This calls for the more active type of intervention involved in skills or the training approach. It occurs, I think, at a time when the child is especially open and undefensive and is receptive to aid, suggestion, and inspirational models. As Viktor Lowenfeld remarked, with characteristic insight, "If we can stimulate the child's unaware production to such an extent that it reaches in his unaware style a creative maturity which will be able to stand the critical awareness which once will set in, we have kept the child from making a sudden change and have protected him from disappointment or shock with regard to his changing imaginative activity."[17]

I submit that both approaches we have contemplated are appropriate. That which accentuates the unfolding displays its particular virtue during the first years of life, from the period of two to seven. With the developmental changes accompanying the years of schooling, a more active and interventionist stance seems advisable, especially in a milieu virtually bereft of societal support for artistic (as opposed to scientific) endeavors. By the time of adolescence, it is in all probability too late to begin a rigorously structured educational program, and if natural development has not exerted its effect by then, it never will. Instead, one hopes that, by this period, the child will have attained sufficient skills and a sense of critical awareness, as well as ample ideas and feelings he wishes to express; then, he can continue on his own to gain sustenance from whichever artistic medium he selects.

Notes

1. For instances of the work of these scholars, see J. Piaget and B. Inhelder, *The Psychology of the Child* (New York: Basic Books, 1968); J. S. Bruner et al., *Studies in Cognitive Growth* (New York: John Wiley, 1966); E. H. Erikson, *Childhood and Society* (New York: W. W. Norton, 1963).
2. For an exposition of Piaget's developmental work, see Piaget and Inhelder, *Psychology of the Child*; and H. Gardner, *The Quest for Mind* (New York: Alfred A. Knopf, 1973).
3. A cardinal feature of a developmental approach is its focus on features that characterize both males and females. The masculine form is used here purely for the sake of brevity.
4. See H. Gardner, *The Arts and Human Development* (New York: John Wiley, 1973).
5. For an introduction to the work of Project Zero, see H. Gardner, V. Howard, and D. Perkins, "Symbol Systems: A Philosophical, Psychological, and Educational Investigation," in *Media and Symbols: The Forms of Expression, Communication, and Education*, ed. D. Olson (Chicago: University of Chicago Press, 1974); and D. Perkins, "Probing Artistic Process: A Report from Harvard Project Zero," *Journal of Aesthetic Education*, VIII (1974), 33-57.

6. On symbols and symbol systems, see N. Goodman, *Languages of Art* (Indianapolis: Bobbs-Merrill, 1968); see also Gardner, Howard, and Perkins, "Symbol Systems."

7. For supporting evidence, see Gardner, *Arts and Human Development*, Chapter 5.

8. See H. Gardner, D. Wolf, and A. Smith, "The Birth of Artistic Activity: The Symbols of Max and Molly," *New York University Education Quarterly*, VI (1975), 13-21.

9. Gardner, *Arts and Human Development*, Chapter 7.

10. V. S. Pritchett, *The Cab at the Door* (London: Chatto and Windus, 1968), 102.

11. See H. Gardner, E. Winner, and M. Kircher, "Children's Conceptions of the Arts," *Journal of Aesthetic Education*, IX (1975), 60-77.

12. See H. Gardner, "Style Sensitivity in Children," *Human Development*, XV (1972), 324-338; The Development of Sensitivity to Figural and Stylistic Aspects of Paintings," *British Journal of Psychology*, LXIII (1972), 605-615.

13. This research is reported in H. Gardner, M. Kircher, E. Winner, and D. Perkins, "Children's Metaphoric Productions and Preferences," *Journal of Child Language*, II (1975), 60-77.

14. On the frequent decline in artistic abilities at the time of adolescence, see H. Read, *Education through Art* (New York: Pantheon, 1945); Gardner, *Arts and Human Development*, Chapter 6.

15. On artistic problem solving, see H. Gardner, "Problem-solving in the Arts," *Journal of Aesthetic Education*, V (1971), 93-114.

16. For example, see H. Gardner and J. Gardner, "Children's Literary Skills," *Journal of Experimental Education*, XXXIX (1971), 42-46; H. Gardner, "Children's Sensitivity to Musical Styles," *Merrill-Palmer Quarterly*, XIX (1973), 67-77.

17. Viktor Lowenfeld, *Creative and Mental Growth* (New York: Macmillan, 1947), 232.

7

The Critical Act in
Aesthetic Inquiry

DAVID W. ECKER

The theme of this book, children's growth and development in art, has a body of literature associated with it that presents us with a perplexing variety of theoretical aims and approaches as well as a diversity of practical advice. I believe, however, that anyone familiar with this literature will recognize a distinction that virtually amounts to a dichotomy. On the one side (I am tempted to say "the good side") can be placed references to the child's "visual thinking," "prelogical experience," "tacit knowing," "qualitative problem solving," and the like. And on the other side can be placed the antonyms of these terms, which refer, presumably, to the child's critical, rational, or logical thought processes. The distinction has impressive intellectual credentials. It is unfortunate that in its practical application in the field of art education it has degenerated into a cliché. I am referring, of course, to the practice of opposing the "visual" with the "verbal" or "merely verbal" aspects of art teaching and learning. Indeed, art room talk is often dismissed as hollow, devoid of meaning, or even antithetical to creativity in art.

I say this is unfortunate because there is evidence suggesting that language functions in a great variety of ways that affect the child's growth and development in art. The choice, I believe, is not whether talking with the child about his art is to be encouraged or avoided (as Kellogg would have it), but, rather, of the kinds of talk that may be distinguished according to their respective functions in creative and aesthetic situations, which function and which kind of talk best serve to bring about the fullest development of creative potential through art. My own research leads me to conclude that children can think creatively in the kinds of language that might collectively be called "aesthetic inquiry."[1] Children not only talk about art, but also talk about their talk; they not only criticize art objects and events, but also reflect upon the nature of the critical act itself. When their powers of imagination and curiosity are unrestrained, five levels of inquiry may be identified. If we count art production and appreciation as the initial level of inquiry, we find children, first, creating and appreciating art; second, criticizing it; third, challenging or supporting the judgments of others, whether adults or children; fourth, theorizing about the nature of art and criticism; and, fifth, analyzing theories and arguments.

The hypothesis I would like to explore is that the critical responses of the child to his own artistic production determine how far he is able to move from what are apparently biological stages toward what are clearly cultural stages, that is, his progress as an artist in the art world. By analyzing the recorded aesthetic inquiry of two subjects—a three-year-old boy and a sixteen-year-old boy—I shall attempt, with no small amount of trepidation, to identify phenomena that have not been, to my knowledge, adequately explained. Before my analysis, however, I feel that it is necessary to make some preliminary remarks about our motives and expectations.

Motives and Expectations

One reason for exploring theories of children's growth and development in art is our belief that artistic creativity could be more effectively promoted, if not directly taught, if we knew more about its nature. Implied in this belief is our assumption that we already know something about creativity: not only can we recognize those who are artistically creative but also we have practical ideas about the kinds of experiences, lessons, curricula, and environment that enhance the creative performance of all children. I share this belief and do not question the assumption. I have an abiding interest in the relation between theory and practice in art education. And I think that professional art teachers (and teachers of teachers) do have a working knowledge of creativity. I suspect, however, that they gain this know-how more from practice than from theory. Future art teachers usually learn how to help others in creating art by creating art themselves and by practice teaching under the supervision of experienced art teachers who were trained in the same way.

Perhaps the art student's first twinges of a conscious need for theory come in a course on methods when more general questions about artistic development require something beyond a report of "how it works in my situation." What happens next depends upon what kinds of questions are asked of a particular theory, and (what amounts to the same thing) what is expected of a theoretical answer. In my research course at New York University I try to encourage reasonable expectations on the part of my graduate students who are mostly art teachers in the public schools.

The kinds of answers sought can readily be identified with the various ways theory and practice may be related. We engage in *the practical evaluation of theory* when a theory is judged adequate to the extent that it conforms to practice, when that theory truly describes, interprets, or explains what we know (at least in part) about artistic practices and their cultivation. The practice is a "given" in the relationship. Or we engage in *the theoretical evaluation of practice*, when the practice is judged adequate to the extent that it conforms to a given theory. The theory may well have been selected because it provides or suggests criteria for assessing teaching and learning in art. Either way of exploring creativity is legitimate if one makes explicit the key assumption—whether theory or practice is the given.

Another pair of procedures, often hard to distinguish from the first, seems illegitimate just because assumptions or motives are not made clear. We engage in *the theoretical rationalization of practice* when a theory is advanced (perhaps unwittingly) because it is consistent with or supports what we are presently doing in the studio or classroom. Conversely, we ignore or suppress those theories that seem to be inconsistent with our practices. Or we engage in *the practical rationalization of theory;* that is, we tend to notice, record, describe, and praise those practices that conform to our theory and overlook those that raise doubts about or discredit our theory. We may suspect such rationalization when examples or illustrations are presented at one point in the theory and at another point are converted to data, evidence, or proof.

A third pair of reciprocal procedures relating theory and practice provokes still other kinds of questions and answers. We engage in *the extension of practice in light of theory* when a theory is used heuristically to help us generate new teaching strategies and curriculum units suggested or deduced from elements of the theory. Or we engage in *the extension of theory in light of practice.* Observations are recorded, anecdotes collected, descriptions classified, and further hypotheses suggested in the presence of art and its creation, the circumstances of its occurrence, and firsthand reports of children, art teachers, supervisors, and observers.

I must admit that I have attempted to relate theory and practice in all of these ways at one time or another—the illegitimate ways, unwittingly, of course.

Yet I did not draw the preceding distinction in order to make a confession but, rather, to delimit my ensuing analysis to the last-identified activity: the extension of theory in light of practice. The theory I shall attempt to extend is the one whose central concept is that aesthetic education is the result of aesthetic inquiry conducted at one or more of the five levels alluded to earlier.[2] I call them "levels" of inquiry because of the fact that language at a "higher level" of inquiry refers to inquiry at a level or levels below it. For example, the fifth level (metatheory) finds its referents in the fourth level (theory), while the third level (metacriticism) finds its referents in the second level (criticism). This fact is basic to aesthetic inquiry because the investigator—whether researcher, teacher, or student—must convert it to a value or control if he is to solve aesthetic problems.

The taxonomic schema I have just outlined, and within which I am attempting to extend a particular theory, actually shows that another cliché—the distinction between theory and practice—can be misleading if not destructive in its popular use. It is obvious that one can "practice" (inquire) at any level of aesthetic inquiry. One can practice how to theorize as well as theorize about theorizing and other practices, such as painting a picture, criticizing it, and criticizing the criticism.

Analyzing the Developmental Data

The three paintings shown here (Figures 7-1 to 7-3) are typical of the more than one hundred paintings produced by Gregory at the age of twenty-nine months to the age of three years. They were painted during three-hour play group sessions directed by a teacher and one parent-assistant. These sessions were held Monday through Friday with approximately ten children involved in the usual outdoor games, while indoor activities included block building, housekeeping, and dramatic play with a variety of materials. The main point I wish to emphasize concerning these paintings is what I find nothing unusual about them: they are aesthetically well organized, spontaneously produced, and highly predictable. They are, in other words, exactly what one expects of a child this age. Gregory worked on these paintings with gusto, assurance, and, evidently, undiminishing interest, as did the other children in the group. Indeed, it is what art educators have come to expect of children the world over when they are provided with paper, brushes, paint, and the freedom to paint.

It is worth noting here that children's paintings would not be confused with the creative work of professional artists at any other period in Western art history but the present era. I have tested this hypothesis by deliberately intermingling slides of children's art with the art of certain contemporary painters and fooled even art students as to the identity of the creators. In my especially perverse moments I have also included slides of monkeys' art. My purpose was not to denigrate professional artists, children, or monkeys, but to test empirically a distinction not generally recognized: the difference between *creative* and *aesthetic* objects and processes.

Some of the paintings I have used in my informal research are found in Desmond Morris's important book *The Biology of Art.* [3] One is identified by Morris as exhibiting the "multiple scribble phase of child art" (p. 121). Another is of a handsome drawing by Sophie, a ten-year-old female gorilla in the Rotterdam Zoo. Six are of work by Congo, a male champanzee "not yet four years of age," according to Morris (pp. 40, 57, 97, 112, 120, 128). Three paintings that are relevant to my thesis I have taken from Professor Janson's essay, "After Betsy, What?" which Elliot Eisner and I included in our *Readings in Art Education.* [4] They are deKooning's *Backyard on Tenth Street,* on exhibit in the Baltimore Museum; an interpretation

Figure 7-2

Figure 7-1

Figure 7-3

of this painting by Alice Jones, age six, a first grader in a Baltimore
public school; and a finger painting by Betsy, a chimpanzee, also
age six, of the Baltimore Public Zoo (pp. 372-373).

Janson was provoked by these three paintings, which originally
appeared in a Baltimore newspaper (in 1957) with a challenge to
readers to identify them correctly. His own response was to review
historically how concepts of art and the creative process have changed
from the Greeks to the present day. In search of a way of distin-
guishing among these paintings, he first insisted that "the making of
works of art is an exclusively human activity." Yet, since "neither
representation nor manual skill are essential to the creative process in
the visual arts"—he cites the collages of Braque and Picasso and the
Dadaist use of chance and the lucky accident—Janson goes on to say

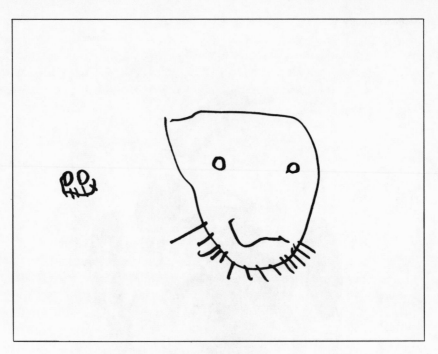

Figure 7-4

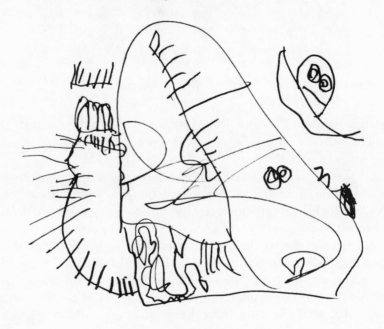

Figure 7-5

that "the exploitation of the accidental is an essential aspect of all art."[5] Janson is saying, in effect, that Betsy was not exploiting her accidental brush strokes for the sake of making art, but perhaps was being exploited by her zoo keeper.

Janson wrote his essay before Morris's book was published and was, therefore, not aware that apes had been drawing and painting under experimental conditions for decades. Thus, for our book of *Readings,* he added a postscript to his essay. He noted that "Morris' observations show that the picture-making behavior of apes follows a surprisingly strict evolutionary pattern, which follows step by step the development of drawing ability in human infants. Both run through the same sequence of stages—up to a point: and that point is reached when the child produces his first 'image' (usually a face), an achievement linked to the development of articulate speech. The world of words, like the world of images, remains beyond the ape's capacity."[6] But what separates the work of monkeys and children from adult professional work is that the former is predictable while the latter is "accident prone." Janson suggests the term "proto-art" for the first category (with "pre-figurative" and "figurative" work separating infrahumans and humans) and "art" for the second category. "Only much later, when he approaches adulthood, will the proto-artist discover that he needs the approval of outside beholders, and will preserve his work in the hope of finding an appreciative public."[7] Janson might well have been talking about the two humans whose work and responses to that work I have chosen to analyze.

I have already characterized Gregory's paintings. In light of the foregoing discussion and my prior analysis of Gregory's responses to over six hundred of his drawings (e.g., Figures 7-4 to 7-5), I now want to claim that the two kinds of activities may be engaged in separately but are often intermingled. Moreover, the data suggest a more refined characterization of the first two levels of aesthetic inquiry, as follows: The first consists of *artistic activity,* in which the child is engaged in the production of an object or event that is perceived by adults as art (or "proto-art," following Janson's lead); the second is *critical activity* (or "proto-criticism"), in which the child is engaged in any kind of response to the product of artistic activity, whether this response is viewed positively or negatively by adults.

Gregory's paintings and drawings would be classified as proto-art and thus taken as evidence of artistic activity. Since all of his drawings were produced at home, however, it was possible to record many of the spontaneous linquistic responses of the child to these drawings, and so we also have ample evidence of his critical activities. It could be argued, of course, that the creative process is, in part, a critical process, that continued artistic production and the directions it takes are governed by qualitative judgments acting as feedback during the activity.[8] Ripping up or otherwise destroying a drawing would also be considered a critical activity. Following is a partial list of the most literal descriptions of critical activities that occurred to me as I reviewed this material.

The first is *naming*. The child identifies objects or events depicted or intended, during or following the artistic activity. For example, a pencil drawing done at twenty-four months of age includes marks named by the subject as "write," "boaten," "airplane," and "bile" (for snowmobile). Upon completion of a multicolored crayon drawing at thirty months, Gregory announced: "That's Ginger" (his play group leader). This depiction of a human figure is the first recognized as such by either child or the parents. Another example is a pencil drawing: "That's Ginger's wagon." The critical response to one crayon drawing on blue paper at this age is perhaps unusual: "This is not an alligator. It is not a spider. It's not a grapefruit. It's not Apple-jacks. It's a drawing."

Other tentative descriptions of artistic activity involving language are the following: *telling a story, acting out, presenting, showing, remembering, incorporating,* and *intending.* Any of these general descriptions could be viewed as categories, which could, in turn, immediately suggest subcategories. For instance, *intending* could be subdivided into fulfilling an intention ("I'll make an alligator"; draws an alligator; states "That's a happy alligator"); modifying an intention ("I'll make an alligator for you. Alligators have sharp fur. This is an octopus. Octopuses have sharp claws . . . "); and failing to achieve what was intended. Yet I feel that calling them descriptions rather than categories is less misleading at this stage of theory construction since premature reduction of complex phenomena to categories is the quickest way toward the rationalization of a theory, which is one of the errors mentioned earlier.

I have been critical elsewhere of those theories which have tended to minimize or suppress references to what the child says about his art as irrelevant to the understanding of his art.[9] I might be accused here of exaggerating the significance of the talk accompanying artistic activity. Protection against both these possibilities is to be found in fuller and more complete descriptions of the event. For example, the following dialogue, which the subject initiated at the age of thirty-seven months, seems essential to the proper appreciation of the drawing that ensued.

> Greg: Draw a jet plane. [Father draws a plane.]
> Greg: That's not a jet plane; it has propellers.
> Father: You're right. Let me try again. [Father draws a jet plane.]
> Greg: That's terrific! Where are the wheels?
> Father: It's a retractable—like our plane. The wheels fold up inside the plane in the air. [A few minutes later Greg draws his own plane with wheels, windows, and people inside the windows.]
> Greg: Here are the wheels, here are the windows . . . .

The first description that occurred to me was *showing that he knows,* and it would be hard to deny that there is cognitive activity here. But one would have to ignore the aesthetic qualities of the drawing itself in order to categorize the event as evidence only of cognition. The drawing demonstration by the father raises further issues. But any theory must account for all aspects of the event to be explained, unless what is to be explained about the event is carefully delimited beforehand.

In order to continue with the more humble task of describing the phenomena to be explained—or, to be more accurate, to suggest by a few more examples and anecdotes the direction my current research is taking—it is necessary to jump ahead thirteen years in human development to our second subject, Scott, a sixteen-year-old junior in a New Jersey high school. Included in this chapter are three of Scott's works. Scott was a potential dropout, failing all of his subjects, including art, until Mr. Thomas P. Fitzpatrick took an interest in him, following the discovery of some of his drawings in a wastepaper basket.[10] What followed was a most unusual artistic development as evidenced in the creation of these drawings—all done with a twenty-nine-cent ball-point pen. Scott is now illustrating a book by a well-known New York writer of surrealistic poetry. In a separate venture, an edition of Scott's drawings is to be printed by a small publishing house.

Mr. Fitzpatrick's initial judgments followed by the positive responses of others in the art world have provided Scott with the impetus for more ambitious undertakings. But what comes through in Mr. Fitzpatrick's interview is Scott's wit, intelligence, and self-awareness—his ability to analyze his drawings in terms of the sources of their inspiration and to assess their merits and defects.

Teacher and student first discuss the origin of *The Snake* (Figure 7-6).

Scott: This is back . . . we'll go back a year ago. I'm in my first year of high school and I'd read *Alice in Wonderland.* Very impressed by the figures they did. So the next day I was in the art class and, as usual, I wasn't doing anything, and I started sketching it out. And I really didn't have anything from the book in mind, but what I did was try to use the same techniques that I saw in the book. . . . And what came out was the small sketch, which later you saw . . . .

Fitz: Um yeah.

Scott: . . . and you encouraged me to do a larger one. Which I didn't think was possible. This is the first one I've ever did this size, this much detail, I never thought I could do it . . . .

Fitz: What did you think about, doing the work on large paper instead of the small work . . . ?

Scott: I was scared. I didn't know what to put in there. But, ah, when I'm trying to do these, I try . . . like I don't have a set idea in my mind . . . only try to just put the, ah, basic concept of the snake and the guy down.

Then Scott attempts a deeper explanation of the work.

Scott: When I started out as a little kid to draw things it was because I didn't have a real rocket ship, I didn't have a real submarine, so I had to draw them. And I had to make my own little movies out of them. What I had to do was choose the best scene out of that little play that I wanted to put on and put it on paper. Then I could look at it and make snake noises, rocket noises. And so we have here the snake that guards the road. This is the idea I originally had. And he is in this enchanted forest . . . and the problem is, they can't get through here. So they choose the brave little person . . . there's always someone in the village that's stuck with the job . . . and not very quick witted, but still, he goes up there and he draws the snake's attention and gets him involved in conversations, like . . . in there, I tried to get him to saying like "Good day, sir." I think that's sort of wearing the village costume there and he's got the snake's attention while the knight is going to come up and clobber him.

Fitz: Why is the knight missing in the large drawing of the snake?

Scott: 'cause this snake is smiling and you never hit a snake in the back when he's smiling.

The second drawing discussed is *The Greenhouse* (Figure 7-7).

Fitz: How do you feel about those people there? Why did you keep outlining them over and over again? Was it for a reason?

Figure 7-6. The Snake

Figure 7-7. The Greenhouse

Scott: Yes, everything here, you're going to have to, uh . . . I forget where I learned that. I saw it someplace and use it now and then. Ah, they stand out and they're supposed to. Those are the two obvious characters. It gives them more of an appearance of reality. I guess, when you do that . . . . They are solid. . . . I can't have everything standing out at once. I've got to draw attention somewhere, so . . . .

Fitz: Do you think those people belong in there?

Scott: Yeah. The basic idea when I started out was, this guy is showing this girl a greenhouse. Maybe his uncle kept it locked for years. He'd inherited it. She came over to clean the house and he fell in love with her and he's showing her the sacred greenhouse. And this is what you'll find in your average sacred greenhouse.

The Graveyard (Figure 7-8), however, provoked the longest analysis. The following is a much-abbreviated transcript.

Scott: Now I can start lecturing on my favorite author, H. P. Lovecraft. I think he's one of the most unrecognized . . . . Well, he's being recognized now; his books are coming out. But at the time not too many people were interested in this whole type of horror . . . . He had a whole mythology. His was always the unnameable, the thing you couldn't put your finger on. That's one of the author's tricks. He never really explains to you what the horror is and he leaves it up to your own imagination. You imagine whatever is scary enough to you to scare you. And it works pretty well.

Now there's nothing horrible here [referring to the drawing]. You've seen graveyards. The story here . . . . It was about a guy who was an apprentice to a professor, and they would journey off to places and they would read in strange books . . . he found in one book a reference to a hidden graveyard . . . . they dug under a certain marked stone. Obviously they knew they were there 'cause the leader of the two had telephone cable with him, and he went down the steps with a light while the other stayed at the top with the telephone listening to him. And at the end you hear him yelling that he hadn't counted on this, and then there's silence. Then this voice says, "Warren is dead." . . . It's always the sense of aloneness that adds to the horror.

At the conclusion of the interview, Mr. Fitzpatrick asked Scott what direction he thought he would take with his art.

Scott: I'd like to try illustration, if someone's got a story about the knights . . . . Right now I'm studying . . . I've got books from the library about the costumes, the buildings. I'm learning architecture, about how they used to build the houses. I'm taking *Prince Valiant* comics out of the newspaper because I think Hal Foster's a very good artist. I'm studying his work and putting it down into notebooks. Hopefully, like I do with present-day stuff, like if I want to draw a 1930 radio, I draw a 1930 radio . . . . I'll know how to put it all down. Once you get all the knowledge inside your head, then all you've got to do is be

Figure 7-8. The Graveyard

impressed by something and you'll know what to put down. Sort of like a computer. It knows which parts to take out and put down . . . . What I'm trying to do is know as much as I can about the way it was back then.

It is readily apparent from this young man's words and deeds— his critical and artistic activities—that he has, in Janson's words, "discover[ed] that he needs the approval of outside beholders, and he will preserve his work in the hope of finding an appreciative public." While Gregory's work was predictable and therefore properly called "proto-art," Scott's drawings seem clearly to qualify for Janson's second category, "art." I would like now to carry Janson's distinctions a step further, in light of the foregoing. I suggested earlier that there is an important difference between creative and aesthetic objects and processes, a difference that is often obscured in the field of art education. I shall conclude by attempting to make this distinction more explicit.

The Creative-Aesthetic Distinction

We can appreciate the need for a correct analysis of the concept "creative art" in theory and practice if we reflect, for a moment, on the meanings of the words "create," "creative," "creativity," and their derivatives as they are ordinarily used. The dictionary says that to create is "to cause to be, bring into being, to make," while "creative" means "having the power to create." Thus, at the very least, the sentence "John is a creative artist" means that "John has the power to bring into being something novel, original, or unique (not something copied or reproduced)." But, surely, while the production of novelty is a necessary condition for calling John creative, it is insufficient in itself. For we do not ordinarily accept a random scribble on paper, an accidental brush stroke on canvas, or a haphazard striking of keys on a piano as evidence of John's creativity. (It must be remembered that, for Janson, while the artist is one who is "accident prone," he is an artist because he can go on to exploit the accident.) It would seem, then, that another condition for correctly calling John creative is that the speaker also perceives the novelty John has produced *as art*, that is, as an object or event similar in at least some respects to objects or events already existing in the art world. The speaker's familiarity with this world seems required. Indeed, one check on the truth of the claim that "John is a creative artist" is to see whether, in fact, the object or event *is* unique when compared with existing art objects or events.[11]

But even if the scribble, sequence of notes, or configuration on canvas is found to be truly unique in the art world, this fact alone is still insufficient. For the object to be called "creative" we would ordinarily expect that the speaker also *valued it* as a unique art object. Thus, in conformity with ordinary linquistic usage, we may incorporate the results of the foregoing analysis in the following statement.

1. *What is done (made, performed) is not ordinarily called artistically creative unless the object or event is seen as art, is thought to be unique, and is valued for its uniqueness.*

And, without getting involved with a statistical sampling of linguistic usage, we may also accept this slightly stronger statement.

2. *An object or event (or series of objects or events) produced by John must be seen as art, thought to be unique, and valued for its uniqueness, before John is identified as a creative artist by those familiar with the art world.*

It can now be noted that much of the classical psychological research on the personal characteristics, social milieu, and education of the creative artist—young or old—depends upon just such prior judgments by "the experts" as to which artists shall be included among the subjects of the researcher's study. That is, researchers adopting this procedure (and a fortiori all theories of creativity grounded in the results of such research) take the gist of the second statement *as given.* And references to "operational definitions," "interjudge reliability," "method of population identification," and so forth, that are found in the literature reporting such research boil down to the following paradigmatic sentence.

3. *Our experts (independently) believe that John is a creative artist because they value the uniqueness of his artworks.*

Although I am persuaded that the results of such research have value for the field of art education, it still makes sense to pursue the question as to whether the following statement is true.

4. *John is a creative artist.*

The following amounts to the same thing in the context of our analysis.

5. *X, Y, and Z artworks (produced by John) are evidence of creativity.*

Those researchers who, in effect, have reason to believe that the third statement is true cannot thereby assume the truth of the fourth and fifth statements because these statements are not implied by the third statement. Any research finding is flawed, moreover, if the phrase "creative artist" appears without quotation marks (as it were) in unqualified statements that the creative artist has particular traits.

What is required to determine the truth of the fourth statement is, (a), an explication of *why* the experts believe that John is a creative artist (not merely the report that they do agree); and, (b), a determination of whether their reasons are consistent and if these reasons justify their belief. In other words, it must be determined, in the terms of the fifth statement, that there are good reasons to support the claim that X, Y, and Z artworks are *valuable* (not merely that they are valued). The point here, is that a determination of the truth of the fourth and fifth statements cannot be restricted to finding out whether someone (an expert or otherwise) holds certain beliefs and values.

I shall quickly indicate how experts may positively value the uniqueness of an artwork and justify their judgments that it is valuable with quite different kinds of reasons. Perhaps the first expert that comes to mind is the art historian, who could readily establish the historical value of Picasso's *Les Demoiselles d'Avignon* (1906-1907) as pivotal in the development of cubism and the understanding of what followed in Western painting. An art dealer, on the other hand, might well establish the monetary value of Picasso's painting on the open market; because it is unique and irreplaceable it could command a huge sum if the Museum of Modern Art decided to "deaccession" it. A contemporary art critic may also positively value the painting, although its first critics, including Matisse, were outraged. Whereas the justifications of historical judgments of art and assessments of monetary worth are fairly straightforward, a special problem arises with the justification of aesthetic judgments. There is a lively dispute among aestheticians as to whether uniqueness can be an aesthetic predicate.[12] The question is, formally, whether the historical fact that a painting is unique can be counted as one of the reasons that presumably would justify the following judgment.

6. *X is a good painting.*

My own argument that it cannot be so counted goes as follows:

Historical judgments of the uniqueness of a particular painting are always *comparative* judgments in which the historian views the painting in the context of a group of paintings (or the history of painting) so as to determine if it presents some visible departure in form, content, or technique to warrant the judgment that it is indeed unique. But an *aesthetic* judgment cannot be a comparative judgment involving other paintings because to judge the aesthetic quality of a painting requires that the critic view it as a totality—as an aesthetic whole—so as then to be able to reflect upon the quality of the experience it afforded. A comparative judgment (historical, economic, political, or sociological), on the other hand, requires that there be established some basis upon which a comparison is to be made. And one cannot at the same time consider the totality of a painting as an aesthetic object while comparing an aspect of that painting with other paintings.

There is another way of making the same point. Imagine two paintings perceptually indistinguishable; one is a fake, a visually perfect copy painted by a master forger of the other, the original, painted by John. The art historian determines which is the authentic painting by X-raying the two canvases to check the underpainting against a known example of John's work. He may well be impressed with the great skill of the forger in re-creating the original, but it is unlikely he would call the forger a creative artist. The art critic, however, is primarily interested in the aesthetic quality of the experience afforded by the object in his perceptual field. Since he cannot determine whether the painting is the fake or the original solely by looking at it, his determination is irrelevant to his task as art critic, even if he learns that John was judged to be a creative artist by the art historian. All things being equal except authenticity, the critic *must* judge the two paintings as having equal aesthetic merit. His justification must be grounded in the aesthetic facts of his experience with each painting, and his description of these facts can be verified by others through their experiences with the same paintings.[13]

The above is my analysis of a distinctive practice of the art historian and the art critic, respectively. The practice of the studio art teacher involves aesthetic judgments as well as comparative judgments of students' work. The only difference in the teacher's practice is the question of the appropriate means of communicating these judgments. When the statement, "John is a creative artist," refers to a sixteen-year-old boy and is justified by comparing his work with the work of his peers, then there are obviously psychological, social, and perhaps ethical considerations that might affect the teacher's decision as to whether—or how—to communicate this judgment to John or his parents. What distinguishes artists, teachers, critics, historians, museum and gallery workers, and other professionals in the art world from laymen is their skill in making and justifying aesthetic and comparative judgments of art objects and events, among other practices. And some of them, the artist and the art teacher especially, have more than a hunch as to what promotes creativity and what denies it in a given situation.

Conclusion

The foregoing analysis of materials provided by just two subjects constitutes only a small part of my efforts to extend a particular conception of aesthetic education in light of the evidence of children's artistic and critical activities—what they do and say in art contexts. Yet I hope I have pinpointed a much-neglected problem: how the critical responses of the child to his or her own artistic production determine how far he or she is able to move toward becoming a creative artist. That the young child is not a creative artist seems evident enough; that a few children become artists is equally obvious. While it is not at all clear how this happens, the difficult transition from biological to cultural stages of artistic development apparently requires aesthetic inquiry at the level of art criticism—a growing sense of one's own artistic accomplishments in the context of the art world. At least my evidence suggests this conclusion.

Notes

1. David W. Ecker, "Analyzing Children's Talk about Art," *Journal of Aesthetic Education,* VII (January 1973), 58-73.
2. David W. Ecker and Eugene F. Kaelin, "The Limits of Aesthetic Inquiry: A Guide to Educational Research," in *Philosophical Redirection of Educational Research,* Seventy-first Yearbook of the National Society for the Study of Education (Chicago: University of Chicago Press, 1972), 285-286.
3. Desmond Morris, *The Biology of Art* (London: Methuen & Co., 1962).
4. H. W. Janson, "After Betsy, What?" in Elliot W. Eisner and David W. Ecker,

Readings in Art Education (Waltham, Mass.: Blaisdell Publishing Co., 1966), 370-378.

5. *Ibid.*, 374.

6. *Ibid.*, 377-378.

7. *Ibid.*, 378.

8. This is basically the argument in David W. Ecker, "The Artistic Process as Qualitative Problem-Solving," *Journal of Aesthetics and Art Criticism,* XXI (Spring 1963), 283-290.

9. See Ecker, "Analyzing Children's Talk about Art."

10. Mr. Fitzpatrick also conducted a forty-seven-minute tape-recorded interview with Scott as part of a project undertaken by Mr. Fitzpatrick while he was a member of my graduate research course at New York University. I wish to thank Mr. Fitzpatrick and his subject, Mr. Scott Kerr, for permission to use the material quoted and shown, which is contained in the unpublished document, "Teaching Strategies for Exceptional Students," May 1974.

11. Every object or event is, strictly speaking, unique to its time and place; hence it would be irrelevant to argue that everything is unique in this sense of uniqueness.

12. Mary Mothersill, " 'Unique' as an Aesthetic Predicate," *Journal of Philosophy,* LVII (August 3, 1961), 421-437.

13. See David W. Ecker, "Justifying Aesthetic Judgments," *Art Education,* XX (May 1967), 5-8.

PART II

The Arts and the Social Context of Schooling

Introduction

Education is a process, and schools are institutions. Because such institutions function in a social context, they are buffeted by the pressures and values that pervade that context. Thus, in a significant sense schools not only reflect the values of the society, but they serve them. Perhaps that is the way it should be. At the same time educational aspirations often exceed the virtues that characterize the society the schools serve. "Ah! but a man's reach should exceed his grasp, or what's heaven for?"

To realize the fondest of our educational hopes will require attention to the circumstances beyond the boundaries of the school itself. Attention must be paid to the forces, both political and economic, that shape the character of the school and give direction to its mission. Educational change, in short, must attend to factors outside the walls of the schools.

The chapters in Part II address themselves largely to the possibilities of reorganizing school programs in the arts and to identifying the social conditions that influence educational priorities. In doing so they provide a complementary dimension to the issues addressed in Part I. The promise of such attention is that it helps all of us concerned with the arts in education avoid those forms of self-deception that tend to reassure us that the arts are increasing in their educational significance in the schools, when in fact they are not. What I believe we are seeking ultimately is a systemic change in our conception of man and hence in our conception of the conditions that will foster his development. This is no modest goal. To aspire to less is to aspire to less than what we can be—after all, what *is* a heaven for?

8

Art, Education, and the Consumption of Images

EDMUND BURKE FELDMAN

> Unlike the reader, the spectator is not free to absorb only what he chooses, assimilating his impressions later, in meditation or reverie; he becomes the prey of what he sees.
>
> René Huyghe,
> *Ideas and Images in World Art*

On the face of it, there does not seem to be any obvious connection between art and education. I say this notwithstanding the existence of the hybrid discipline art education and despite the widespread conviction that, since art and education are both good things, they must somehow be related. But the fact is that art, as classically defined, is a superior form of work, whereas education has more to do with the molding of character, the transmission of information, and the development of skills. If we take just the last item in that definition—the development of skills—and use it as a rationale for art education, we arrive at something close to the current state of practice in the profession, although, to be sure, art educators also make pious sounds about their commitment to the objectives of liberal education: the acquisition of knowledge and the development of character. They are, nevertheless, committed in practice to more or less good work with artistic materials, the product of which is supposed to be enhanced moral and intellectual development. There is little convincing evidence to support them in this claim.

The discrepancy between practice and educational rationale is easily explained by recourse to the classical theory of art. The Greeks understood that the artisan is a workman, and they valued his product. They even suspected that the very structure of the cosmos was echoed in the organization of his finest works; this was because his work was designed according to fundamentally mathematical, that is, geometric, rules. Thus, if the artisan knew geometry, he was a superior sort of workman—capable of exercising his mind as he endeavored to uncover the mysteries of the universe locked in the microcosm. But this is an exalted definition of the artisan's role, a role that impressed Sir Herbert Read to the extent that he advanced what he called a Platonic theory of "education through art."[1] Still, that austere and aristocratic bachelor, Plato, had no use for artists in his *Republic;* he feared they might miseducate children by exposing them to what is untrue, dangerous, immoral, or ugly. Like other Greeks of his class, he appreciated the educational importance of art, that is, the cognitive and aesthetic values of seeing beautiful sculpture or listening to harmonious music. But he would have been shocked at the prospect of educating the future leaders of society by teaching them to practice a craft like an ordinary *banausos,* or workman. Children might sing and play; they might study suitably edited poems and stories, mainly so that their imaginations and emotions would be shaped in conformity with the good, the true, the just, and the beautiful. But they should not be trained as practitioners of painting, pottery, and sculpture—not if they were going to function as free citizens and wise governors of the polis. Free citizens, the future rulers of the state, must know what is good in art or morals in order to exercise intelligent judgment in these matters. But such knowledge (we would call it critical expertise) was gained through practice in the art of dialectic, the Socratic method of examining questions and ideas through argument. Since Greek artisans were mainly slaves or menial laborers, they had no opportunity (that is, no leisure time) to study goodness and truth; hence, though they might be good workers, they would not necessarily know the *reason why* a work was good. Sir Herbert Read notwithstanding, Plato believed that the practice of an art or craft unsuits a person for a life of reason and reflection. It hinders the development of dialectical skill and hence of critical judgment. We, on the other hand, are convinced that systematic instruction in artistic performance, especially at elementary school levels, is an essential part of the general education of each child. And it is not only for the sake of play or exploration with materials that we hold this conviction: we believe that painting, modeling, carving, printmaking, and other similar activities develop problem-solving skills, creativity, wholesome character, appreciation of beauty, good habits of work, and psychological health. As was mentioned above, however, there is no real evidence that this is so.

Why do we insist, in the face of the educational traditions we inherited from ancient Hellas, that the practice of an art is aesthetically, morally, or intellectually desirable? Perhaps the working-class origin of Christianity contributed to an upward revision in the status of the worker: Jesus had worked as a carpenter; many of his followers were slaves and manual laborers. Although the Old Testament appreciated the importance of work and the human dignity of the worker, the Jewish tradition was very similar to the Greek in setting the study of law or dialectic above the skilled making of things. By the fifth century, therefore, Jesus was presented to the Romans as a first-class Talmudist rather than a carpenter who did some preaching on the side. And so we have carved sarcophagi showing Christ among the doctors and Christ discoursing on the law. Early Christianity still shared the old Jewish attitude about the essential inferiority of manual workers: its artistic products were embarrassingly crude (unless made by Greek, Syrian, or Roman artisans). The quality of Christian art began to improve only during the late Middle Ages when it became apparent that the newly converted tribesmen of Europe were more impressed by visual images than by verbal exhortation or written texts, which they could not read. But during its first seven or eight centuries, the church treated artisans and workmen as the Greeks and Romans had—somewhat better than peasants and serfs, but hardly with the respect reserved for lawyers, men of letters, or even illiterate knights. By the time of the high Gothic period, however, the senior stone carvers, master masons, and image makers employed in cathedral construction had emerged as an upper class of workmen almost on a par with ecclesiastics. Here as with the best Greek artisans, it was knowledge of geometry that moved them upward in the hierarchy of the building and decorating trades. Until the twelfth century, however, we can find no evidence on the status of the artisan to make us believe that he was regarded as well suited, by virtue of his training and experience in a craft, to exercise leadership in the councils of government, trade, or war. Highly esteemed though he might have been among other workmen, the artisan did not belong to either of the powerful and respected orders of medieval society, the clergy or the knightly nobility. With the exception of a few master masons, the artisan was not a learned man.

It was not until the Italian Renaissance that the artist emerged from the artisan class and began to be regarded as something of an intellectual, a person who could mingle on terms of equality with humanists, on the one hand, and clergy on the other. I shall not go into all the reasons for this change in the status of the artist (Arnold Hauser is the best source on the subject[2]). For our purposes, it is enough to point out that the Quattrocento witnessed the admission of certain image makers to the rarefied atmosphere cultivated by the learned men and women of Florence, Milan, Urbino, Ferrara, and Naples. The majority of artisans, however, remained more or less well-paid workmen. Even the outstanding artists were still attached, by virtue of their training as apprentices and their guild membership, to the ethos of the craft tradition.

The princes, bankers, and churchmen of the fifteenth and sixteenth centuries were learned as well as rich men. Furthermore, the art they commissioned was intended mainly for their private pleasure and contemplation, as opposed to the instruction of the masses. Artists who sought their patronage needed to be acquainted with the humanistic and Neoplatonic ideas that were modifying or replacing the legacy of medieval Christian thought that survived among the masses. Thus the sophistication of the former artisan led to the phenomenon of the "universal man," the artistic genius who is more than a humanist or mere technician. The test of his knowledge and craft was simultaneously visible in his art. But since the Renaissance set a premium on the man of action, intellect was not prized for its own sake; it had to be accompanied by concrete performance and graceful expression. The heroes of the age were admired because they knew how to *do* things. The artist could be a hero, no less than the statesman, because he, too, was a knower and a doer. It is clear that he had come a long way from the more or less servile status of the skilled but ignorant workman.

The modern notion of the artist is much indebted to the ideal of the artist-intellectual established by a few Renaissance men of genius, such as Alberti, Brunelleschi, Leonardo, Raphael, and Michelangelo. Modern art education has taken these men of the Quattrocento and Cinquecento as models for its efforts on behalf of children and young people in schools, colleges, and universities. To be sure, the Renaissance ideal of a synthesis of knowledge and craft in the education of an artist has been diluted by the romantic ideal of inspiration as a means of bypassing both technical apprenticeship and academic study in the cultivation of genius. The result is that we have today many artists who are neither craftsmen in the Greek sense nor intellectuals in the Renaissance sense. Many of them sit on university faculties, however, and call themselves professors. All this testifies to the touching desire of our society to support excellence without undertaking the liberal and humane studies that would enable us to know what excellence in art, or anything else, looks, sounds, feels, and tastes like.

One other consequence of the modern or Renaissance elevation of the artist's status was the creation of a gap between the populace as a whole and the most gifted men of the age. There was now a serious conflict between the tastes and aspirations of the progressive elements of society—the newly enfranchised artists and humanist intellectuals—and the masses of laymen who clung to essentially mystical and irrational ideas based on late medieval art and theology. In this conflict we see the origins of our contemporary notion of an avant-garde consisting of artists and cultural arbiters whose position *in* the avant-garde is confirmed by the resistance of the populace to their creations. Since this clash appears to be a conflict between the educated and the uneducated, enlightened persons tend to become automatic advocates of vanguard movements in art or anything else. In these cultural struggles, the ideological position of art education is clear: it aligns itself with "the tradition of the new," as Harold Rosenberg has called it.[3] Art educators perceive their mission as the evangelical promotion of favorable conditions for the celebration of what is most advanced, that is, most recent, on the creative scene.

The tendency of art educators to proselytize on behalf of avant garde art is a recognition—for the wrong reasons perhaps—of their responsibility for the kind and quality of images that students ingest or consume. That is what education in its best sense is all about. Teachers in any humanistic area have the same responsibility: to shape the images inside the heads of their students. But we recognize that the teacher's part in the entire process of creating, disseminating, and consuming images is not as crucial as it once was. That is, other agencies and modalities—mainly the mass media—are more powerful and more effective than teachers in urging images, hence values, upon the public.

The Image and Compulsory Assent

Much of the political struggle that goes on in an advanced industrial state revolves around access to the social organs of image dissemination. It is generally understood that control over those who fashion images, together with the ability to facilitate or prevent their distribution, is the key to power—in office seeking, the creation of markets, the merchandising of commodities, and the diffusion of ideas. But if power seekers instinctively appreciate the value of images, they do not necessarily understand the processes through which images compel assent.

An important asset of the image in the world of power and persuasion is that it transcends the usual methods of communication. This is not to say that visual images bypass our organs of intellect. They do, however, *reverse the order* in which ideas are normally received and evaluated. The image is first of all received by our organs of sensory and motor activity. This is to say that they oblige viewers to do a certain amount of physical work *before* any kind of cognitive, that is, logical and semantic, analysis is undertaken. And so the human organism already has made an investment in the image by the time it is ready to scrutinize it critically. The same cannot be said for literary and oral communication. Even when words succeed in creating mental images, as in poetry, certain kinds of prose, and colorful speech, they are received as logical structures that the reader or auditor can analyze *as* he reads or listens. The images created by verbal language, on the other hand, are almost always perceived *after* their logical and semantic dimensions have been analyzed and understood.

One reason for this difference between the perception of visual and verbal imagery lies in the fundamentally sequential structure of speech and writing as opposed to the almost simultaneous perception of visual forms. Second, because of our phylogenetic heritage, the visual image establishes connections with different—one might say "older"—portions of the brain than verbal structures. The feelings experienced in the presence of visual images are more difficult to control or resist than those dependent on language. Because language (especially the complex linguistic forms of modern man) evolved after the development of visual perception in the phylogeny of our species, we are equipped with older, possibly less sophisticated, biological equipment for the apprehension of images. We cannot so readily defend against what a picture seems to tell us to do or feel. Third, our knowledge systems and our educational institutions have been organized almost exclusively for the transmission and reception of linear structures. It is obvious that these institutions find themselves in crisis when nonlinear, that is, visual, sources of imagery are perfected and made cheaply and instantly available. To complicate the problem further, it is possible that the most technically sophisticated mental operations on which an advanced civilization depends cannot be learned except through linear, sequentially organized meaning structures. But for the engineering of public assent, the encouragement of nonreflective behavior, visual imagery is ideal.

If visual images are relatively invulnerable to logical and semantic scrutiny, how can we account for the extraordinary influence of verbal slogans in religion, politics, and advertising? The explanation is simple, and it reinforces our argument concerning the compelling power of the visual image: the effectiveness of a slogan depends on repetition, and the function of repetition is to convert a logical sequence into an image. In fact, the repeated slogan becomes a motor image—one that we find difficult to forget, like the lyrics of a bad song or a frequently heard advertising jingle. So long as a slogan can be analyzed semantically it can be resisted. But once it has been drilled into the popular consciousness in the form of a patterned reenactment, there is no way to prevent many compelling transactions, that is, automatic acquiescence, from taking place. Thus the slogan becomes part of our involuntary behavior.

Several questions then arise. First, how can teachers, specifically art educators, regain what might be called their pedagogical authority so far as the consumption of images is concerned? Second, is it essential that art educators themselves be influential creators of imagery? Third, what is the most strategic position for the art educator to occupy in the structure of creating and disseminating images? Fourth, assuming that the traditional job of teaching in schools continues to represent a viable role for art educators, what changes in curricular content and teaching method seem to be called for? I shall discuss these four questions in some greater detail.

Pedagogical Authority of Art Educators

The pedagogical authority of the art educator can only be restored, I believe, if teaching art in the schools is redefined as the critical study of visual images. To be sure, such images arise from many sources, including the images created by children and adolescents as well as by professional artists and designers. We cannot, however, afford to spend as much time as in the past on the training of that gifted minority of students who are themselves destined to become professionals. To continue along the present path is to be condemned to increasing irrelevance and, finally, to educational oblivion. In order to gain a position of genuine educational influence, the art educator must assume a role vis-à-vis man-made imagery that is analogous to the role of the teacher of reading and literature. The reason we believe we can evaluate ideas, spoken or written, is that we learned certain literary and dialectical skills at a fairly early age. And, to the extent that we acquired these skills as children, we were enabled to extend and enrich our subsequent living and learning. There is no comparable form of education dealing with the visual imagery that swamps children from the time they are born and preoccupies adults until they take their last breath. Thus there is a vacuum in the education of persons growing up in an age increasingly characterized by the consumption of nonverbal images.

Art Educators as Creators of Images

Great artists are influential creators of images. But influential creators of images are not always artists. And rarely are they teachers of art. Today most influential creators of imagery are what I call "media impresarios." Their work consists of, in brief, originating, packaging, selling, and distributing the images created by skilled artisans whom they employ. Typical media impresarios are film and record producers, television producers, advertising executives, book and magazine publishers, and the heads of the major architectural and industrial design firms. It is obvious that none of these impresarios is a teacher in the narrow sense of the term. The art educator engaged in the creation of paintings, prints, sculpture, and crafts can, therefore, view his artistic activity in three ways: he can regard himself as one who is continuing to practice an ancient art according to the highest possible standards; he can regard himself as a part-time professional who transmits to students the results of his firsthand experience as an artist; he can regard himself as a kind of psychological experimenter conducting inquiries into his own creative processes so that he can better guide the creative work of others. I submit that these are the principal rationales for the artistic activity of the art educator, and I confess to having advanced such arguments myself in the attempt to convince others of the artist's worth in the educational scheme of things. Such rationales are honorable and are germane to art education programs as presently conceived and carried out. But these programs seem increasingly unrelated to the processes of creating and consuming images in our culture. Hence, while the traditional reason for artists creating art remain valid, their connection to education grows more and more tenuous.

Strategic Position of Art Educators

So far as the strategic position of the art educator in the image-consumption process is concerned, there is nothing fundamentally wrong with the role of the schoolteacher. The function of teaching within the institutional structure of a school seems impotent vis-à-vis the activity of the mass media only because the skills cultivated in most school curricula pertain to obsolescent modes of image exchange and consumption. That is, schooling tends to be print oriented whereas pupils are increasingly image oriented. This is not to advocate abandonment of studies dealing with the grammar and rhetoric of letters. Educators who wish to influence values cannot, however, afford to neglect the grammar and rhetoric of images.

The power of the mass media to gain unquestioning acceptance of their images is not necessarily due to the inherent excellence of these images (although they are often impressive from a technical standpoint). Rather, they prevail because they operate in a critical vacuum: the analysis and evaluation of the images that govern our daily lives are conducted by the mass media themselves. Unlike the traditional artist who is mainly concerned with the creation of objets d'art, modern manufacturers of images publicize and distribute their products and create new occasions in the media for praising their work and celebrating their victories over the populace. Thus they hold a virtual monopoly over the imaginations of the people who alone are in a position to exercise political control over the managers of the various media: film, television, the record industry, magazine publishing, and so forth. So far as power over the image-consumption process is concerned, the situation appears to be tightly held and managed. The most influential image makers are substantially cut off from effective criticism by the various publics that make up our society.

In circumstances so fraught with danger for a democracy the art educator seems particularly well situated to develop the popular skills in analyzing and evaluating images that might function as a countervailing force. And the performance of such a function would be in keeping with the traditional role of liberal education, that is, the education either of elites destined to be rulers or of free citizens preparing for the responsibilities of self-governance. Hence, the problem of the art educator is not structural; the position of classroom teacher (with all the ancillary support that it commands) can be exceedingly influential when we consider that it operates over a period of schooling that lasts at least twelve years and penetrates every part of the nation. In other words, our problem remains the classical one of devising appropriate curricula and implementing them with suitable teaching techniques.

Changes in Curriculum and Teaching

The specific substance of necessary changes in art curriculum and teaching would fill several volumes. There are, however, a few general principles that should guide the construction of art education curricula as they relate to image consumption. First, some negative strictures should be given.

1. We should not base art curricula exclusively on the imagery of children and adolescents.

2. We should not present the cultivation of artistic proficiency as the sole or principal goal of art programs.

3. We should not evaluate creativity only in terms of originality in artistic, spoken, or written expression.

4. We should not base the visual "literature" of the art program on the work of contemporary artists alone. Neither should we confine our study to art in galleries.

5. We should avoid the trap of aestheticism, that is, the promotion of the idea that art instruction is solely aimed at the creation or appreciation of beautiful things.

6. We should not confuse art criticism with connoisseurship.

Following is some positive advice.

1. We should stress the function of the image as a cognitive vehicle and as a hypothetical model for behavior.

2. We should emphasize talk about images more than talk about ourselves; we should study art more than artists.

3. We should study critical procedures more than critical conclusions.

4. We should learn to see the visual elements in the small- and large-scale environment as expressive forms.

5. We should learn to defend critical interpretations by recourse to visual evidence rather than citation of art authorities and art publicists.

6. So far as curricular scope is concerned, we should try to deal with the major kinds and styles of imagery rather than the entire history of imagery.

7. In terms of curricular sequence, we should begin with contemporary images (the most familiar visual products) and move across cultures and historical periods to the examination of images that are comparable from the standpoint of appearance, style, function, material, or affect.

8. We should encourage artistic performance as a fact-gathering, image-organizing, and material-forming activity. The culmination of an art experience should be a sharing, a public exercise in visual persuasion, explanation, and display.

9. We should organize art teaching practices so that they entail the use of verbal and written expression as well as the selection and shaping of visual materials. We should, in other words, stress the role of art in multimedia communication.

Conclusion

As educators we stand in an adversary position vis-à-vis the contemporary culture of images. It cannot be otherwise if we wish to associate ourselves with the humane traditions of the West. But opposition does not constitute a program; certainly it does not give us the materials of a curriculum. What an adversary stance *does* urge is the development of visual literacy. If we believe that unfettered human intelligence is adequate to deal with the problems of a postindustrial civilization, then we are obliged to cultivate the tools that will enable intelligence to be free and to cope with the new problems of information and education posed by our civilization. The forces arrayed against us are impressive: the vast technologies of the mass media controlled by a few, virtually anonymous, frequently unscrupulous impresarios; the substantially unregulated operation of broadcasting, cinema, advertising, and publishing mainly for the sake of maximizing profits; the new alliance of technocrats, bureaucrats, and industrialists determined to maintain their authority, on the one hand, and their markets, on the other, by keeping the popular imagination in a condition of vassalage to the media of mass persuasion. We have little reason to believe that our politics or our economics will succeed in breaking up these powerful combinations against the existence of a free and decent imaginative life for the masses. Perhaps an education that is directed toward genuinely liberal and humane ends would make a difference. It would be morally refreshing to see this begin to happen in the field of art education.

Notes

1. Herbert Read, *Education through Art* (New York: Pantheon Books, 1945).
2. Arnold Hauser, *The Social History of Art*, 2 vols. (New York: Alfred A. Knopf, 1959).
3. Harold Rosenberg, *The Tradition of the New* (New York: Horizon Press, 1959).

9

The Politics of Arts Education in California

LOUIS P. NASH

Aristotle was right. "Man is by nature a political animal." He went on to say in his *Politics* that while reading, writing, and drawing should be taught for their utility, music and drawing are avenues to leisure activities, and the noble employment of leisure is the highest aim of man. As in Aristotle's time, public education today is highly influenced by politics. The lives of our children are often molded, not by the finest in educational expertise, but by political deals or the sincere but misguided fancies of elected officials.

Was it the result of educational research or Sputnik that centered our national priorities in education on mathematics and science in the late 1950's? Was it local initiative, a ground swell of parents' concern, that gave us the federal education acts of the middle 1960's with their categorical funding?

Politics and Arts Education

In the spring of 1975 there was discussion in California on the topic "Learning Your ABC's (Arts Battle in California)—Color Them Brown." California, with a new, ingenious, young governor (Jerry Brown), was in the throes of a great arts controversy. Substantial public support for the arts had been generated by a state senator who had helped to provide considerably increased state support of the arts. When he proposed controversial changes in the state's support of the arts, the governor took the legislation into his own hands, which resulted in a substantially reduced program that was completely under the governor's control. Thus the arts program will closely parallel the governor's taste in art or will follow the directions provided by his advisers. The state senator, who is sincerely concerned with the need for support of the arts, lost his leadership role by advocating a controversial program without the political power base to make it a reality.

Some years ago a legislator introduced major changes in the program for the preparation of teachers. California's governor, the father of the present governor, requested another legislator, who was highly respected by the education community, to lend his name to the bill. Although this former educator believed the bill would be harmful to education, his political needs indicated that he should support it. He did so and thus helped change teacher preparation in the state.

A decade ago the legislature became enamored of foreign languages and made it mandatory for all students in certain grades to study a foreign language. School districts poured millions of dollars into the program. They hired teachers who were specialists in the field and purchased television sets for in-school viewing and other instructional materials. Not only were funds diverted from other programs, but most arts programs for those grades were eliminated or drastically reduced in order to make time for the required language classes. After several years the law was repealed, leaving television sets unused, language teachers without positions, and arts programs demolished.

One more example should suffice. Since 1967 arts consultants in California schools have dropped from 408 to 112, while almost every school district and country with any administrative staff whatsoever now has a project director to handle federal funds and to write projects.

The above illustrations are not intended to suggest that politics is dirty or that legislators and other elected officials are stupid or misguided. They are meant to emphasize the need for the education establishment to form close ties and communication links with those in political power. We have allowed these educational disasters to come about through our ineffectiveness in dealing with political realities.

If the arts are to survive in public education, arts educators must join with all other educators in learning to work and perform in the political arena. The remainder of this chapter will discuss trends in arts education at the national, state, and local level. It will also make some suggestions for participation and direction for those concerned with education in the arts.

Trends in Arts Education

President Johnson's signature on the law establishing the National Endowment for the Arts opened a new era for the arts in this country. Comparisons with other nations may, of course, belittle America's efforts. But it must be recognized that the succeeding years have seen phenomenal growth in public support for the arts. The Artists-in-Schools Program, which was sponsored by the National Endowment, was inaugurated in 1969. From miniscule beginnings, it has grown to the point where, in 1974, 1,750 artists were placed in 5,000 schools in the United States.

The Artists-in-Schools Program cannot take the place of a basic arts curriculum, and I confess that my own impressions of the program were extremely negative until I became directly involved with some of its activities. In San Francisco the efforts of one highly talented and dedicated artist-parent in one school has grown in seven years to a highly diversified project involving forty schools and thousands of students. In Orange, California, the whole community is dancing, thanks to an Artists-in-Schools dance program, which is now in its second year.

Dr. Thomas Bergin of the University of Notre Dame, chairman of the National Panel of the Artists-in-Schools Program, remarked at the opening session of the panel:

It is difficult to exaggerate the total thrust this program can have . . . the boundless opportunity it represents . . . and above all, what it might yet become.

I know I speak on your behalf when I say we intend to work at it. We believe this program provides a whole new dimension for the arts . . . a whole new communication system or network, one which enables us to reach out to all our young people across the Nation . . . and at the same time sensitizes teachers to the great rewards which the arts bring to their teaching and the whole educational endeavor. On many different occasions and in many different ways, John Kennedy used to say: "We must begin with our young if we truly want to bring about lasting change . . . whether it is in greater appreciation of the arts . . . greater human dignity, better citizenship, or whatever, our young can change the world." Surely, Artists-in-Schools is on that track.[1]

A second national program to emerge in the last decade is the Alliance for Arts Education, which links the United States Office of Education and the John F. Kennedy Center for the Performing Arts. The alliance has two main purposes: first, to utilize the Kennedy Center as a national showcase for arts education and provide expert assistance to the nation in that field; and, second, to strengthen arts education throughout the nation by assisting in the formation of state committees to bring together all the diverse elements of arts education in a unified effort.

Now in its third year, the alliance has had tremendous impact upon the whole nation. With minimum financial support from Congress, but with the efforts of a highly dedicated staff and the prestige of national leaders in Congress and the arts, the alliance has touched all of us and has affected the lives of millions of boys and girls. The activities of the California State Committee, which are supported nationally, strongly influenced the creation of the position I now hold—consultant in arts education in the California State Department of Education—a position for which arts educators had been struggling valiantly for years. In every state, with varying degrees of success, arts educators are working together toward a common goal: improving arts education. And many of them are meeting each other for the first time on state committees.

A third emerging element on the national scene is the John D. Rockefeller 3rd Fund. Dynamically led by Kathryn Bloom, formerly with the U.S. Office of Education, the fund has as its goal the development of comprehensive arts education programs and their infusion into the mainstream of the curriculum. To accomplish this goal the fund suggests strengthening individual arts education, developing interdisciplinary programs, and utilizing community resources.

Charles B. Fowler, distinguished arts consultant, described comprehensive arts education as follows:

The idea of infusing the arts in the curriculum—the interdisciplinary context—
causes problems. To view the arts comprehensively causes apprehension because
we fear the loss of our claim to our private world. But that claim is fictitious.
Operating separately as we have, we never had much freedom. The English
teachers have it; so do the science and the mathematics teachers. At least they
have *more* of it. They are far more their own masters. They don't have to
continually wage a fight for a place in the curriculum, or an assured slice of the
budget, or a chance to reach all the students, or a need to achieve status with
the power structure. And they don't need to spend precious energies writing
hundreds of articles and position papers justifying their existence. They operate
far more independently than the arts. And for good reason. They are all
together. Biology teachers are not threatened by physics or chemistry. They
represent the sciences. We think of mathematics, not algebra, geometry, and
trigonometry; a comprehensive posture for the arts can provide a new sense of
release for arts educators. With that changed posture will come other important
differences in the way we operate. We will no longer need to give art shows in
order to impress the administration, nor concerts for the purpose of showcasing
the music department. Such public displays become occasions to share learning
and achievement, not ways to impress or gain status or personal rewards. It is
then that we will begin to teach for true leisure.

I also have an idea that as we reach out and join hands and as that process
is multiplied in reaching beyond ourselves out into the community, we will also
find that our elitist orientations will quite naturally subside in the process. This
joining of forces brings a whole new attitude of *inclusion*. The cooperative
venture will preclude whole programs that exclude and, instead, begin to make a
place for every student in the arts. When we are able to relax into less protective-
ness, we will open ourselves more willingly to others. The old music program,
which started with everyone and gradually eliminated people and music in a
great converging pyramid that ended at its apex with a doctor who could only
enjoy the last quartets of Beethoven (and there were very few people left),
could be inverted, so that it started with everyone and enlarged their horizons
to enjoy a continually wider range of music.

I think this is the case with all the arts, and I for one look forward to
the day when arts educators have succeeded in these efforts. I favor more meetings to these ends and more efforts toward alignment, until the arts, as a cooperative venture, make the impact on American lives that those lives have a right
to.[2]

The JDR 3rd Fund has worked with a number of school districts
and agencies, but its major thrust lately has been to assist state
departments of education in developing arts education programs. In
California the fund was a major catalyst in devising a plan for arts
education. For several years Pennsylvania has received support from
the fund; that support has been as much in the form of direction and

guidance as of funding. Because of that help and the dedicated efforts of the proponents of arts education in the state who have had the wisdom to pursue every avenue of support, including the fund, Pennsylvania has truly become one of the leaders in the field of comprehensive arts education.

The fund's latest project has been to organize a consortium of ten states that have begun to develop comprehensive arts education programs. Representatives from these states have been meeting regularly to refine the process, share some triumphs and failures, and develop models that may perhaps provide guidance for other states as well as to assist one another. The ten states provided leadership in the recent national meeting of the Alliance for Arts Education at the Kennedy Center in which all states were represented.

The fund has served in an advisory capacity to the alliance; together they conducted at the Kennedy Center last year a planning session for the development of comprehensive arts education programs for individual states. The remarks by Charles Fowler, quoted above, were excerpted from those proceedings. A measure of the fund's influence is recorded in this year's grants proposal information from the alliance, which reflects the philosophy of the JDR 3rd Fund toward arts education: "all the arts for all the children."

The work of the Ford Foundation and the Rockefeller Foundation is well known and need not be repeated here. These foundations and many smaller but equally supportive organizations have had great influence in directing federal funds and those of many major corporations toward support for the arts and arts education. The Arthur Fels Foundation, which is less well known than some of the giants, has been extremely helpful and, I might add, patient as we in California spent several years developing a Humanities Framework, a proposal that is perhaps unique in education today.

National activity such as the National Endowment for the Arts, the National Endowment for the Humanities, the Alliance for Arts Education, and the JDR 3rd Fund all affect directions in individual states. Though each state is unique, it has many things in common with the other states; these common aspects often reflect national directions.

No mention has been made of federal programs in education, which have also affected arts education, not only through Title III innovative programs but also, indirectly, through Title I support.

Numerous projects, funded under Title III, have produced a wealth of materials that have been shared among the states.

The greatest problem in state and local education today is finance. Inflation and declining enrollments are forcing schools to cut educational programs severely. This is understandable since taxpayers are not wildly enthusiastic in their support of increasing taxes for schools when their own budgets are strained at the local supermarket.

Arts education has not received a substantial part of state arts council grants, except perhaps in an indirect way of supporting arts projects that may or may not benefit children. Appropriations by state legislatures to arts councils are not keeping pace with inflation; thus, little in the immediate future can be gained from them. In the long run, however, the impact of each state alliance for arts education will expand the activities to education, and so we can look for more state arts councils to provide support for arts in the schools.

Recently in California, though, opposition by the large arts organizations scuttled proposed arts legislation directed toward the "little man" and with a large component for arts education. Leaders in arts education in the state are now developing legislation specifically for arts education, and in Michigan a major effect has been expended to give arts education a portion of that state's education appropriation.

National and state surveys indicate a major interest and support for the expansion of arts education. It is easy to respond to a survey; it is an entirely different matter to reach into a pocketbook.

In spite of surveys, pontifical pronouncements, and the like, the arts are being eliminated in schools by default. Teacher certification no longer requires arts courses in many states, and pressures for teaching the basic subjects give many elementary teachers an easy out for neglecting the arts. Harrassed teachers, pressured by parents, administrators, and even the federal government, can find few precious minutes to teach the arts, even if they desire to do so. Until laws make the arts mandatory in the curriculum, they will continue to be neglected.

Arts education leaders in many states are beginning, albeit a little late, to get into the political arena. They are finding tremendous community support at the local school level. An arts council, a few artists and patrons of the arts, or even one dedicated parent can cause great things to happen. In one community, three "music mothers" brought about substantial changes in the school district's program in spite of the low ranking of the arts in the educational priorities as assessed by the community. A few band boosters improved the music program in another community. One committed parent in another district led such a strong campaign that the school board succumbed and hired specialists. A desert community, through the support of the arts council and the local university, helped to pass a tax increase that enabled ten arts specialists to be hired.

These are isolated examples, but they indicate a direction for all communities. Arts educators often wait too long to muster support, and, once programs are eliminated, or even threatened, it is too late. Arts educators, regardless of the strength of their programs, must seek support and build a solid public relations program before the ax falls. Each community contains a very small group of individuals who constitute the city's power structure. Support from one such individual may be all that is needed to affect major changes or to maintain solid arts programs.

We have, then, three avenues for the support and development of arts education. First is encouragement for arts education at the state and national levels through local support and enthusiasm for existing programs and the inauguration of legislation directed toward initiating arts education.

Second is to follow the lead of the JDR 3rd Fund to infuse the arts into the basic curriculum so that they will not be on the periphery and thus easily eliminated. (In line with this thinking, the reader will note that "arts" rather than "art" has been used throughout this chapter.)

Third is to get into politics. To some, politics has been distasteful, but both before and since Aristotle politics has been a noble endeavor, and politicians are, in the main, dedicated to providing a true representation for the people they serve. Whether on the local school board, city council, state legislature, or in Congress, these representatives are listening and want to hear their constituents. It is up to each individual to make his or her concerns heard. If Aristotle was right, stand up and be a "political animal."

Notes

1. United States Congress, House, *Congressional Record*, 93rd Cong., 1st sess., from remarks of John Brademas of Indiana, November 19, 1974.
2. "Summary Report and Reactions to the Comprehensive Arts Planning Project at the J. F. Kennedy Center, October 1974," by Charles B. Fowler, journalist and consultant in the arts.

10

Crystal Gazing, Forecasting, and Wishful Thinking: The Future of the Arts in Public Education

HILDA P. LEWIS

> Heaven from all creatures hides the book of fate.
>
> Shakespeare

Neither I nor anyone else can say what the future holds. The future cannot be known, at least not in the same sense that we know the present and the past. Neither of the two time-honored roads to knowledge—reason and observation—is adequate in dealing with the future. The future cannot be perceived. Nor can we enter into it by following the path of logic. Nevertheless, as far back as history can take us we find people seeking ways to predict the future.

All societies have their diviners. The word "diviner" comes from the Latin word for a god. People believe that the diviner has access to knowledge not available to ordinary people. I am greatly honored and much abashed to find myself, at least for the moment, a part of this tradition. But I must confess that I am not clairvoyant; nor do I have a hot line to the deity. Though I do not know how to use the techniques of my illustrious predecessors, I may serve some of the same ends. Let me explain.

In ancient Greece when someone wanted to know what fate held in store, he went to the temple at Delphi over which a goddess, the pythoness, presided. But the pythoness spoke in riddles that the petitioner had to solve. Literature is full of tales about the consequences of misinterpreting these riddles. When Croesus asked the oracle how long his kingdom would last, he was told "until a mule is king of the Medes." Taking it to mean the kingdom would last forever, Croesus made war against the Medes and Persians. He was defeated by Cyrus, whose mother was a princess of Medes and whose father was a Persian subject. It was Cyrus who was, metaphorically speaking, the mule—the hybrid issue of such a union. Macbeth, emboldened by the witch's prophecy that he would be king until "Birnam Wood comes to Dunsinane," unleashed his ambitions, and, secure in the illusion of his own invincibility, embarked on the course that destroyed him.

Diviners are of many varieties. The ancient Hebrew prophets and their counterparts in all ages claim special knowledge of the moral judgment of God and sound warnings against behavior that would anger him and cause him to wreak havoc upon the earth. Crystal gazers are seers—or see-ers—who, as the name suggests, claim a gift of extraordinary vision. They sit in a quiet, darkened room, free from pictures, mirrors, ornaments, or bright colors, and fix their eyes upon the crystal ball until it begins to look dull or cloudy with small pinpoints of light glittering within, like tiny stars. Then their visions begin to appear, and they speak. When a lady goes to a fortune-teller and hears that she will meet a tall, dark stranger, she decides to get some new clothes, get her hair styled, and shed a few pounds. Because she looks better and feels ready for romance, her prospects are thereby greatly enhanced.

People seek knowledge of the future in order to act wisely in the present. They relate what they hear to their desires. Their deeds affect the future. They must, however, build on what exists. Past, present, and future are bound together.

Inherent in the idea of predicting the future is the concept of an orderly universe. The planets moving in their predetermined orbits are seen by astrologers as part of a larger plan involving life on earth. People with extraordinary powers need only a glimpse of a fragment of this orderly pattern to be able to describe the rest. The *I Ching*, the lines on the palm, the way tarot cards fall, the arrangement of tea leaves at the bottom of a cup—all these manifestations are not considered random events but part of a hidden design, which when properly understood, are clues to the rest.

People with an aversion to the mystical reject the predictive value of such omens. They look for and believe in other signs, those that fall more comfortably within a scientific philosophy. They rely on scientifically based forecasting. In forecasting, data are analyzed so that one can make statements about the probability of occurrence of certain events.

The most ubiquitous forecast is the weather report. It is reliable because, as the old saying goes, "everyone talks about the weather but no one does anything about it." The weather can be predicted with a high degree of confidence because human intervention is, at present, rare. In the old days, weather reports were stated in terms such as "fair and warm," "intermittent showers," "snow in the mountains." Nowadays weather forecasts are stated in terms of probability—"the chances are seven in ten that it will rain." Forecasting deals with the probability of occurrence of alternative futures.

Probabilistic inferences from scientific data and theory offer a way of knowing about the future without recourse to divination or clairvoyance. The ancient concept of the future as a fate, that is, a predetermined course of events, gives way to the notion of a variety of possible alternative futures. The new field of futures research aims at helping policy makers choose wisely among alternative courses of action. Choices are made in the light of objectives; thus, we first decide on the future we want, and then we plan how to achieve it. Scientific methods are thus placed in the service of wish fulfillment.

Through the ages people have sought knowledge of the future as a guide to action. Hopes and expectations affect deeds. Aspirations, wishes, and dreams are first steps in planning for the future. Wishful thinking is not just an idle pastime but a source of goals that can be actively pursued. The self-fulfilling prophecy works because it subtly molds behavior. The future we envision acts as a lodestone; it moves us toward it.

It is important for educators concerned with the arts to project a state of affairs that seems both possible and desirable and then to act consciously to achieve their goals. It can be said that there are those who do, those who are done to, and those who just sit and watch. For too long education has been done to. In recent years, change has too often come about by legislative actions, student protest, funded programs, budget cuts, and the like. It is time for the profession itself to take the initiative.

I shall now describe arts education as I would like it to be, identify some influences that favor development in this direction as well as some that oppose it, and suggest ways that might move us closer to this vision of the arts in education.

A View of the Future of Arts Education

I would like to see all the arts offered to all children and young people. By this I mean every elementary school, middle school, and secondary school would conduct programs that include not only music, the visual arts, and creative writing, but also dance, drama, and newer art forms including film, photography, television, multimedia productions, and, indeed, whatever art forms emerge in the years to come.

I would like the arts to enjoy a status in the curriculum comparable to the basic skills and the sciences. By this I mean that the arts will be considered as essential to the development, well-being, and future of students as any other area of the curriculum and that the allocation of financial resources, human resources, and instructional time will reflect this high esteem.

At present we are far from this goal. In all too many elementary schools few of the arts are taught; those that are taught are given meager time allotments and tend to be regarded as diversion rather than education. Conditions are even worse in the high school. Few schools offer a wide choice of arts courses, and those that are offered are taken by a small minority of students. The final report of *A Survey of the Status of the Theatre in United States High Schools*[1] begins with the sentence "Few United States high schools offer classroom instruction in the theatre arts." Curriculum overcrowding, limited funds, and unavailability of qualified teachers, in that order, are the reasons most frequently cited for the absence of courses in theater.

The study goes on to say that the chances of such courses being offered increase in proportion to the size of the school's student body. It also reports the alarming fact that nearly 18 percent of the teachers who direct high school plays do so without any previous college course work in directing, acting, or the technical aspects of theater and design. The study clearly shows that unless a faculty is very large it is not likely to include a drama teacher, and, surely, not a dance teacher or a teacher of filmmaking.

The situation is somewhat different for music. Some music is generally offered in the schools, but the courses are taken by only a small minority of students. The *Report on a Study of Music Programs in U.S. Elementary and Secondary Schools—1972-1973,*[2] conducted by the American Music Conference with the cooperation of the Music Educators' National Conference, dated February 1974, notes the following: 69 percent of the students take no music at all in the years of high school; only 10.4 percent of the high schools require music for graduation; 88.1 percent of the high schools do not offer a major in music; only 4.5 percent of high school students were enrolled in general music in the academic year 1972-1973; at the elementary school level, 83.4 percent reported a decrease in the music budget, and 50 percent reported that the art budget had also been cut.

The pattern for visual arts courses, as with music, is that they are offered by almost all junior and senior high schools, taken by a relatively small proportion of the students, and are almost never required.

With meager arts programming as the starting point and gloomy economic conditions to contend with, is it realistic to anticipate expansion of arts programs? Are there any data to support an optimistic view of the future of arts education?

Public Support for the Arts

In recent years interest in and involvement in the arts have grown. According to the nationwide Harris poll taken in January 1973,[3] 49 percent of the public sixteen years or older attend art shows, museums, and other visual arts exhibits. This figure is 2 percent greater than attendance at spectator sports. Forty-eight percent attend the theater, movies, ballet, or modern dance performances, opera, the circus, or other pageants. Forty-three percent reported that they engage in creative activities such as photography, painting, sketching, woodworking, and weaving. Thirty-seven percent attend musical performances. The young, the affluent, and the educated are the most dedicated in their pursuit of the arts. Furthermore, 89 percent of the population feel that the availability of museums, concert halls, and theaters is important to the quality of life.

The Harris poll also reveals that Americans are highly supportive of the arts in the schools. The majority of the public thinks the schools should be offering more courses in the arts. Ninety-four percent feel that playing a musical instrument should be taught in the local schools. Ninety-two percent favor the teaching of weaving, woodworking, pottery, and other crafts in the local schools; 89 percent think that art appreciation should be included in the curriculum; 81 percent feel that acting should be taught; 77 percent are in favor of teaching dancing.

These figures are national averages. A state-by-state analysis would, of course, reveal where support is stronger and where it is weaker than the average for the nation. For example support for the arts in California is stronger than it is nationally. The Harris poll for that state revealed that Californians are more likely to be involved with the arts than the average American elsewhere.[4] Three out of four Californians engaged in some form of artistic activity, and many more said they would like to do so. Californians are also more likely to attend theater and dance performances.

An article in the San Francisco *Chronicle* of April 18, 1975, reports that nine out of ten Californians agree that

arts and cultural activities are as important for a community to have as libraries, schools, parks and recreational activities . . . .

Most want more performances and museums (three out of four also agreed that a live stage experience is more meaningful than watching it on TV), with better accessibility (more important to Central Valley residents) and cheaper admissions (varying by income group, of course). A majority of every demographic group (72 percent overall, 79 percent of blacks) think that government (at some level), as well as businesses and corporations should support the arts. Even 67 percent of those who did not attend a single performance last year, and 62 percent of those who never attend favored government support, so important do Californians regard the arts for the quality of life.

Legislators, elected officials and corporation executives will have much in this study to guide them as they consider arts support. In the light of this report, boards of education should really reexamine their consciences and the terrible recent history of cutbacks in arts education. The public clearly wants the opposite results. 91 percent said that it was important for children to be exposed to the performing arts. Large majorities want the arts taught in the schools for credit as part of the core curriculum, four out of five saying that arts and crafts courses should be paid for from the regular school budget. . . . the public is speaking out clearly for the kind of life in the arts it wants.

Skeptics might argue that it is easy to respond to an interviewer in a way that makes one appear to be more favorable to the arts than is actually the case; that these data need to be taken lightly; that behavior in the voting booth may not always be consistent with values expressed in the poll. Acknowledging this objection, we can divide each percentage responding in favor of the arts into two groups: one group that unequivocally supports the arts; the remaining group that feels it ought to support the arts. The latter group needs encouragement and persuasion to be consistently supportive of the arts. The former group is our allies.

It is ironic that evidence for public support of the arts and arts education comes to light at a time of shrinking financial resources. While we can hope that the present economic crisis will soon end, we cannot rely on it. Plans for a universal, comprehensive education in the arts cannot assume an expansion of funds commensurate with the expansion of function. The challenge is to develop excellent programs within budgetary constraints. This means fuller utilization of present resources.

All of the arts can be brought into every school without adding staff or extending the school day by trying new approaches to the content, staffing, and financing of arts programs. One way of accomplishing this is by integrating offerings and resources in a comprehensive arts program keyed to the total curriculum and making optimum use of present materials, space, and talent in the schools and in the community.

Integration is a time-honored solution to the need for curricular expansion. The social sciences, for example, have been unified for instruction in the elementary school for many years. The concept of social studies goes back to the 1880's. By 1921 the strength of the movement for unification was evidenced in the formation of the National Council for the Social Studies. In the following decades the teaching of history, geography, and civics as separate subjects was superseded by programs of social studies. In a similar way, the recognition of the interrelatedness of reading, speaking, writing, and listening and their dependence on vocabulary, grammar, usage, spelling, and punctuation gave rise to programs in the language arts. It is clear that the time has come for those who teach the arts to acknowledge that integration can facilitate richer, more varied programs, permit more effective use of instructional time, and eliminate wasteful competition over the access to resources.

An integrated arts program emphasizes what is fundamental to the arts. All the arts have a common core. All involve forms that are aesthetic, creative, and expressive. All bring into existence something that was not there before. All embody and communicate human aspiration and feeling. All are rooted in ritual and symbolism. All require a body of skills that are developed through practice.

The need to identify goals and content relevant to a number of arts directs attention to significant learning and steers programs away from the trivial and frivolous lessons that undermine the status of the arts in the curriculum. There are many strands common to all the arts that might be used to tie them together for instruction. The arts can be related by a shared expression of an emotion, by a common theme, by analogies of form, or by a common origin in a particular culture. It is not difficult, for example, to find works of art, music, poetry, stories, ballet scenes, folk dances, rituals, and the like whose theme is valor, bravery, or heroism. The love of mother and child finds frequent expression in the arts. Learning experiences might also be built around the similarities and differences in formal elements such as line, rhythm, color, space, or pattern, as they apply in various art forms. Or the arts of a culture could be considered along with its history, geography, and anthropology. For example, a study of Mexico could involve Aztec and Mayan myths and legends, traditional music, folk dance and costumes, and modern and traditional painting and sculpture.

The commonalities among the arts can illuminate children's own creative work as well. Children might, for example, express the theme of mechanization through movement, musical composition, constructions, multimedia productions, and other art forms. It is possible to relate the arts in many ways that stimulate imagination and deepen enjoyment. I am, however, especially drawn to a process orientation. This orientation focuses primarily on what goes on in the learner as a consequence of what goes on in the work of art that is being created or experienced. The basic processes are a set of outward behaviors and inner experiences that are common to all the arts and are the foundation of aesthetic experience. They include perceiving, responding, understanding (knowing), creating, evaluating (valuing), developing skills.

The processes can be useful in unifying the arts for instruction. For example, a series of experiences can be offered to develop perception involving still objects (painting, sculpture, photographs, natural forms), moving objects (dancers, film, kinetic sculpture, light), sounds (instrumental, electronic, vocal, natural), and whatever else the imagination of the teacher can devise.

Each of the processes has its own extension; they undergo a course of development that begins in early infancy and can continue throughout the life span. Perception, for example, develops from the infant's recognition of people and objects to the sustained and discerning attention of the connoisseur; evaluation grows from accepting and rejecting to informed, discriminating, and well-articulated judgments.

Processes interact with one another. Growth in one process motivates other processes. Thus, the development of skills expands the creative range; to distinguish the extraordinary from the mediocre requires knowledge of the art forms under consideration.

The development of aesthetic sensitivity depends on the maturing of the basic processes, all of which are involved in the aesthetic response. Performance and enjoyment of the arts rest on the ability to experience (perceive and respond) fully, on knowledge and skills of the various art forms, and on the competence to judge one's own work and that of others.

The Place of the Arts in the Curriculum

In addition to offering all the arts to all the children, I would like to see the arts become central rather than peripheral in the curriculum. This means, first, that the arts program exists as a self-sustaining component of the curriculum, parallel to the social studies, language arts, sciences and mathematics, and, second, that the arts enter into all other areas of the curriculum with which they share content and processes. To infuse the arts into all areas of the curriculum is to restore the content of separate disciplines to their natural state. If this appears to be a difficult task, it is probably because educators have compartmentalized their own thinking and practice for so long that the artificial barriers seem natural and the natural relationships are no longer evident.

The potential links between the arts and all other areas of the curriculum exist and are waiting to be rediscovered. For example, the geometric designs in the weaving of the Navaho could provide one focus for bringing together mathematics, anthropology, and the art of weaving. The Aztec or Mayan calendars involve painting and sculpture respectively, as well as mathematics, astronomy, and mythology.

What I am suggesting is that we view the arts, the humanities, and the sciences as complementary manifestations of how people deal with the natural and social environment, that we dismantle the wall separating the affective from the cognitive, that we reform the curriculum by unifying the teaching of the arts around the basic processes that bring together the arts and other disciplines. This approach requires, of course, responses to the perennial problems of schools—staffing, scheduling, financing, preparation of teachers, use of human and material community resources, and the like. Below is a sample of ways in which schools might organize to meet new needs.

Organizing for New Arts Programs

Few schools are currently staffed to offer all the arts. High schools usually have a music teacher, an art teacher, and an English teacher who offers creative writing. Few elementary or middle schools are staffed with people who are able to teach drama, dance, film-making, or any of the other arts traditionally missing from the curriculum.

If the situation were ideal, schools and districts could hire teachers fully prepared to function in a comprehensive, integrated, community-based arts program. This may not be possible, however, since the school may not be in a position to add or replace faculty or a specialist competent in all the arts may not be found. How can the need be filled?

Districts could develop teams that are able collectively to teach all of the arts. The teams could serve the whole district, several schools, or a single large school. The teams need not have a full-time person for each art form. Some team members might be interested in working only part time in the schools in order that they might have time to practice their art. Other team members might be able to teach more than one art form, combining, for example, drama and movement or filmmaking and creative writing.

When there are vacancies to be filled, faculty can be employed to work in arts programs in various ways. In schools with open classrooms teaching teams can be set up to include the competencies necessary for the program. Or, a school could engage a resident specialist in the arts who works with all teachers and classes, helping teachers to plan for teaching the arts in all curricular areas and working with teachers in offering all of the arts.

Schools can also look to the community for assistance. They can, for example, enter into cooperative arrangements with museums, performing groups, and artists, bringing together the expertise of people in education and in the arts in joint planning and implementation of programs. In such a venture, each party acknowledges the complementary character of the relationship in a spirit of mutual respect. Each one recognizes that the joint efforts of the group can be far more effective than what either could do alone. The arrangement is truly a merger, not a takeover. As Lydia Joel points out,

arts organizations . . . need to pay more attention to the educational needs and concerns of the schools and to the realities of the school environment. Bringing the arts into the schools has to be the joint responsibility of artists and arts educators. On the one hand, educators must be sensitive to the needs and constraints of artists. On the other, artists must temper their professional ambitions with sensitivity to the school audience and to school personnel. Arts organizations need to try to match their offerings with students' needs, classroom teachers' competencies, and the schools' curricular concerns. This means not only carefully tailored programs, but also much more flexibility in presentation formats and more attention to carefully prepared materials for classroom teachers to use.

Effective lines of communication must be established between the staff of a school and visiting artists. This is necessary not only to ensure mutual understanding of professional concerns, but also to prevent mix-ups concerning scheduling, logistics, and equipment. Such mix-ups can prove very costly in terms of resources wasted and goodwill destroyed.

When the chief concern of an arts organization is simply to provide opportunities and security for artists to "do their own thing" rather than to translate an arts performance into a learning situation for school children, such performances are likely to have little lasting significance in the schools. Interest in children and in their capacity to learn is very important, as is the ability to relate to the particular age level of an audience. Engaging, outgoing, and enthusiastic visiting artists have made more inroads than detached, removed performers. Artists who were open to questions and flexible enough to let children participate have had a greater impact. . . . The project's most positive achievements have developed with artists who came to work in the schools without a set performance repertoire and were flexible enough to shape what they had to offer to the needs of the schools.[5]

Colleges and universities engaged in teacher education need to prepare arts teachers for schools, museums, and other educational agencies. Programs must be developed that orient artists to the world of the classroom and introduce prospective teachers to the world of the arts. Educational institutions ought to prepare candidates for arts teaching in a variety of settings. The educational staffs of museums and other arts organizations need people who are knowledgeable in child growth and development, able to plan curriculum and instruction, and skillful in dealing with the young. Artists working in schools may need help in finding effective ways of communicating their insights to children. Although some artists fit easily into the elementary school environment, many can benefit from systematic preparation for a teaching role. Preservice and in-service programs could be useful in orienting artists toward the way in which schools function, the total curriculum, and the relationship of their area to programs as a whole. Such programs could help artists to become cognizant of the developmental level of the learners, the unique qualities of individual children, and their capacity for artistic learning.

In addition, provision must be made for elementary school specialists in the arts. As more and more schools move toward open classrooms with differentiated staff responsibilities, specialized preparation becomes desirable. Teacher training institutions ought to address this need.

As schools and other agencies of arts education move in the direction of cooperative functions, there is likely to be sharing of personnel, space, and equipment. Joint offerings can take place on the school site, the museum site, in public auditoriums, in neighborhood arts centers, or elsewhere in the community. I can envision jointly sponsored programs housed in institutions such as the Exploratorium in San Francisco or the Lawrence Hall of Science in Berkeley in fields such as art and technology, traditional and electronic music, holography, kinetics, or optics. Such programs might be offered during or outside of school time. Regardless of the time and place, however, they remain part of the educational offering of the schools and are viewed as instruction rather than diversion; they are paracurricular rather than extracurricular.

The use of the community in schooling vastly expands the range of available alternatives. Neighborhood arts centers might provide the space, equipment, and human resources for arts programs the school is not prepared to handle, such as filmmaking or television production.

Such programs could serve as apprenticeships for some students. Apprenticeships with performing groups or individual artists might be advantageous for promising young musicians, artists, actors, and dancers. The school can guide students into a wide variety of programs at a cost far below what it would take to offer them at the school site. In addition, students and other young people working with performing arts associations might constitute a traveling group of players offering theater, dance, concerts, lecture-demonstrations, improvisation, storytelling, and theater games to the schools.

By now it may seem that I have forgotten about the need to keep costs down. How can human and material resources be augmented without a corresponding increment of cost?

Some community agencies are able to offer services without charge. Docents, for example, volunteer their time. Space in public auditoriums is often available during the day at minimal or no cost to schools. Neighborhood arts centers might allow schools to use their staff, space, and equipment at a cost far below that of duplicating them for the exclusive use of the schools. Schools need, however, to find ways of meeting expenses that cannot be absorbed elsewhere, such as the cost of transportation to museums. Funds can be sought from a variety of sources. Schools can explore the possibility of raising money from individuals in the community, local businesses, private foundations, or government agencies. Success in funding is more likely if a well-planned program is presented when the request is made. To delay program planning until funds are assured is to reduce the likelihood of curricular change.

In order to move from a program in which the arts are ornaments on the curriculum to one in which they are essential, school and district personnel must regard the change as both possible and desirable. The attitude of people affected by change is a critical factor. Change is not likely to succeed if it arouses apprehension—if people feel inadequate to the new demands and fear failure, loss of respect, and loss of status. Properly conceived, change will be regarded as an opportunity to grow in a desired direction, to be more effective, and to find greater personal satisfaction.

Changes in the way we deliver educational services will require changes in the structure and membership of professional organizations. When art educators, music educators, drama educators, museum educators in the arts and sciences, and individuals from a variety of institutions share professional concerns, it makes sense to provide machinery for communication and concerted action through professional organization. The old slogan "In unity there is strength" should be a call to action for arts associations in the years ahead.

The essential criterion of the value of an educational offering is its effect on the learner. In a proper educational setting, children and young people will commit themselves to learning in the arts with high spirits and earnest intent. They will learn habits of concentration and industry needed for achievement in any area. They will develop skills in a variety of arts, knowledge about the arts, and the capacity to create within or to enjoy art forms. They will become more sensitive to feelings and more aware of the emotional and physical environment in which they live.

In addition to the benefits to students, there could be far-reaching social effects. First, a community that provides training in the arts would constitute a vast audience and source of support for theaters, museums, and arts programs. Second, talents that might otherwise have been neglected could be developed. There would be a broad base of artistic activity supporting excellence in all the arts. By increasing the number of people working seriously in the arts, the possibility of the emergence of truly great works is increased.

To accommodate a program such as I have been describing, the schools will have to change. A community-based, personalized program offering many options will not fit into schools that are rigid and bound by regulations. Schools and communities will need to find new ways of working to allow arts programs to grow.

There will be many problems. There are always problems when one departs from the familiar to find something better. We can always see these problems as insurmountable and thus justify continuing in the old ways for as long as "they" let us. Change is disturbing. Old habits and routines are broken, and old habits, like old shoes, are very comfortable. No matter how good the new shoe, it seldom feels as good as the old one. Most of us change reluctantly. But change is inevitable. Everything changes around us, and we are caught in these changes willingly or not. If arts educators can set their sights and work for the kind of program they want, they will be far better off than if change is imposed.

I cannot predict the future, but I have described what it might be. This future offers all the arts to all the children; places the arts at the center of the curriculum; is individualized; offers many options to students; is flexibly staffed; and is planned and carried out jointly by the schools and other community agencies. It may seem an optimistic view for these times. The future rests on present deeds. If, as a profession, we conceptualize a desirable future and work toward it, our vision may come to be reality. And so, the future of the arts is the responsibility of us all.

Notes

1. Joseph H. Peluso, *A Survey of the Status of the Theatre in United States High Schools* (Washington, D.C.: Department of Health, Education, and Welfare, 1970), 9.
2. American Music Conference, *Report on a Study of Music Programs in U.S. Elementary and Secondary Schools—1972-1973* (Chicago: the Conference, 1974).
3. National Research Center for the Arts, *Americans and the Arts* (New York: ACA Publications, 1974).
4. National Research Center for the Arts, *Californians and the Arts: A Survey of Public Attitudes toward and Participation in the Arts and Culture in California* (Sacramento: Office of Procurement, Publications Section, n.d.).
5. Lydia Joel, "The Impact of IMPACT," *Dance Scope,* VI (No. 2, 1972), 13. © American Dance Guild, New York, New York.

11

School Art: The Search for
an Avant-Garde

AL HURWITZ

The choice of topic may seem a strange one inasmuch as the concept
of the avant-garde is customarily associated with the world of the
artist rather than that of the schools. Or, to put it another way, why
confuse art history with what happens to children in our classrooms?
Why not, indeed? There is, after all, a respectable body of opinion in
art education that has, for some time, viewed the artist as a model
for both pupil and teacher, and the aesthetic education movement
has added to this concept the figures of the historian and critic as
further models for consideration. Many of us, therefore, are already
in the business of establishing closer linkages between the art
education of youngsters and the professionals themselves. The "real"
artists, it is believed, are closer to the wellsprings of art and, therefore,
represent a process of dealing with both the creation and the understanding of art works. This can provide a teacher with a more
valid basis for selecting those tasks which enable young people to
move toward a more fulfilling existence, that is, toward an education
through art.

I believe the above to be true, and I do not find the idea limiting
or insensitive to the needs and nature of children. One cannot name
a single function or view of art, however contextual (to borrow a

phrase from Elliot Eisner), that does not find some echo in the real world of art. If I were to consider the most important goal in art education as therapeutic, the intense subjectivity of expressionism and a host of artists would come to mind whose work must be linked with neurosis of some kind. (For example, would Van Gogh have been a better painter if he had had access to a guidance counselor?) If I believed one of the major goals of art education was to enhance *visual literacy* or the development of *perceptual acuity,* my mind would immediately turn to the work of op artists, to segments of the basic design course of the Bauhaus, or to a Gestalt critic such as R. Arnheim. If I felt that art education is most potent when it is directed toward the reordering of one's environment, I would think of all the architects and planners who shape our lives in this country or who draw us to foreign shores each summer. If I thought that the best use of school time lay in dealing with the power of art to provide vivid and unique means of objectifying feelings and ideas, then my points of reference could move from the content of museums to that of local movie houses.

In other words, it is not terribly risky to draw upon the behavior of artists as sources of validation for what can happen in the classroom. My only quarrel with this theory is that it is rarely taken far enough. A major concern of my own work has been to take ideas of artists seriously, to try to narrow the uncomfortable gap between the shifting, emerging insights of visual performers and the sluggish pace of change of that most conservative of educational figures—the average art teacher. (If it appears that I am overstating the case, let me pose the question of what would happen if art teachers were asked to undergo the amount of retraining similar to that of physics, mathematics, and social studies teachers of the last decade.) The training the art teacher receives in art school or university usually sets the pattern for thinking about art for a lifetime of teaching, and it is not likely to undergo any substantive change unless someone provides the mechanisms—the means of change. That is where supervision or leadership from some source comes in, and that is basically the vantage point from which I speak.

It will become obvious, if indeed it has not already, that this chapter is not designed for the researcher or the scholar. I began as a teacher, moving from elementary to junior to senior high school. For most of my life I have worked with children and teachers as a supervisor, employing whatever means were at my disposal, whether persuasion or money—using formal or informal means—moving system-wide or with individuals, to achieve the kind of special ferment that makes an art room an exciting place to be. I like to think that some of us are creating our own avant-garde, which brings me back to the title of this chapter.

I have always been drawn to what lies beyond my own immediate view of an art program. I have looked at what artists were doing and asked, "If it is good for them, why not for us?" Teacher training institutions, however, have not always shared my enthusiasm, and, as a result, most art programs have still to catch up with their past, that is, with arts' history. The collage, now considered an overworked cliché by many, was thought to be very fashionable and even avant-garde just before World War II. And yet Picasso and Juan Gris were experimenting with the idea in 1912. Although Julio Gonzales was working with the technology of welding before the 1920's, most senior high school sculpture programs are still dealing with clay, wood, and cardboard.

At this point it would probably be helpful to review the meaning of the term "avant-garde" and some attendant attitudes before discussing its feasibility as a means of dealing with school art. The term is difficult to use without lapsing into a kind of dated romanticism, and time, of course, has its own way of dealing with words. "Doing your own thing," the catch phrase of the 1960's, was another way of restating the hallowed iconoclasm of the artist—that uncompromising hewing to visions that were bound to be misunderstood by a philistine world. The idea of rejection by the middle-class "boobocracy" (to use H. L. Mencken's phrase), even if it led to a life of poverty, was also part of the mystique because, after all, one was bound to be exonerated by history. Indeed, the more the artist was mocked by his enemies, the more reenforced was he in his state of self-imposed existentialism. There were also stereotypes of personal behavior that inevitably related to it—sitting on floors, hairstyles, clothing styles, even prescribed modes of interior decoration—and hard-core avant-gardists rarely deviated from the accepted accoutrements of the group. While this is a classic bohemian view which dates from the Paris of the turn of the century, its contemporary echo should be unmistakable.

What does all this mean to the teacher in the schools? It is

significant to me because the avant-garde stance has much in common with the adolescent's way of thinking. As an example, if children
are going to develop a visual life-style according to their own rules,
the art teacher should not only accept it, but should honor it in some
way by building upon it in the art program. The teacher cannot,
however, stop at this level, but must go on to larger issues. The schools
can also do without the self-defeating negative aspects of avant-
garde behavior. We do not need nihilism or anarchy any more than
we need the Cassandras of the avant-garde who proclaim the death
of art. I also reject experimentation carried on strictly for kicks without attention being paid to content, meaning, or any formal considerations.

It may appear that I am being selective in describing my own
kind of avant-garde. But selectivity is, after all, essential in education in general. As in other areas, the schools force one to thread a
path through a series of constraints: time, money, and nature of school
and community. The avant-garde that one seeks must be appropriate
to one's means. I have discussed what I reject about the avant-garde;
now I shall present what I feel is acceptable.

I accept wholeheartedly the idea of questioning conventionally
conceived categories of art and have never found the accepted modes
of imagery—sculpture, printmaking, painting—to be limiting factors.
While I believe in continuity, when that is possible, I also like the
incongruous—the disjunctive—the extension of awarenesses that lie
beyond what exists at a given moment.

There is also the general problem of changing perceptions, of
moving children beyond ways of thinking and even feeling that have
been imposed upon them, unwittingly or otherwise. If a child asks
someone to draw a horse, he will expect to see a profile facing left.
If one draws a horse as seen from a helicopter, it will look like a
cello, and it takes some time for the child to realize what is happening. My own search for an avant-garde involves, then, the stretching
of sensibilities—the jarring of perceptions, the search for tasks and
situations that involve multilevels of awareness. Because I am basically
an artist, I think in visual terms. I am aware, however, that we can
operate from within any of our sense modalities as a prelude to the
creation of more varied and complex sets of experiences. I like to
think that although I begin as an artist I cannot be sure whether the
group will end up as performers, as entrepreneurs of multimedia enterprises, or as participants in some totally unanticipated coalition of art
forms.

As Clement Greenberg reminds us, "wherever there is an advance guard there is a rear guard."[1] What then does the rear guard represent to the teacher who is eager to man the aesthetic barricades? As it turns out, the rear guard is wherever one happens to be before continuing the advance. Everyone has to be someplace, and that place is an area bounded by the experience, knowledge, and beliefs of the moment. The cutting edge for all of us rests upon the parameters of our experience and knowledge. An example of this concept can be found in studying the progress of technology of the art program. The traditional and still the most popular means to increase youngsters' perceptual powers is through drawing, which involves the technology of the pencil, the crayon, the stick of charcoal. Bartlett Hayes came to the conclusion some fifteen years ago that the processes of perception were far more complex and added to the pencil the technology of the camera in his Visual Perception program.[2] Since then others have suggested that filmmaking could provide a more extended sort of visual awareness, and now some of us are trying to discover where video porta-packs and computer graphics fit into the picture. In the meantime, most teachers still continue to render objects with pencils, partly because it is cheap and convenient, partly because that sort of imagery is still rich in possibilities and in its own way goes where computers fear to tread. However promising the conté crayon is, it still only taps one level of awareness, whereas the other kinds of technology I have mentioned extend our perceptions in ways that drawing could never pretend to do. One way to view the avant-garde, then, is to search for any means at one's disposal, to enlarge the student's view of life and of himself. The question inevitably arises: "Is what you are doing art, and, if so, how do you know?" My criteria run somewhat as follows: if some sense of coherence is evident, if meanings and feelings are conveyed, and, if these meanings and feelings could not have existed without some visual dimension, then whatever emerges will lie within my purview of art.

Whatever the nature of art, it is a peculiarly human activity involving a variety of organizational strategies for various purposes. When one speaks of the death of art or even of anti- or non-art, he can only refer to art in its most limited sense since the problem of confronting life through objects and images can obviously never disappear. No one has yet definitively limited the materials or the problems involved in dealing with images, and it is in this very openness that the seeds of an avant-garde await the venturesome teacher.

The following brief descriptions demonstrate how some of my

colleagues and I have gone about extending the awarenesses of children and adolescents through periodic reexaminations of our programs. All of the projects, unless otherwise noted, take place in the schools of Newton, Massachusetts.

Group Documentation

A media specialist and a drama teacher take a class of eighth graders to a local gas station. They have a full array of equipment and spend several mornings carefully documenting the life, the rhythm of the gas station. Drawings are turned into slides; super 8-mm film records action; cassette tapes capture special sounds; a video porta-pack allows them to interview customers. The students even function as station operators as another means of absorbing the environment. They also study the physical activities that are peculiar to gas stations and create pantomimic exercises for both camera and television. Black-and-white photography adds another dimension to the study, and, at the end of the week, a mass of data is accumulated. The problem now is to assemble the information into some coherent final production. Working as a group, we will have to study the balance of images and the structure and flow of sound and sight; in short, we will study design and continuity within the context of multiple imagery. The students, it is to be hoped, will realize the multitude of visual possibilities that lie within customarily mundane subject matter.

Working with a Conceptual Sculptor

A class of ninth-grade students assists a conceptual sculptor in assembling a huge flying machine. On the first day they make the components of the structure, and on the second day they assemble huge sheets of mylar and helium-filled weather balloons on the plaza in front of Boston's new City Hall. The machine does not operate properly; it gets off the ground, but not quite into the sky. No one considers the event a failure because for two days the attention of the children has been riveted upon the process, held by the idea of pure suspense. They have worked with adults in a partnership and have shared an experience they will long remember. What they produced was a kind of sculpture, which was radically new and fraught with drama.

Attending to Each Other through Art

A mixed group of children and adults are blindfolded and seated opposite each other. Large balls of clay are placed between the two partners, and in complete silence they create a piece of sculpture, working only from the shape of the clay and the touch of their partners' hands. When the object is felt to be completed, blindfolds are removed and everyone is surprised at both the integrity of the design of the clay and the identity of their partners. In the second stage, with the participants working without blindfolds, all pieces of sculpture are joined together into one large piece, and in the final phase each participant makes a small human figure and finds a home for it in the total work, which suddenly turns into a fantastic environment for lovers, readers, sleepers, conversationalists, and so forth. A metamorphosis of form and function has occurred as each operation prepares the student for a succeeding stage.

Environmental Problem I

This environmental project occurs in a school in Brookline, Massachusetts. A senior high art teacher is assigned a large space to convert into the school art center. She dispenses with the syllabus for the studio class and designs a curriculum out of the problem of converting the room. Three murals, woven curtains, modular furniture, and total color coordination are some of the problems the class confronts. Art is thus used to make the school a pleasanter place to inhabit. They have learned that design can enhance the quality of life and in the school environment at that!

Environmental Problem II

Another senior high art class takes a totally empty room and converts it into a fully functioning art center through the use of one material: three-ply cardboard. Desks, easels, chairs, storage units, critique areas—all are created from the same material. When it is finished, the room is taken apart and moved outside, where all of the components are reassembled into three-dimensional forms. From industrial designers the students have been transformed into sculptors and have discovered that art can move from one form to another, using previous stages as raw material for what follows. They have learned that experience is open ended and can lead one into unexpected directions.

Environmental Sculpture III

A group of seventh graders turn a jungle gym into a three-dimensional loom and, after a number of weaving experiences, decide to connect the structure to the rest of the playground equipment—swings, seesaws, and so on. More yarn and rope are used, and, for planar variation, sheets and old clothes are soaked in plaster of paris and added. The entire playground eventually is converted into one huge rambling piece of sculpture, and the students have jointly designed a work that far exceeds their own human proportions.

Community Service through Sculpture

At Phillips Academy in Andover, Massachusetts, a group of boys conduct a study of playground needs in their community. They present the city aldermen with a plan of action and a budget and are now on their way to creating novel sculptural play equipment for the children of the community. They are living with the social and political dimension of art.

Art through Technology

Also at Phillips Academy a teacher trained as a sculptor re-educates himself in skills of technology that are new to him, such as motors, electronics, synthesizers, circuitry, and kinetics. He creates a new course in sculpture wherein his students combine these skills to form objects that behave in ways totally new to them. The materials may be new, such as illuminated Plexiglass, but so are the ways in which the materials behave. He has thus attempted to close the gap between the Center for Advanced Visual Studies at the Massachusetts Institute of Technology and his own art room.

Light Activity

A group of fifth graders have a darkened gymnasium to themselves for an afternoon. Using media equipment common to most elementary schools, they experiment with a number of light show techniques: designing projected images on slides, making animated films without cameras, combining cut shapes of theatrical gelatins with silhouette shapes, and so forth. They project on hard surfaces (cardboard sculptures) and soft surfaces (parachutes). They are exercising new controls of images involving the brilliance of light on a grand environmental scale. Up to this point they have thought of color primarily in terms of pigment and crayons. They have also learned that equipment that was purchased primarily to convey information can be used to create art.

Film Animation

A group of junior high students have made their first 16-mm animated film. They have formerly thought of art activity as a single-image object; now that object is just the beginning. It has taken on a life of its own as it progresses through a scenario. They are now dramatists in that ideas must be communicated through the structure of plot, climax, denouement, and so on; they have accomplished this by mastering camera and sound equipment and by developing infinite patience. They have learned to work as a team, to pool ideas, to assist each other in the search for the proper sounds.

A Perception Center

In the schools of Warminster, Pennsylvania, a supervisor and his superintendent receive a grant to build a center especially designed for the training of perceptual acuity. The children come to a dome-shaped structure where they participate in programs that are intended to test their ability to discriminate in a variety of visual situations. They may compare groups of images, or they may break down one artwork into multiple images. The act of positive looking has become an exciting educational event.

Development of Contemporary Graphic Images

A senior high teacher, bored with the traditional modes of printmaking (linoleum, collographs, woodcuts) and unable to afford an etching press, develops a working relationship with the graphics teacher in the industrial arts department. Working as a team, they help students study the work of contemporary printmakers. The students, applying the design skills learned in the art program, extend their graphic imagery through the use of photo silk screen, offset printing, phototypesetting, and a variety of techniques for pattern repetitions, reductions, or enlargements.

Conclusion

The gist of my argument has been that, while an avant-garde can exist even within the limited confines of the public school program, most teachers appear reluctant to seek it out. There are many sources of ideas for extending the content of curriculum, and, to my mind, one of the most promising is the professional artist whose task it is to extend the perceptions of society through the shifting process of discovery, expansion, reformation, communication, and so forth. Since it is one responsibility of art educators to act as mediators between schooling and the world at large, the potency of the ongoing visual revolution ought not be ignored. The fact that the work of many teachers does not reflect the real world of art attests to a sluggishness born of ignorance and a desire to perpetuate the convenience of the known and tested. It also reflects the conservatism of that subsociety we call "the schools." By reaching for the untried, teachers can achieve either success or distinguished failure. (The freedom to fail, after all, is yet another characteristic that teachers can share with artists.) The waters of the avant-garde can be murky, but the thrill of navigating them can make the difference between a program that is alive with promise and one that is tediously safe and banal.

Notes

1. Clement Greenberg, *Art and Culture: Critical Essays* (Boston: Beacon Press, 1961), 9.
2. Phillips Academy, Andover, Massachusetts.

12

Bridging the Gap between
the Arts and Education

JUNIUS EDDY

As it must to all fathers, the opportunity came to me a few years ago to attend the first PTA meeting of the year in my daughter's junior high school. Before we all were dismissed to wander through the halls trying to follow our children's class schedule, with ten minutes allotted to each class, an earnest and dedicated lady was given a short time to make a plea for financial support of a cultural organization called Young Horizons.

This, she told us, was a nonprofit organization of parents in our town that provided free professional performances of music, dance, and drama for our children during school hours. She said the programs were varied to suit age and interest levels from kindergarten through eighth grade. Her plea went something like this: "With your help, we will be able to offer a wide range of exciting events, and you will have the satisfaction of helping with an unforgettable series of cultural experiences that will truly widen the horizons of our youngsters." Finally, she said, all details would be handled by her group, "without bothering the school staff or meddling in the curriculum, and without adding extra tax dollars to our hard-pressed school budgets."

Everyone present nodded approvingly, and I suspect very few

parents in that somewhat well-to-do suburb failed to contribute something to this worthwhile effort. I found the incident both saddening and challenging for it illuminated the attitudes that seem to exist in most schools, among most parents, and in the community at large regarding the place of the creative and performing arts in our educational system today. Pat the arts gently and approvingly on the head, but do not let them interfere seriously with the regular, prescribed work of the schools. Widen the horizons of our children through an "unforgettable series of cultural experiences." But do not bother to involve the school staff in the process, and do not interfere with the really important learning that goes on in the classroom. And, by all means, do not ever let these activities add extra local tax dollars to the school budget.

Prior to the 1960's the typical way in which young people were exposed to quality experiences in the arts, if it was done at all, was through such groups as the Young Horizons Program. Beginning in about 1966 the schools, and education generally, found another sponsor with seemingly limitless resources. Although these resources were derived from tax dollars, they were not local tax dollars. They were dollars from Washington. With the passage of the Elementary and Secondary Education Act of 1965, unheard of amounts of public funds were allocated to support activities dealing with the arts in general education. Because they are well known I shall not elaborate on the provisions in Titles I and III of the act under which a wide range and variety of arts programs were undertaken by local school systems.

Now, some years later, although the funds available through that act are still impressive, the situation with respect to federally supported programs and projects in the arts is gradually returning to normal. I am writing in general terms, of course, which puts me somewhat ahead of the story, but I think that many of these early efforts under ESEA tended to perpetuate and feed the kind of one-shot, randomly organized "cultural enrichment" approach that schools such as the one my daughter attended took with respect to the role of the arts in general education.

That incident, in fact, illustrates in large measure the point that underlies my general thesis: for generations in this country a broad chasm has tended to separate the world of education from the world of the arts in American schools, and, undoubtedly, in our society as a whole.

Bridges *across* this gap are necessary. Though they are now being built, many are still rather rickety, constructed perhaps more tentatively than we might wish. But the important thing is that construction is going forward despite poor economic conditions and the spiritual (and humanistic) uncertainty of our times. Thus, the outlook is optimistic for all those with an interest in the arts and in the education of the young—educators and cultural leaders alike. Such an interest is no longer a futile enterprise, but one well worth time, effort, and devotion.

I must confess at the outset to a certain uneasiness at being included among the authors in this book. I think I am the only one who is not, strictly speaking, either an educator or an artist. I have, however, been a little bit of both in my time. I was trained in the theater and earned my living for a time as a playwright and a director. And I have worked as a professional screenwriter of documentary and educational films. There was a period when I taught these subjects, both at the college level and, at the other end of the spectrum, in a neighborhood settlement house in Cleveland, an unusual interracial arts center called Karamu House (meaning, in Swahili, "the center of the community").

But in this essay I am neither an artist nor an educator, but one of those mysterious creatures—a foundation man.

And I am a foundation type that appears to be in relatively scarce supply these days because I am not merely concerned with "The Arts" nor with "Education" but with the connections between the two. There are few foundation programs directed explicitly toward this dual purpose. In fact, I know of only one: the JDR 3rd Fund's Arts in General Education Program, which is alluded to in Jerome Hausman's chapter.

But, for the most part, in foundations, and indeed in governmental agencies at the federal, state, and local levels, "Education" stakes out its territory in one place, and "The Arts" carves out its domain in another. Only with difficulty do we find it possible to bridge the gap.

I might interject here that my work in recent years, in two large, national foundations (Ford and Rockefeller) and before that with the U.S. Office of Education, has, in spite of its frustrations, provided me with an extraordinary opportunity to study the whole area of arts in education in some detail. It has enabled me to travel widely throughout the United States, to see something of what has been going on, to become acquainted with a wide variety of programs and projects and to know many of the people responsible for them, and, from this vantage point, to develop a broad sense of the emerging forces that either sustain or inhibit constructive efforts in this field. But the opportunity has, at the same time, placed me somewhere in the middle—neither an artistic fish nor an educational fowl—hanging in midair over the chasm, with no firm locus on either side, but with my interests embracing both.

I assume it is not necessary to convince readers of this chapter that the arts are fundamental to the education of the young. Other authors will deal with the underlying rationale for fusing the educational experience with the arts experience in order that learning can begin to take place, in children and in young adults, within this broad aesthetic domain that many believe is fundamental to the development of fully functioning human beings. But, as has been stated previously, what is important here is the gap, the ways in which it institutionalizes itself, and the guideposts that might be helpful in finding our way across it.

For the past ten years, since the creation of the National Endowment for the Arts and since the movement for state and local arts councils has begun to grow and flourish across the nation, it seems that an unusual phenomenon has emerged. A curious kind of standoff has grown up between these Johnny-come-lately agencies and institutions devoted to the arts and those long-established institutions concerned with the education of children and youth.

In Washington, when the Arts Endowment was first established, the two empires remained essentially separate with respect to educational matters. Although this general situation continues today, there is considerable evidence that it is beginning to change. It may be that a major cause for this separation is simply one of money: the education agencies had and have much larger budgets available to them than do those concerned with the arts. I remember, in 1966 or 1967, when Roger Stevens, the businessman and Broadway producer who was the Arts Endowment's first chairman, came to the Office of Education to discuss joint ventures with us. He always spoke wistfully about the billions in HEW's and OE's budgets as compared to the few millions he was able to pry out of Congress at that time. As a result, he felt that USOE should contribute the larger share to joint ventures of the OE and the National Endowment in the field of arts in education. And, from his standpoint, this made sense. His priority was not education, in the formal sense of school-based activities, but artists and the arts, and his modest budget was only a drop in the bucket in terms of those needs all across the country.

It was to Steven's credit that he cared about public education. And he worked devotedly with the OE on a major project—the Educational Laboratory Theatre—to bring top-quality theater to thousands of high school students in three major U.S. cities in the late 1960's. This program consisted of a three-year project in Providence, Rhode Island, which embraced high schools throughout the state; in three school districts in and around New Orleans; and in high schools throughout the city of Los Angeles. The program enabled secondary students beginning in their sophomore year to attend four professionally produced plays a year for three years. Many subprojects were also involved—experiments with different kinds of plays, varied staging techniques, selection of plays, a host of supplementary materials, preparation and follow-up activities, special projects for students, and a wide range of teacher retraining approaches—and the entire enterprise was monitored and studied by CEMREL, the regional educational laboratory in St. Louis. The results were compiled in a four-volume set of reports that are still available from CEMREL. These reports provide invaluable information for anyone seeking to establish similar theatrical experiences for high school students. The guidelines, warnings, and recommendations could short-cut the usual trial-and-error process and prevent both money and time being wasted when these projects are undertaken.

The Arts Endowment supported the theater elements, and the Office of Education, under ESEA Titles III and IV, supported the educational and research elements. It is probably the largest single federally supported arts in education program in the nation's history (some $6,000,000 was spent on it over a four-year period). It is indeed unfortunate that more performing arts organizations and more school systems are not aware of this seminal enterprise and, therefore, do not avail themselves of CEMREL's report on it.

But, it must be admitted, there have been few cooperative ventures on this scale, and, despite the national Artists-in-Schools Program in which the Arts Endowment has been engaged for the last three or four years, the endowment's educational activities have largely been conceived in *artists'* terms and not educational terms. For one thing, with the exception perhaps of some theater and dance residencies in schools and the Filmmakers-in-the-Schools Program, they have generally concentrated on children on a random classroom basis and have usually ignored the classroom teacher. In most states, in fact, the visual artists (painters and sculptors) are informed in their guidelines that they should be artists and not teachers—and certainly not the teachers of teachers. Fortunately, this situation is changing to some degree, but most artists who come to work in the schools for short periods of time still operate under the general approach. While this is understandable, given the mandate of the Arts Endowment and the small percentage of the nation's schools that can be touched by the program, it serves to perpetuate the "enrichment" syndrome rather than dealing with fundamental educational change in the public schools.

The same dichotomy as at the national level seems to exist between many state arts councils and their educational counterparts, the state education agencies. Here, too, the modest budgets of the state arts councils, compared to those for education, combined with the differing mandates of these two agencies, accounts for most of the problems between them. Because the needs of the arts are so great in most states, it is unusual if more than 10 percent of the budgets of state arts councils is allotted to educational activities. And when these agencies do engage in educational work, it is generally on their terms, related to the needs of their artist clientele. Seldom is such work undertaken as a cooperative effort with the schools—with joint planning and development between both parties as its essential ingredient.

In the world of foundations, the same separation obtains. When I went to the Ford Foundation in 1969, I thought that it might be possible in such a nonpublic institution to do something about the situation. I soon discovered, however, that Ford's Division of Humanities and the Arts was responsible for "the Arts," while the Division of Education and Research was responsible for "Education." With a few notable exceptions—projects that some of us managed to work out jointly during the years I was there, and several others since that time—it is only with extreme difficulty that one group enters the other's domain or attempts to tackle *together* an issue that involves both fields.

I spent four years there trying to work across those lines and evolve a joint program aimed specifically at the varied needs of the arts in education. For the most part, however, programs that were primarily in the arts were handled by the arts division and those in education by the education division. While we did talk back and forth and advise one another to some extent, we largely went our own ways and evolved our own projects apart from one another.

The situation has been somewhat more encouraging at the Rockefeller Foundation. Although I was brought in as a consultant to the Arts Program and have had to husband carefully the very modest part of that program's annual budget allotted for work in the arts in education, there has been a genuine recognition among officers and trustees there that the arts should be made more central to education and that this field should be given some priority in a program directed toward "the creative person" in America.

As mentioned above, the funds are modest, but we have tried to focus what little has become available, in this period of economic stringency, on the needs of teachers and school administrators with respect to the arts. These funds have mainly been in the form of small planning and development grants designed to assist forward-looking institutions of higher education to restructure their work in teacher education. They have emphasized the needs of the class-room teacher, at both the preservice and graduate retraining levels, for broader training in the arts and their multiple uses as teaching tools.

A brief description of a few of these grants might be helpful. During the first year of the program a grant went to Webster College in St. Louis to help its education department establish a program for Master of Arts in Teaching in Aesthetic Education; this is an in-service degree that experienced classroom teachers can work on over a period of twenty-seven months. The School of Performing Arts at the University of Southern California has received a grant to encourage its faculty to work with an arts-centered neighborhood elementary school and to provide the information gathered in this project to the faculties of arts and education in order to improve teacher education at USC. A third grant went to New York University to assist a group of top-level faculty members in the newly created Division of Arts and Arts Education—within NYU's School of Educa-tion—in planning a major reorientation of its teacher education program. Several other small planning and development grants, to higher education training institutions, and to several unusual arts resource groups, are now in the works. These efforts will not, of course, change the situation overnight. They may, however, begin to point the way to something different and to make nationally visible a few institutions where classroom teachers can obtain a more comprehensive kind of training in the arts and aesthetic education.

I have mentioned only these two large foundations because they are the ones I know best. But, in point of fact, few national and local foundations are substantially involved in this dual-interest area. Some make occasional grants in the field; others, like the Rockefeller Brothers Fund and the Edward John Noble Foundation, have begun to pay increasing attention to it. But, so far as I am aware, only the JDR 3rd Fund has established a specific *program* to foster developments in the arts in education.

Institutions of higher learning are also due their share of criticism. While there is increasing evidence that efforts are being made to bridge the gap between the arts and education, the dichotomy remains in many colleges and universities. The fine and performing arts, with students working in studios, build their empires in one place, and education in another. Arts education is often taught in the school or department of education, and the students have only minimal access to the studio faculty. That faculty would, in turn, rather be preparing the serious artist than working with people who will use the arts for some other purpose—for education, for therapy, or for social work, and so on.

And so, it seems to me, the gap continues to exist, and the bridges remain to be built. What it appears to have produced at the classroom level in our schools is a kind of uneasy relationship between artist and educator. I recognize, of course, that there are exceptions to this generalization. In some schools the blend is indeed occurring with striking effect, and I believe an increasing number of such projects and programs can and will begin to take place. I shall mention, below, a few of the reasons why I am more hopeful now, perhaps, than I have been before that we are on the rising crest of a major educational wave in this field.

In order to take advantage of this wave, we must bend all our efforts to breaking down the historic barriers between artist and teacher, between arts-oriented teachers and other teachers and school administrators, between the separate fields of art, and between the public and private institutions in our localities, our states, and in the federal arena that have been established to meet the urgent needs of the young in our society.

For, in actuality, it really *is* the business of those in the arts fields—the professionals and their organizations and the agencies attempting to sustain and support the artist in our society—to be concerned about the young and about the processes through and by which they learn. In the long run, it will be to their ultimate benefit as well. Arts organizations seeking to cultivate the young audience must, however, come to realize that, to succeed in these efforts, they will have to do more than provide six tickets for the price of five, an occasional youth concert, or a field trip to a museum once each term. It can only mean more if both parties to the process begin to work more closely together, to develop approaches with some sequence and continuity that exemplify the fundamental role of the arts in the entire fabric of education. This means seeking out and involving in education—both formal schooling and learning outside the classroom—those fine artists who also care about children and are not upset by the conventional academic establishment.

I have become increasingly irritated by those who look upon artists as uniquely qualified to "save" our children, who regard the school as a kind of jail from which young people must be liberated through the simple humanity of the creative artist, who want to go into schools and "do their thing" but who often have contempt for the school environment and those who work there.

A growing number of artists and arts organizations have indeed gone beyond this attitude. They respect the creativity in our best teachers and are seeking ways to work with them as partners in a larger enterprise. We must identify more and more of these people and make it possible for them to work with teachers and offer children the best of what both professions can bring to the learning process. And—by the same token—we have got to begin breaking down what often seem to be the largely irrational attitudes of many of our teachers, administrators, and parents toward the professional artist. It is unfortunate but true that our schools are often not places where creative people of any kind, and artists in particular, are apt to feel welcome and at home. The jargon and the "educationese" of the professional in education often sound like sheer nonsense to the professional in the arts. The rules and regulations, the disciplinary practices, and the need to set goals and meet learning objectives annoy and frustrate those in the arts who want to work in educational settings.

Thus, it is clear that, if the partnership is to be genuine and fulfilling for all concerned, professional educators must examine carefully the kinds of environments and conditions that obtain in their places of learning, and every attempt must be made to open up the school in humane and educationally rewarding ways. The two groups will need to meet and plan together to make all kinds of artistic experiences available to children, both in and out of the school, in terms that take account of the individual learner's own growth and maturation level. The time is fast approaching when schools can no longer afford to "buy" from the outside artistic marketplace a random assortment of "enrichment" experiences without any real regard for sequence and continuity, or sometimes even substance. The problem has got to begin to "bother" the school official, to "intrude" on the curriculum, and to gain a greater share of the local tax dollar.

Artists-in-Schools Programs need to develop a whole series of orientation sessions, acquainting artists with schools and with the teachers they may be working with. Conversely, teachers, supervisors, and administrators must be oriented to the artist and to what his or her presence in the school can really accomplish for teachers as well as children.

At the training level, colleges and universities must begin to examine the kinds of education in and about the arts that are offered to prospective teachers. In this era, when there is an increasing oversupply of classroom teachers, something more fundamental can and must be done to make the prospective teacher more at home in the arts and more sensitive to the entire aesthetic domain generally. Those future teachers who find jobs in a tightening market will often be those who have more to offer in these and other fields than is normally gained in the conventional methods course in art or music.

At the graduate level, schools and departments of education—and their counterparts in the arts fields—will need to review carefully what they can offer to the classroom teacher who may return for special training in an arts or aesthetic education field. And the programs that prepare the art and music specialist—and perhaps one day similar numbers of specialists in theater, dance, and film education—

will need to give increasing attention to the question of enlarging the skills of the specialist to include more than one art form. The multi-arts specialist may soon come to be in real demand as school systems face the inevitable limitations on personnel and services.

Finally, in order to deal with governmental institutions at the state and federal levels, articulate spokesmen from education and the arts will need to become increasingly political. It will be necessary for them to look beyond their own local needs and to put greater pressure on their state arts agencies and education agencies to make arts education a major and a joint priority. It is remarkable what can happen when a chief state school officer (or a state arts council executive) bluntly says that the arts are, indeed, fundamental to education. This has already happened in a few states, and the reverberations have been felt down the line until it finally becomes "legitimate" for local school leaders to pay attention to the arts and to put money into programs in art and education.

Representatives from ten such state education agencies met in Chicago, May 19-20, 1975, to consider this entire issue. This meeting, supported jointly by the Rockefeller Foundation and the JDR 3rd Fund, was organized by the fund's Arts in Education Program, which has been exerting considerable effort recently toward helping state education agencies develop comprehensive plans for the arts in education. The Chicago meeting laid the groundwork for what promises to be a major undertaking aimed at collaborative efforts by the state agencies.

There are other signs, too, that the necessary bridges are finally being built between the arts and education. Because there are so many projects, and each is so complex, I shall do no more than mention a few of them briefly.

First is the newly established Alliance for Arts Education, which received modest funds from HEW in FY 1975 and is being administered by the Kennedy Center for the Performing Arts in Washington. It is an effort to bring together, at the state and local levels, those who believe it is time to forge new partnerships between art and education. Teachers, professors, state leaders, artists, arts educators, and others are being encouraged to join forces in a united effort to achieve the desired goals.

Second, a major long-term Study of Schooling in the United States has been established under the direction of UCLA's Dean

John Goodlad at the Research Center of the Institute for the Development of Educational Activities (I/D/E/A) in Los Angeles. A substudy on the arts in precollegiate education, supported jointly by the Rockefeller Foundation and the JDR 3rd Fund, is a significant part of the overall study design.

Third, the American Council for the Arts in Education is organizing—under the leadership of David Rockefeller, Jr.—a national panel of outstanding citizens from all walks of American life to consider the problems and prospects for the arts in education for individuals of all ages. The effort is similar to that of the Rockefeller panel ten years ago on "The Performing Arts: Problems and Prospects," which focused on the arts per se in American society. The panel's deliberations, when finally published, could have a major impact on priorities and policy development at all levels.

Fourth, the National Endowment for the Arts and many state arts councils are, despite their problems concerning budget and mandate, becoming increasingly involved in planning and working substantially and comprehensively in this hybrid field.

Finally, many school systems across the country, spurred to some extent by the early impetus of ESEA's Title III and Title I arts projects, are taking this entire issue more and more seriously. These school systems are developing productive alliances with arts organizations in the community and devoting greater in-service time to orient and retrain classroom teachers in the arts. Interdisciplinary teams of faculty members are planning new kinds of curriculum strategies that specifically include the arts.

As was stated at the outset, the bridges between art and education are often rickety—but, increasingly, I believe, they are being given firmer and more substantial foundations. And the dedicated people, on both sides of this learning equation, are at last starting to conduct the essential dialogues which, one hopes, will one day make this age-old chasm virtually nonexistent.

It seems appropriate to end this chapter with a quotation from a booklet the American Council for the Arts in Education published a few years ago called *We Speak for the Arts*. This publication effectively sets forth an essential rationale for making the arts a basic element in public education. It states:

The arts cannot make people good, or wise, or honest or powerful, but the arts can make them whole in certain wonderful ways—and that could be the beginning of the way back to a world fit to live in. Having been so deeply disappointed by the triumph of technology, why not now try to foster the other side of human beings so long neglected? Folk art or fine art, education needs each desperately, but the time is late, and the omission has been inexcusable. Can this society still think that the arts are ornaments to life? They are among the best things life has to offer. What indeed is America waiting for?

13

Elitism in the Arts and Egalitarianism in the Community—What's an Arts Educator to Do?

JEROME J. HAUSMAN

Memories of Schoolyard Duty

Perhaps it is a sign of my advancing years and growing simplemindedness, but of late I have been drawn to images and memories that to all the world might be seen as insignificant and unworthy of note. One such image has me as a young junior high school art teacher (about twenty-five years ago) assigned to "yard duty." As everyone knows, young adolescents have a way of devouring their lunches with great gusto and speed. School cafeterias or lunchrooms are not designed to contain the bursts of physical energy that usually follow lunch, and so, on a rotating basis, teachers within the school were assigned to "supervise" rather open-ended, unstructured activity of students within the more spacious confines of the schoolyard or playground. While the rest of my colleagues were left to enjoy their sandwiches, cottage cheese, and coffee in the relative peace and quiet of the teachers' room, I found myself (whistle in hand) watching over the unstructured, seemingly chaotic play of our student body.

A common occurrence in "schoolyard life" is the "chase." It has various points of initiation: one youngster hits another; a bat or book or scarf is grabbed; verbal taunts or facial grimaces raise the ire of another student. Whatever the point of instigation, what follows

is a chase—one youngster sets out to catch another. It is this phenomenon that was of interest to me. There I stood as a representative
of authority as kids went running after each other. I shall not discuss
the professional ethics or educational soundness of my position, but
I just watched—as a matter of fact, it was an interesting event—one
youngster winding his or her way as quickly as possible among the
many other students in the yard, while in hot pursuit there was
another youngster bent on catching him or her. So long as the gap
between the two was tolerable, that is, so long as the pursuer held
forth hope that he or she could catch the other student, the chase
continued. There were, of course, those who were easily caught. And
there were those who were rarely caught. What interested me was the
dynamics of the chase.

Putting aside the specifics of my schoolyard observations, I
think that one can readily see all kinds of parallels for some of the
chases in which we all engage. To be sure, it is not the circumstance
of having a hat or book taken; nor is there the necessity to engage in
actual physical pursuit of another human being. What does occur to
me is that all of us engage in responding to or creating circumstances
in which there is a gap between where we are and where we want to
be; there is a gap between perception of current realities and aspirations
directed toward hoped for realities. The chase for each of us involves
a sense of what we aspire to, the context in which we exist, and the
capabilities for resolving the ambiguities implicit in what I am
referring to as the "gap." I do not mean to oversimplify what are
surely complicated processes by which values and directions are
established or how the dynamics of our perceptions or motivations
are manifested. What I am interested in establishing is the very
simple point that these dynamics of our perceptions or motivations
are manifested. I am also interested in establishing the very simple
point that these dynamics are interrelated within a larger context
(my analogy was the schoolyard). The interplay of components is one
in which there are tensions to be maintained between ourselves and
other persons or things as we seek the resolution of problems or the
"closing of the gap." Given changing circumstances or events and
the factors of what constitutes an interesting or worthwhile "chase"
can be quite different. It is as if there is a continuing need to set
goals, reach new solutions, and then set new goals. We deal with
tensions and resolutions of tensions throughout our lives. Maybe

that is why we refer to a life of sustained tension and ambiguity (with no resolution or satisfaction) as a "rat race."

Tensions, the Resolution of Tensions, and Aesthetic Form

A number of my friends whose work is in the biological sciences have provided additional "models" that make clearer my observation that there are connected tensions and resolutions of tensions as we move through life. For example, one can point to homeostatic mechanisms (in which an organism seeks physiological equilibrium); one can also refer to the necessary mechanisms that provide the tension toward disequilibrium or imbalance. Even so simple an occurrence as standing upright requires a force and a counterforce that make it possible to achieve a sense of balance. Thus, standing upright requires our dealing with forces; being "in balance" involves the continued resolution of these tensions.

Within the visual arts, there are all too numerous examples of the conscious use of tensions and the resolution of tensions. I can recall many of Hans Hofmann's critiques in which he referred to the visual dynamics of "push" and "pull." Johannes Itten's foundation course at the Bauhaus stressed the conscious awareness and control of polarities and analogies. The list is known to all those who engage in foundation design concepts and exercises. Contrasts such as large-small, broad-narrow, thick-thin, horizontal-vertical, light-heavy, loud-soft, and dark-light provide the means for consciously conceived resolutions. Itten observed; "As the life and beauty of our earth unfolds in the regions between the North Pole and South Pole, so gradations between the poles of contrast contain the life and beauty of the worlds of contrast."[1] Still another example of the kind of thing I am pointing to is the balance between "content and form" referred to by Piet Mondrian: "To create this unity in art, balance of the one and the other must be created."[2]

What does all of this have to do with art or art education, or, more specifically, any topic dealing with elitism and egalitarianism? It is obvious that my first point seeks to establish a sense for the artist who deals with the tensions and resolutions of tensions (his work) within a particular time and context. Artists enter the stream of time with its given factors of language, values, and customs. No one can be said to be a completely "free agent" responding only to inner circumstances and direction; rather, each person's life extends from a point of entrance, responding and creating within the circumstance of that life. As was observed by George Kubler, "good" or "bad" entrances are more than matters of position in the sequence. They also depend upon the union of temperamental endowments with specific position. Every position is keyed, as it were, to the action of a certain range of temperaments. "Thus," Kubler goes on to observe, "every birth can be imagined as set into play on two wheels of fortune, one governing the allotment of its temperament, and the other ruling its entrance into a sequence . . . . By this view, the great differences between artists are not so much those of talent as of entrance and position in sequence."[3]

What does it mean to deal with the given factors of an artist's entrance and position in today's context? There is, of course, no simple answer. Why is this so? First, the multiple images and forms of past and present converge upon our consciousness. Second, new technologies and media, such as film, video, and computers, have been added to the realm of possibility as an artist seeks the expression and realization of ideas. Third, all of this is to say nothing of the "institutionalization of the avant-garde"[4] via our media and educational agencies. In today's context great value has been placed upon being creative, original, different, and innovative. Leonard Meyer has characterized our period as one of "fluctuating stasis," that is, "a steady-state in which an indefinite number of styles and idioms, techniques and movements, will coexist in each of the arts."[5]

Role Expectations for Artists and the Forms They Create

One should consider the role of an artist in other times and cultures. What were the role expectations of an artisan in the Old Kingdom working on the pyramid near Gaza or of a craftsman carving for the Parthenon or the Basilica of St. Peter's in Rome? Artists were far from being free agents obeying their own wills; their situations were more rigidly bound by a chain of prior concepts and expectations. It was not until the fifteenth century that significant steps were taken to elevate the Western artists from responsibilities to relatively predetermined crafted forms. During succeeding generations shifts in forms of patronage and personal values of artists have continued. Writing of rebels and revolutions of the nineteenth century, Geraldine Pelles observed:

Many artists, whether or not they participated directly in the social and political eruptions, regarded art itself as an avenue of revolution, personal and social. Still fired by the ideals of the Enlightenment and the Great Revolution, they hoped to find means of emotional and intellectual restoration through the arts as an area of timeless and timely verities.

Youths did not visualize themselves as painters, composers, or writers merely in terms of the work they did standing before an easel or meditating at a desk. Their very association with this type of work seemed to be a declaration of independence against the ordinary life of the times and an affirmation of the mythical free individual who had become an ideal in the intellectual and political developments of the past hundred years. For a feminist like George Sand, this sort of attraction was particularly strong. She recalled in her autobiography, "To be an artist! Yes, I wanted to be one, not only to escape from the material jail where property, large or small, imprisions us in a circle of odious little preoccupations, but to isolate myself from the control opinion . . . to live away from the prejudices of the world."[6]

Thus, it is possible to come to today's context influenced by a rather romantic view of the artist. The artist is seen as one who courts alienation in the service of deeply held beliefs. There are implied commitments that reach to the core of personal integrity and the responsibility to one's own art even in the face of a community that would be receptive to other forms and values. Sarah Charlesworth makes this point in observing that "the history of modern art has been a long revolution against the complacency, sentimentality, and tedium of bourgeois culture, a rebellion against the self-assuming and rhetorical aspects of traditional forms, against the threat of subsumption or diversion of political or social non-art concerns—a veritable march of progress in the name of freedom, of individuality, of *art.*"[7] In Harold Rosenberg's terms, the American vanguard artist of the 1940's and 1950's took to the white expanse of canvas as "Melville's Ishmael took to the sea."[8] This is the circumstance within which Adolph Gottlieb and Mark Rothko responded to remarks by the art critic Edward Alden Jewell about their paintings in the Federation of Modern Painters and Sculptors Exhibition in 1943: "We feel that our pictures demonstrate our aesthetic beliefs, some of which we, therefore list:

1. To us art is an adventure into an unknown world, which can be explored only by those willing to take the risks.

2. This world of the imagination is fancy-free and violently opposed to common sense.

3. It is our function as artists to make the spectator see the world our way—not his way."[9]

Let me return to my use of the terms "elite" and "egalitarian." As artists set a course toward creating forms that could be said to be remote, more personalized, and responsive to their own more sophisticated concepts, their art could be said to be "elitist."

"To escape," "to isolate oneself," "to live away from the prejudices of the world"—these can be seen as "elitist tendencies," and, I would add, have given rise to a certain kind of individuality and diversity in art forms.

"Egalitarian," as I am using the term, refers to those tendencies that would take art "off the pedestal" and seek to make it more available to everyone. It is a point of view that asserts the equality of all men in the matter of opportunities for receiving and responding to art.

It is interesting to note that there was a counterthrust in American art to balance the evolving formalism of abstract expressionism in the 1950's. The more elitist tendencies, which are best articulated in the writing of a critic like Clement Greenberg, were countered by such forms as environments, happenings, and then pop art. Writing about his own work that was shown in an "Environments, Situations, Spaces" exhibition at the Martha Jackson Gallery, New York City, in 1961, Claes Oldenburg stated: "I am for an art that does something other than sit on its ass in a museum. I am for an art that grows up not knowing it is art at all, an art given the chance of having a starting point of zero. I am for the art that involves itself with everyday crap and still comes out on top. I am for an art that imitates the human, that is comic if necessary, or violent, or whatever is necessary. I am for an art that takes its form from the lines of life, that twists and extends impossibly and accumulates and drips and spits, and is sweet and stupid as life itself."

More recently there have been major exhibitions of artists like Francis Bacon (at the Metropolitan Museum of Art) and Leon Golub (at the New York Cultural Center). Hilton Kramer characterized the Bacon exhibition as a sign of "new conservatism in taste." In his review he observed that "the time may indeed be ripe for Mr. Bacon's triumphal entry into the consciousness of American Art, for he is undeniably one of the classiest conservative painters on the world scene."[10]

I do not wish to dispute Kramer's assessment of Bacon as an artist. All would agree that he is an artist who uses recognizable subject matter—indeed, a subject matter that can be characterized as grotesque, even sadistic. What is also of interest is Kramer's observation that this exhibition is a "significant symptom of a shift in aesthetic loyalties . . . ."[11]

In the *New Yorker* Harold Rosenberg reviewed both the Golub and Bacon exhibitions: "In their rejection of abstract art, both painters raise fundamental issues about the power of painting to deal with the essential experiences of the times. Their case against abstraction rests on its incapacity to pin down the violent and destructive forces by which modern man is threatened and which have become part of him . . . . Their challenge lies in affirming what most art-world opinion has continued to overlook; namely, that what makes a work of art important is its imaginative content, not its conformity to formal standards, on the one hand, or its eccentricity, on the other."[12]

It would be all too simple to suggest that the shift from the formalist critical stance of Clement Greenberg to the Happenings of Kaprow or the drawings and sculptures of Oldenburg or the paintings of Golub or Bacon is reflective of a change from an elitist to an egalitarian orientation. The shifts taking place in criticism during the past fifteen years stem from some rather fundamental changes in the orientation of artists themselves. I would observe, however, that the forms (or events) created in the pop art or the figurative or new realist movements still have been remote from the receptive understanding of a mass audience. What is interesting to me is that the content or subjects of these works are derived more from commonplace images and ideas. These works are thus more accessible by virtue of that content. Closing the "gap" between such artists and their public brings attention to social and personal meanings of the forms created as well as their formal attributes. Hence, it is no wonder that Kramer could observe:

if one looks these days into a journal like *Artforum*, which, month after month, year after year, during the 1960's, published quantities of the most learned and disputatious formalist criticism, one finds that it is the sociology of the art world that now commands the greatest interest. Not the aesthetics of contemporary art, but its socialization is the issue of the moment—which is another confirmation that the so-called "vanguard" is in the process of peaceful assimilation. If the age of criticism is coming to an end in the art world, it is for the same reason that the age of criticism in the literary world—the New Criticism—came to an end a generation ago: its task has been completed, it has placed us in possession of the essential issues raised by the art in question and no longer seems to have any pressing functions to perform.[13]

One could argue that my evidence is taken as much from the shifts in critical writing as the shifts in the forms of art themselves. It can be observed, moreover, that the current state of diversity in art criticism is almost as great as the diversity in art itself; hence, it would be possible to point selectively to evidence in support of contrary points of view. I am drawn to the generalized feeling, nevertheless, that we are in a period of fundamental change in the orientation of artists. The hard-line formalism of an elitist art is giving way to other more public and social concerns. This is reflected clearly in the roles now being assumed by artists.

Artists and Society

There is currently a strong force toward the involvements of artists with social institutions—schools, community art centers, environmental planning groups, housing projects, even the business community. Louis Harris reports that "49% of the public (16 years and older) or 71.3 million people indicated that they attend cultural events. In fact, more people attend such events than attend spectator sports." The Harris report observes, "The American public sees cultural activities and facilities as important assets to the quality of life and to the business and economy of the community."[14] Allan Kaprow states:

On the whole, this widening interest in art stimulates its practice as statistics amply confirm. It echoes not only a pluralistic aesthetics, but it suggests that the range of reason people now have for being interested in contemporary art is sufficient for art's admissibility to the public domain. Not every artist can benefit from all of these reasons, just as the converse is obvious. But the artist is in a position to turn the welcome signs to his advantage; for, in any case, people are taking advantage of the artist.

Essentially, the task is an educational one. The artist is faced with an involved public, willy-nilly. It is not bent on hating him, and so it is better to be loved well than loved to death. The duties of instruction in love fall primarily to the artist himself. His job is to place at the disposal of a receptive audience those new thoughts, new words, the new stances even, which will enable his work to be better understood. If he does not, the public's alternative is its old thoughts and attitudes, loaded as they are with hostilities and stereotyped misunderstandings.[15]

And so it seems to me that all of this signals a new set of attitudes that invite active engagement between artists and others who work in community service. Schools, community centers, hospitals, homes for senior citizens, housing developments, indeed, all places of social exchange, need to be seen for their potential in exhibiting works of art, inviting artists to work or perform, or sponsoring arts events. Not all artists can work in every situation, as all situations are not appropriate for each artist. But the essential thrust for the arts that I see in the future is one of engaging communities in the very processes, structures, and substances of the arts.

Engaging others is not going to be a simple matter of artists' saying "come to my studio" or "performance." It will not involve merely giving a lecture or demonstration and collecting a fee. Rather, "engagement," in the sense that I am using the term, will require an exchange and sustained encounter. Artists working in schools will have to develop knowledge and understanding of the educational context: What is being taught? To whom is it being taught? Why is it being taught and with what consequences? Their own actions should be responsive to an ongoing situation. Musicians or drama or dance groups need to have a feeling for what they are doing in relation to an existing educational program. Teachers, on the other hand, must be sensitive to and supportive of what it is that the artist is doing.

To be sure, there was once a time when the arts were dispensed as something added to or tacked onto the school day. Putting on a good show constituted "dazzling" an audience with technical skill and virtuosity—"that's entertainment"—but it is not enough in today's context.

I am reminded of Ad Reinhardt's statement about "the next revolution in art" (written in 1964) in which he prophesied: "The next revolution will see the fading away of all old, unschooled, 'school of hard knocks' artists telling young artists they need not go to school, and the casting to the dogs of all schooled artist-company-men and the techniques of their trade—brushworking, pan-handling, backscratching, etc.... The next revolution will see the emancipation of the university-academy of art from its marketplace fantasies and its emergence as 'a center of consciousness and conscience.' "[16]

Toward a New Sense of Community

Seen from the perspective of artists and teachers of art addressing themselves to the needs of the community, the seeming "issue" of elitist versus egalitarian orientations dissolves as another of those "academic" ploys so useful for a public lecture but a trap as a real choice in establishing how we ought to behave in life's situations.

The nature of art draws us to the unusual, the unique, the realization that takes us beyond the ordinary to the extraordinary. Art is not life or nature. It is not ordinary experience; it is not the commonplace *except* as the stuff of life or nature, ordinary experience, and the commonplace are seen or understood and organized in a way that helps us to transcend customary modes of perception and understanding.

At the same time, our times are calling for a way of thinking and acting that makes it possible to engage communities in the qualitative dimensions of the arts. This is the concern of those of us who are in art education. If I am correct in my assessment that artists' roles are turning more toward community involvements, then I think it a corollary that art educators and artists must seek cooperative and supportive relationships. All of this will invite widespread involvements with other people and ideas. It suggests other ways to think about the orientation and procedures of our work.

The orientation must be one in which there is a continuing commitment to the qualitative dimensions of the arts. The essential difference is that there will be a repositioning away from formalist orientations toward artistic activity as an integral part of creative community experience. This means, of course, that greater attention will be given to interdisciplinary involvements and the use of materials and resources from within the community. The emphasis being sought is that of artist as "synthesizer" rather than "solitary hero."

In regard to the procedures to be followed, there is the need to begin at the point where we are. The media and circumstances about us afford rich possibilities for action. We should be willing to engage others in the substance of the arts. There is the necessity to think and act comprehensively.

In his book *RSVP Cycles* Lawrence Halprin describes his interest in "scoring" as a way of thinking, planning, and communicating about processes of social interactions. "Scores," for him, "are a means to symbolize exchanges in all fields of human endeavor." What is as important, his work articulates an attitude on the part of artists and their audience (or, one might say creative citizens and their communities). This approach

places great demands on the audience, the theater audience, or the community planning 'audience' or the human relationships 'audience.' If the audience wishes to become involved, there are consequences to this commitment. There are two sides to this relationship. The audience-as-community has an increased opportunity to affect what happens. This can be tremendously exciting and dynamic and far-reaching; but within the excitement there can be many failures and errors along the way. At the same time, this focuses a new series of demands on both the artist as scorer and the audience as community and participator. These new opportunities will lead to new results, to the degree that the audience members become responsive and enter into their role with energy, passion, and responsibility. It means that people can disclose information, respond with feeling states, reveal their needs, be alert to what is going on around them, and take on the role of active participants . . . . There is a mutual relationship and trust involved here between audience and artist that can be called ecological in the broadest sense of the term. If the true function of the artist is seen as an energy thrust which evokes the peak condition of awareness and output within the community, then he functions as an essential ingredient in an on-going energy chain, driving toward the highest potential of his ecological system.[17]

Now, as in the past, artists should follow the dictates of their own sensitivity and skill. What I am calling for (and what I believe the times are mandating) is a clearer commitment for engaging in community effort. A major problem in today's context is the failure to recognize the urgent and overriding human and social needs (for example, articulation and communication of ideas and feelings or the need to enhance the quality of human life). It is sufficient to say that there can be many "scores" for appropropriate response by artists and teachers. The role possibilities include: artist-teachers in and out of schools, artists in residence in housing units and in businesses, artists commissioned for public projects, individuals as participants in arts administration, people working in the design and creation of instructional materials, and artists as designers of video or film communications. It is important to keep in mind that the creation of art is not just adding another commodity to our supermarket of objects or events. Creation in the arts is an assertion of aesthetic value.

I shall return to my image of students in a schoolyard and the dynamics of their lives. What is to be the nature and direction of the classes in which they will engage? What does it take to gain sustained commitments? Indeed, what is the purpose of our chase as we pursue some elusive target? In the end, there is the matter of quality in the encounters we experience—the sounds, movements, sights, tastes, dreams, and feelings that constitute the fabric of our lives. For those of us who engage in setting the pace, what are the responsibilities for sustaining an encounter with those whose lives we seek to influence? The tensions that I would seek are those of persons creatively involved in pursuit of aesthetic form and realization; those with the skills to make this possible have a very special responsibility to their community.

Notes

1. Johannes Itten, *Design Form—The Basic Course at the Bauhaus* (New York: Reinhold, 1964).
2. Piet Mondrian, *Plastic Art and Pure Plastic Art* (New York: Wittenborn, Schultz, 1947).
3. George Kubler, *The Shape of Time* (New Haven, Conn.: Yale University Press, 1962), 7.
4. See Hilton Kramer, *The Age of the Avant-Garde* (New York: Farrar, Strauss and Giroux, 1973).
5. Leonard B. Meyer, *Music, the Arts, and Ideas* (Chicago: University of Chicago Press, 1967), 172.
6. Geraldine Pelles, *Art, Artists, and Society* (Englewood Cliffs, N.J.: Prentice-Hall, 1963), 18.
7. Sarah Charlesworth, "A Declaration of Dependence," *The Fox*, I (No. 1, 1975), 3.
8. Harold Rosenberg, *The Tradition of the New* (New York: Grove Press, 1961).
9. As quoted in catalogue for "Subjects of the Artist—New York Painting, 1941-1947," exhibition at the Downtown Branch of the Whitney Museum of American Art, New York, April 1975.
10. Hilton Kramer, "Signs of a New Conservatism in Taste," *New York Times*, March 30, 1975, Section D, 31.
11. *Ibid.*
12. Harold Rosenberg, "Aesthetics of Mutilation," *New Yorker*, May 12, 1975.
13. Hilton Kramer, "The Revenge of the Philistines," *Commentary*, LIX (May 1975), 40.
14. *Americans and the Arts* (highlights from a survey of public opinion) (New York: ACA Publications, 1974).

15. Allan Kaprow, "Should the Artist Become a Man of the World?" *Art News* (October 1964), 37.

16. Ad Reinhardt, "The Next Revolution in Art," *ibid.* (February 1964), 49.

17. Lawrence Halprin, *The RSVP Cycles* (New York: George Braziller, 1969).

14

Implications of the New Educational Conservatism for the Future of the Arts in Education

ELLIOT W. EISNER

Since educational values frequently flow from visions of educational virtue that logical discourse finds difficult to render, I shall try to create a vignette, a rendering of an educational situation that I would value. I shall try to capture the qualities of schooling that I would like my own children to experience.

An Image of a School

The school I would like my children to attend would have a sense of intellectual excitement about it. Things would be happening there. When I entered that school I would hear a quartet playing in the corner of the building, like the wafts of freshly baked bread, its aromatic quality would permeate the atmosphere. Children would be moving about, some intent on projects that had captured their imaginations and therefore their souls. Others would be working in small groups, collaborating on an experiment in science or engaging in a debate about a fine point in a book about social justice and fair play. Still others would be reading alone, transported to another time. Engagement is the quality that pervades this school, immersion in activities that have deep, personal meaning. These children are actually turned on to what they are doing.

The school I would like my children to attend would have an array of cozy places, small nooks and crannies in which small children could hide, medium-sized children could share, and big children could protect, places that children could make their own, on which they could stamp their own personality, imprint their own signature. Private places are important, and this school would have them.

The school I would like my children to attend would be a visual delight. Paintings, sculpture, prints, and murals would vitalize the spaces. Ink-splattered kids would provide evidence of people literally into their work. Walls would shimmer with the profusion of color and form of work in progress. Unfinished paintings would not signify disinterest but rather complex problems still to be resolved; the subtle aroma of casein and linseed oil and turpentine would make a fine partner to the counterpoint of a quartet or a cool rock transition coming from the space down the way. What we have in this school, this place of life, is a center of human enterprise, a mixture of energy and imagination, a treat for the senses, a celebration of the mind, a realization of the curiosity, the power, and the competence of growing young minds.

Teachers would be around this school, and because it is the kind of place it is they would really be in touch with the children as people. What is even more important, the students would know the teachers as people and not need to play roles, wrap themselves in tinfoil, providing a cardboard image "to the professional staff." It is amazing how skillfully the young learn to play the games of adults, how competently they learn to camouflage their feelings, to feign enthusiasm, to provide compliance, to read the system, and to play by the rules, even when those rules engender meaningless charades. In this school children have genuine educational options, they are encouraged to cultivate their interests deeply, to pursue ambitions, to devote their attention to problems, projects, and ideas that win their interest. This school provides both the physical space and, even more importantly, the psychological space for emerging interests to be pursued. Perhaps that is why one seldom finds the whole class working on a single project or topic or lesson. There are times when the class functions as a community, but more often natural small groups form. Interested children develop interests. Time is organic rather than mechanical; body time rather than clock time determines the pace and length of activities. The ebb and flow of interests and work set the pace for life in school. And when groups are formed around interests, interests rather than age or grade level become the basis for grouping. The young can learn from each other as well as from books and teachers. Furthermore, the direction is not always downward.

The school I would like my children to attend would take seriously the idea that human beings, regardless of their abilities in reading or mathematics, are inherently worthwhile, that life is precious, and that people need not be measured on a common scale. Differences can be valuable, and competencies can develop at different rates and in different forms for different people. This means in practice that what each youngster does will be recognized and, when appropriate, honored. Over in the corner of the room sits Harry. His ability to read is less developed than most of his age-mates, but that fact is not a source of discomfort or stigma. What is important is that as he engages himself in projects that are significant to him, that really touch his core, his need to read will be kindled and his ability to read will be fostered. Harry is quick witted, has the best sense of humor in the class, and has as much independence and social competence as almost any child in school. Harry is seven.

The school I would like my children to attend would have stage crews building scenery and dance troups creating choreography. Musical compositions would be created by composers in residence— Harold and Carol, ages nine and twelve—to be performed by three ten-year-old virtuosos on tape recorder, rubber band strings, and ash can percussion in the presence of the resident critic, Ernestine, who in the school paper critiques this new composition along with two others performed the previous week. In this school the arts are important, the imagination is cultivated, and competence is respected. In this school the arts are natural; they suit the structure; they fit; they relate in an organic way to the life of the place. Could any school have it otherwise?

The answer to that question is most definitely yes. Very few schools approximate the image I have sketched. Most schools— indeed the overwhelming majority—operate in an organizational structure that makes it difficult to adapt to the organic and changing interests of children or to allow for the development of intellectual or aesthetic commitment.

The Current Situation in Schooling

I wish I could say that the picture, at least for the short term—the next two or three years—looks better. I wish I could say that as a result of my travels, my observations of the national educational scene, my conversations with school superintendents, specialists in early childhood education, and teachers, I foresaw a different future for the arts in education. I do not. What I see at present is a growing rise of educational conservatism, a back to basics movement with basics defined as they have seen traditionally defined—reading, writing, and arithmetic. At the secondary level basics also include discipline, not the discipline of anthropology, of history, of psychology, of cinematography, or of playing the English oboe, but discipline in the old-fashioned sense. Parents want the schools to keep the young under control. For example, in Palo Alto, California, an educationally enlightened community, parents rated discipline among the highest of priorities for junior high school students.

Some children and adolescents are apparently hostile toward the school, which results in an increase in vandalism: more windows are being broken, equipment is being stolen, and teachers are threatened. And so, as every decent, well-brought-up citizen knows, the way to solve the problem is through more discipline.

We read in the newspaper that children can no longer do mathematics. The new math is the culprit. It is not important that children understand mathematics, but that they learn to compute. And apparently they cannot compute as well as they could a decade ago. The remedy being suggested is not more opportunities to develop computational skills but the elimination of the effort to enable them to understand mathematics. Somehow, with less understanding and more drill, things will improve.

I have talked with superintendents of county districts that have thirty or forty school districts within them. One such county superintendent in southern California stated that he would be surprised if as many as 10 percent of the elementary school teachers were still teaching social studies. Why is this so? Because these teachers are so preoccupied with skills in reading and arithmetic, social studies can claim little space in the curriculum. Performance in reading and arithmetic undergoes state evaluation. California uses standardized tests to measure achievement in these areas. The evaluation tail, therefore, wags the curriculum dog. Teachers and principals know what is to be counted, and they do what counts. Social studies is not counted; hence it does not count.

I have talked with professors of early childhood education in San Diego, California, and they have expressed concern that the early childhood education program, which is funded by the state, endorsed by the General Assembly, and supervised by the State Department of Education, is diminishing rather than enhancing the quality of education for young children. What is the problem? Reading and arithmetic are squeezing almost everything else out of the curriculum. Even at the kindergarten level, the bookshelf is replacing the playhouse and the dress-up corner. The imaginative life will not measure well on state tests. Although the initial legislation for Early Childhood Education provided for attention to the so-called affective side of educational life, the guidelines state evaluation teams use emphasize the so-called cognitive areas. The observation schedules they employ devote a disproportionate amount of space and attention to reading and "cognitive development."[1] The message that comes through quite clearly to teachers and administrators is that if their ECE programs are going to be evaluated positively, early reading and early mathematics must be given priority. The State Department of Education claims that evaluation of "affective" areas is difficult and that the technology for evaluating the "cognitive" areas is available; hence, the latter will be emphasized. The consequences, as one might have predicted, are not surprising. What is measurable is evaluated, and what is evaluated is emphasized.

The growing emphasis on measurement has caused such alarm among elementary school principals that their national association has devoted its journal of March-April 1975 to the theme, "The Myth of Measurability,"[2] an issue that identifies some of the liabilities of guiding educational planning and teaching on the basis of measurable outcomes. It also points out the millions of dollars the testing companies make in selling their wares in 19,000 school districts serving 53,000,000 students.

The rise of educational conservatism is not restricted to the public schools. Stanford University—one of the great universities in this country—recently became alarmed about the so-called escalation of grades. Too many students were receiving high grades. The way to correct that situation was to reinstate the D.[3] If too many students do too well, then something must be wrong.

Some might feel that I have misread the educational scene today as a result of a professional blind spot concerning the future of the arts in the schools. Is it not true that there is an upsurge of interest in the arts? There are arts festivals and crafts fairs almost everywhere. As a matter of fact, no self-respecting middle-class community would be without them. The density of crafts vendors has become so great in Union Square in San Francisco that they are now being prohibited from setting up their stands. It is estimated that last year there were 700,000,000 visits to museums in this country. [4] The latest Harris poll conducted for the Associated Council on the Arts paints a much different picture than the one I described.[5] In that poll of a selected sample of over 3,000 people, it was found that in the sample for California two out of three people favored the teaching of arts courses for credit as a part of the core curriculum, like English and mathematics. A total of 86 percent said that playing a musical instrument should be taught in schools for credit, 83 percent thought that drawing, painting, and sculpture should be taught for credit, 77 percent felt art appreciation should be taught for credit, and 79 percent said the same for music appreciation, 71 percent thought that pottery, ceramics, and crafts should be taught for credit, and 69 favored the teaching of ballet, modern dance, and movement for credit.

The survey also found that 85 percent of those who visit museums frequently had taken arts courses as children or as adolescents, as compared with 50 percent of those who did not go to museums in the past year. The survey concludes that the arts in education have had an apparent influence on the aesthetic habits of adults.

In light of these data we might have good grounds for expecting an artistic renaissance in American schools. According to public opinion, at least as sampled by Louis Harris and Associates, Americans not only value the arts in general and would be willing to pay more taxes to support them; they also value them in the educational programs provided for the young. Why then has the renaissance not occurred? Why are educational tendencies directed toward other goals? Why are there different views of what is important? Why is it that in California the number of school district art supervisors has dropped from 408 in 1967 to 115 in 1973.[6]

There is no single, simple explanation, but there are to my mind some persuasive hypotheses.

Sources of Educational Constraint

In the first place, and this may be the most general overall factor, our culture and the culture of much of the Western world tend to view the arts as something that is nonintellectual. Art, generically speaking, is considered the product of talent, something that issues forth from the emotions rather than from the intellect. Since schools and education are by definition involved with thinking, the arts can only occupy a marginal or peripheral place. Schools are places concerned with works of the mind and not with works of the hand. Schools are places that should cultivate ideas, not images. Schools are places that should focus upon intelligence, thought, and cognition, and not upon soul, emotion, or imagination. In short, the overriding, general conception of mind and of the school's role in its development is itself parochial and represents a fundamental mis-conception of what is involved in thinking.

These are harsh words. Is there evidence to support them? One piece of evidence deals with the dichotomy we make in educational jargon between cognition on the one hand and affect on the other. Cognition is supposed to deal with thought, and affect is supposed to deal with feeling. The distinction, once made for heuristic purposes, becomes reified; it becomes real. Psychologists proclaim it, and measurement experts operationalize it. Teachers are supposed to emphasize the one, but give at least a passing nod to the other in order to maintain some semblance of balance in the curriculum. Thus in some classrooms cognitive activities take place in the morning and affective activities are left for a part of the afternoon. When is mathematics taught in most elementary schools? When are the visual arts taught? Obviously, if you have to think, the morning is better than the afternoon. In the afternoon children might be tired, and, on Friday afternoon, if they are not tired, they are anticipating the weekend break; thus, there is no better time for art.

As long as the arts are considered areas of enrichment in the curriculum they will be viewed as marginal niceties—good-time friends, but when the chips are down, they will be among the first to go.

In the second place we still labor under the illusion that the public views schools as having something to do with education. As everyone knows, schools are educational institutions, places that cultivate people's positive attributes, realize their potentialities, nourish their spirit, liberate their imagination, engender visions of the good life, and foster a love of learning, a respect for truth, and a sensitivity to beauty. Or are they? Are these the values that animate our schools and motivate our communities to support them? I doubt it. Schools are looked upon by most citizens as places to be used to get ahead in the world. Schools are the ladders (whether in actuality or in belief) up which one moves to achieve success. Economic mobility and social mobility are largely influenced by how well one does in school and how far one goes. And, as more and more people go to school longer and longer, *where* one goes will become as important a factor as *whether* one goes was in previous years. People know that, especially in upper-middle-class, well-manicured, polite communities. Parents in these communities are very interested in how well their children do in school, and, compared to national norms, their children do well indeed. The children in such communities will, in general, be educational winners. They will have access to the college of their parents' choice.

I am suggesting that schools in our society function not so much to cultivate the virtues I described earlier, but rather to select out of the population those who can play the game by the rules through which it functions. That is one of the reasons why upper-middle-class parents are so concerned that their children do well in third-year mathematics in high school; it is needed for admission to prestigious colleges and universities. I cannot convince myself that they believe sentential calculus will really be more useful in pursuing the good life than, say, in-depth work in one of the arts. I cannot remember the last time I inverted a fraction or calculated the truth of a geometric derivative, let alone basked in the memory of a whole, unified, coherent, and moving experience in which those once-held skills were acquired. The fact is we teach what we teach because the subjects are passports through our system, not because we have reflected on the nature of education and judged them necessary.

When schooling becomes a mechanism for economic and social mobility a number of consequences follow. First, if schools are in the business of selecting the able from the less able, then there cannot be a majority of winners. Selectivity means weeding out as well as screening in. When everybody is somebody, nobody is anybody. Second, if schools are conceived to be productive in the industrial sense, they need a product.[7] That product becomes education. Some get it; others do not. What is more appropriately viewed as a verb—a process to be engaged in, a journey one embarks upon—becomes a noun. Education becomes objectified. Once objectified it becomes capable of being measured, or so the argument goes. Thus test performance on third-grade reading tests mandated by the state and college board examinations provides the official index of educational quality.[8] Schools have become institutions concerned at least as much with processing and certifying as they are with educating. The public knows this. It is not that education in its grandest sense is not valued. It is that, given the game, it is not terribly relevant. Education in the grand sense of the word is a leisure-time activity. It not only requires a sense of engagement, but it takes time. It is to be savored, rolled over the tongue, cherished. We are more concerned with efficiency than with leisure. The instructional engineer, the cost-benefit analyst, and the educational accountant are the school district's educational specialists. Does any school district employ a philosopher of education? The thought alone makes one smile.

While the public might like a more generous conception of education, at present they realize they cannot afford it. It is not in the monetary sense that they cannot afford it, but in the sense that to provide such an educational environment might jeopardize their children's chances for meeting the criteria by which schools now select and reward.

Admission to the University of California is a good example. The University of California is the highest prestige public institution in the state. To gain admittance to the university, one must be in the upper 12 percent of his class; he must also have taken four years of English, two years of a foreign language, two or three years of mathematics, two or three years of science, and three or four years of social studies. These are the required subjects. If a student is educationally ambitious, he or she will take three or four years of science or mathematics, four years of social studies, and three years of a foreign language. Any time left over in the schedule can then be devoted to such nonessential courses as the arts. If one wants to attend a less prestigious institution, the state colleges, for example, those courses required for admission to the University of California need not be taken. How much data do students and parents need to figure out what counts? The message is clear. It is communicated in writing at the seventh- and eighth-grade levels, but it is understood by some parents when they enroll their child in kindergarten.

Thus, we must recognize the dominant function and the pervasive quality of schools. The major function is to certify and to select. What they produce is "education" according to the limited criteria they invoke. Their pervasive quality frequently borders on the image of the industrial plant; try to find a soft surface in a secondary school. They are organized bureaucratically with growing tendencies toward a form of simplistic accountability that has little or nothing to do with the educational process. Administrators have separated themselves from the teaching profession, and teachers increasingly view administrators as management. Administrators complain about unionization and grumble that the union is not interested in education, only in salaries. Teachers complain that administrators do not care about teachers. Administrators are excluded from teachers' unions, and teachers are excluded from administrators' organizations. Each group defines the other group almost as an adversary. School boards, meanwhile, want to see demonstrated payoffs, and the state legislature in California passes laws designed to improve the quality of education by mandating an evaluation program for all certificated personnel while allocating no funds for this to be done.

I have painted the educational picture in this country in broad strokes as I see it. I have tried to get across the point that the problem of making the arts an equal partner in school curricula will require some fundamental changes in our conception of mind and in the functions we want schools to serve. The root problems are both epistemological and social. They are epistemological because they relate to our narrow conception of what it means to know; they are social because schools do not exist in a vacuum. Their current priorities are reinforced by commercial interests and by institutions of higher education, and they are sustained by technically oriented professional educators and psychologists who have made a heavy investment in a set of tools that define education in terms that the tools can treat. In short, the problem of generating an educational environment in which the arts play a significant role is a systemic problem, not a local one; another art or music teacher here or there will not be sufficient.

At the same time I hope I have not projected the feeling of hopelessness. I continue to be optimistic. What *will* lead to hopelessness is a failure to recognize the depth of the problem and the extent to which it is sustained by cultural agencies and vested interests. What *will* lead to hopelessness is our willingness to deceive ourselves into thinking that another art class or two is the answer. Let us take a leaf out of the arts themselves and pay attention to the entire ground on which our schools participate; let us look at the forest as well as the trees.

What We Can Do to Bring about Educational Change

I continue to be optimistic because there are things that we can do to bring about change; we have allies. For example, recent work in neuropsychiatry is providing increasing evidence that human consciousness is a function of two hemispheres of the brain: the left hemisphere, which deals with linear, logical, and discursive forms of thinking, is complemented by the right hemisphere, which deals with analogical, visual, spatial, and metaphorical thought.[9] This research demonstrates that thinking does not reside solely in the functions of the left hemisphere; it is a product of the right hemisphere as well. What is lyrical, holistic, synthetic, and metaphorical, what comes to consciousness in the forms of icons or images, is largely a product of the thinking of the right hemisphere. Such processes, central to human adaptability and creativity, could be fostered through programs that are genuinely educational. We are thus aided by the work being done in this area.

We also have an ally in our potential ability to give the arts a visibility within the school and the community that most other areas do not have. The arts in the school have to be taken out of the classroom and "demonstrated" in the public eye. The hallways, courtyards, auditoriums of our schools and the shopping centers and the universities of our communities—these are the places the arts need to pervade with materials, perhaps in written form that enables the public to understand what they are about, and what they mean educationally.

Our own artistic skills can be used to develop the case for arts education by creating portrayals of the arts in the schools that can be shown to school boards, PTA groups, Kiwanis, Rotary, and other such groups; these portrayals would illustrate the contributions of the arts in the educational development of the young.[10] We could, for example, use films, slides, and work samples collected over time that illustrate children's educational development; videotaped critical analyses of arts teaching would help lay people begin to understand the kinds of demands, intellectually and aesthetically, that work in the arts exact. We can use tape-recorded interviews with students in which they discuss what they have learned from their work in the arts. We can work at demolishing the myth that the arts are only for the talented or the academically dull.

These efforts, as useful as they might be for increasing the visibility and understanding of the arts in education, will, however, not be adequate. There are several other things that need attention. Those of us who work in one of the arts in education need to establish a coalition with others working in other areas of the arts. Music educators should develop plans with those in art education. Both groups ought to cooperate with those in drama, dance, and in the humanistic aspects of English. All of us have a common stake in the arts and share a common belief in their importance in the education of the young. All of us have so far worked alone, as if other groups did not exist. That needs to be changed. We badly need a plan through which a unified and articulated position can be formulated, and then we must make our voices heard.

In some cases this coalition may lead to the development of transdisciplinary courses in the arts in schools. That is all to the good. In other cases it will lead to a stronger educational image and a more powerful political force. We cannot afford the seductive luxury of isolation.

In addition to a coalition of educators in the arts, we need to locate in the communities within which we work those people who are now responsive to the arts and who value them. We need to identify a constituency. Citizens who now value the arts in their own lives are the most likely to value them in the education of the young. That constituency could become vocal and could exercise the political influence necessary to remind school boards that the arts are not frills but central ingredients in the educational process. School boards are responsive to community input, as so many communities have already demonstrated. We need such a constituency to serve as advocates for the arts in education.

In order to ensure citizens that they are not jeopardizing their children's educational chances by advocating an adequate role for the arts in the schools, requirements for college admission need to be broadened. One place to start is with the University of California.

One can imagine the impact on school programs if that university required courses in the arts as a condition of admission. One can imagine the impact if the college board entrance examination required a portfolio, a recorded musical performance, an original musical composition, a piece of verse, a filmed ballet solo, or the like. We can begin to plan the ways through which the narrow conception of relevant educational experience is broadened so that those who want to work in the arts can do so without jeopardizing their chances for university admission.

I believe it will take a major coordinated, unified effort to engender a paradigmatic shift in our conception of education. But, in the long run, that is what is necessary. Although this shift can start with modest beginnings, we should not delude ourselves that either the effort or the goals are modest. They are not. What we seek is a basic, systemic change in thinking about the educational process and about the school's function in its pursuit.

This effort is not only conceptual; it will be political as well. I believe the goal is worth the effort, and, even if we fail, the struggle in behalf of good causes will contribute to the realization of our own humanity. And besides, in the final analysis, we might succeed.

Notes

1. These schedules are used by monitor and review teams that visit schools receiving funds from the state of California for early childhood education programs.
2. *The National Elementary Principal*, LIV (March-April 1975).
3. The reinstitution of the D has occurred not only at Stanford University but at a host of other universities concerned with "grade escalation." I have seldom seen a thoughtful educational rationale for this decision.
4. George Goodwin, "The Role of Public Education in Three California Art Museums: A Survey of Trustees' and Staff Members' Views," doctoral dissertation, Stanford University, June 1975.
5. Louis Harris and Associates, *Californians and the Arts* (New York: ACA Publications, 1974).
6. These data were issued by Louis Nash, state consultant in arts education, California State Department of Education, 1975.
7. For a penetrating analysis of the product orientation to schooling, see Ivan Illich, *Tools for Conviviality* (New York: Harper and Row, 1973), *passim.*
8. These scores are frequently published in local newspapers in rank order for each school in a school district.

9. Michael S. Gazzaniga, "The Split Brain in Man," in *The Nature of Human Consciousness*, ed. Robert E. Ornstein (San Francisco: W. H. Freeman, 1973).

10. For an elaboration of artistic approaches to the description of educational outcomes, see Elliot W. Eisner, "Toward a More Adequate Conception of Evaluation in the Arts," *Peabody Journal of Education*, LII (April 1975), 173-179.

E DUE